CW00751215

AN INTRODUCTION TO GAME STUDIES

GAMES IN CULTURE

AN INTRODUCTION TO GAME STUDIES

GAMES IN CULTURE

Frans Mäyrä

SAGE Publications
Los Angeles • London • New Delhi • Singapore

© 2008 Frans Mäyrä

First Published 2008

Apart from any fair dealing for the purposes of research or
private study, or criticism or review, as permitted under the
Copyright, Designs and Patents Act, 1988, this publication
may be reproduced, stored or transmitted in any form, or by
any means, only with the prior permission in writing of the
publishers, or in the case of reprographic reproduction, in
accordance with the terms of licences issued by the Copyright
Licensing Agency. Enquiries concerning reproduction outside
those terms should be sent to the publishers.

SAGE Publications Ltd
1 Oliver's Yard
55 City Road
London EC1Y 1SP

SAGE Publications Inc.
2455 Teller Road
Thousand Oaks, California 91320

SAGE Publications India Pvt Ltd
B 1/I 1 Mohan Cooperative Industrial Area
Mathura Road
New Delhi 110 044

SAGE Publications Asia-Pacific Pte Ltd
3 Church Street
#10-04 Samsung Hub
Singapore 049483

Library of Congress Control Number: 2007927907

British Library Cataloguing in Publication data

A catalogue record for this book is available from
the British Library

ISBN 978-1-4129-3445-9
ISBN 978-1-4129-3446-6 (pbk)

Typeset by CEPHA Imaging Pvt. Ltd., Bangalore, India
Printed in Great Britain by Ashford Colour Press Ltd

FSC
www.fsc.org

MIX
Paper from
responsible sources
FSC® C011748

CONTENTS

CONTENTS

LIST OF TABLES AND FIGURES

TABLES

FIGURES

LIST OF BOXES

ACKNOWLEDGEMENTS

I want to thank all my colleagues in Hypermedia Laboratory at the University of Tampere who have over years contributed greatly to my thinking about digital games and game studies, as well as to that knowledgeable and wide-reaching international community of scholars who have worked with me in DiGRA. Particular thanks to Aki Järvinen and Olli Sotamaa who read the manuscript and made many very useful comments and suggestions. And my warmest thanks go to Laura who has been both a co-author and an inspiration in many of the key ideas that have now taken the form of this book. It has been an adventure and it is nowhere over yet!

ACKNOWLEDGEMENTS

1

INTRODUCTION: WHAT IS GAME STUDIES?

> If we apply to science our definition of play as an activity occurring within certain limits of space, time, and meaning, according to fixed rules, we might arrive at the amazing and horrifying conclusion that all the branches of science and learning are so many forms of play because each of them is isolate within its own field and bounded by the strict rules of its own methodology. (Johan Huizinga, 1938/1971, *Homo Ludens*)

Making sense of games

Playing games can be interesting and fun, but also challenging in many ways; game studies shares the same characteristics. The aim of this book is to guide its readers into the path of analytical appreciation and enhanced understanding of games. This is a textbook of game studies, which is a new field of study focusing on games, particularly in their different digital forms. As an introductory text on contemporary subject matter, it is best thought of as a 'portal in paper': it is designed to give a compact overview of the field, and equip its readers with the key tools necessary for continuing into more detailed and advanced lines of inquiry. Therefore, it will provide several information boxes with pointers into sources of further information, with more such information provided in the accompanying website (*www.gamestudiesbook.net*). The book is also designed to be used as a companion piece in an introductory course of game studies, and to facilitate that use, as well as self-study, at the end of each chapter there are concluding chapter summaries and a few sample assignments, with notes on related methodologies, which are also discussed further in the final chapter.

The structure of the book is both conceptually and historically organized. Some of the history and key approaches of game studies are introduced in the two initial chapters, after which the book will attempt to familiarize the reader with the key historical phases of game culture and related, most important game forms. Rather than aiming to be encyclopaedic or generic, the discussion of games contained in this book is based on individual and concrete representative examples of games, chosen to open the road into more comprehensive appreciation of the diversity of the field. The historically and thematically oriented chapters each introduce key concepts that are useful for understanding a particular type of game; the discussions of this kind of specific concepts are embedded at the points where they are useful within the overall historical framework. The main framework focuses on distinctions between gameplay and representational aspects of games, and on discussing various dynamic aspects of games.

There are many ways how games and their study could be presented, partly owing to the breadth and diversity of games themselves, partly because the discipline is a newcomer, and there are several perfectly valid approaches to the study of games. My own twisty road as an academic trained originally in textual and art studies, who then moved into teaching and studying digital culture and then into heading an interdisciplinary research laboratory on game studies, has of course an effect on what kind of approach is adopted here. Rather than being mostly a book about making games, or one analysing only their structures or functions, or a study that investigates the business or legal aspects related to games, this work's principal starting point is on *games as culture*. This means that the artistic and creative dimensions of games are taken rather seriously, but since the concept of 'culture' has undergone many changes as researchers from several disciplines have contributed to its formation, the view presented here is necessarily and inherently interdisciplinary. The views that intersect in this book can be grouped into (1) study of *games* (2) study of *players*, (3) study of the *contexts* of the previous two (see Figure 1.1). In reality, these three spheres of inquiry cannot be separated, but must be seen both as mutually interacting and complementary, and informed by historical processes. In some earlier studies (Juul, 2005: 37) a three-partite division focusing on relations between the game, the player and the world is used, but here 'context' is used as a more general concept that includes multiple frames of reference, and thus also multiple possible realities.

A context relevant for understanding a game might be informed by the developments within and between particular genres, while in order to understand typical practices of play it might be necessary to take into account a certain way that distinctions between private and public spaces influence playing practices,

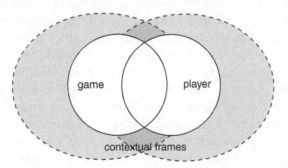

Figure 1.1 The focus of game studies in the interaction between game and player, informed by their various contextual frames.

for example. The *vision of game studies* informing this book can be described as multidisciplinary and dialectical; if and when we understand anything, it is by making connections that open up new directions for thinking about games. Bringing into contact existing but previously separate ideas, concepts, and frames of thought, we can proceed to create a synthesis of them, and see our grasp of things evolve. As new concepts are introduced, they will also re-contextualize our understanding of game–player relationship. In this way, analytical studies of games can also have an effect on the way we play games or perceive each other as players. During the course of this book, this starting point will be examined from multiple viewpoints, all contributing to a view of *games in culture* – that is, a particular model of sense-making for digital games that is aimed to help distinguish the multiple layers and processes of meaning involved in playing and discussing them.

This basic dialectical structure applies to the aims and structure of this book as well. To start, there are at least two key terms any practitioner of game studies needs to be familiar with: that of (1) *game*, and that of (2) *study*, as in scientific and scholarly practice – both of them rather complex and diverse concepts. One only need to compare a classic board game like the Chinese *Go*, *Dungeons & Dragons*, a fantasy role-playing game, *Solitaire* (style of card games popular also as a digital version installed with the Windows operating system), and a contemporary video game like *Grand Theft Auto III* (Rockstar Games, 2001), to realize that many concepts that are very useful for describing one game can be rather useless when describing another. Similarly, scientific practice has evolved into numerous forms and there are many different approaches which one could apply into the study of games and produce interesting and valuable outcomes. Thus, even if this book presents certain concepts and approaches as useful starting points for game studies, the most important lesson it should provide for its readers relates to the fundamentals of scientific research itself: when systematically applied and critically tested, there are multiple ways into knowledge. Scientific practice is continuously created, maintained and corrected by the academic community, and the never-ending 'approach to truth' describes it much better than a declaration of any single absolute truth.

A friend of games should find this basic character familiar enough, since deep down, *science and scholarship are much like games*. Players are drawn into games because of their challenges, and playing involves creating, testing and revising strategies as well as the skills necessary for progressing in the game. Academic study can captivate in the same way, and largely for same reasons: it requires facing challenges by setting up hypotheses, forming research questions and strategies, and then revising them, as even the most promising directions can lead into blind alleys. And even the occasional discovery or breakthrough usually opens up doors into new directions and new challenges.

At the same time, it is important to realize the differences and institutionalized limitations to the 'play impulse' within scientific work. The quote of

Johan Huizinga opening this chapter is illustrative; the 'horrifying conclusion' of science becoming 'merely a game' is quickly dispelled by Huizinga: he points out that scientific work is not confined in its own reality or 'magic circle' (see Chapter 2), and the 'rules' of its play are constantly challenged and results tested against those from alternative approaches (Huizinga, 1938/1971: 203). Thus, rather than just playing a ready-made game, the work of a scholar is actually much more like that of a *game designer*, who must develop and implement a systematic structure for new ideas and then see how the creation is 'played with' by members of the academic community. The aim is that by the end of this book, the reader will have a better conception of the key elements and steps that are required to successfully engage in academic study of games. Particularly, the last chapter will provide further directions into the practical and methodological issues related with embarking on a game studies project.

Game studies is a young discipline, and there are scholars who would not grant it the name of 'discipline' at all and would rather prefer to talk about a multidisciplinary research field that is focusing on games. Regardless of how we call it, game studies has reached the point where it has become established both as a field of scientific inquiry and as a branch of knowledge that is formally taught at universities. It has its own subject of study – games and playing in their multifarious manifestations – and also its own theories, methods and terminology, which have entered into the usual process of academic application, evaluation and reformulation. In institutional terms, developing into a discipline means that a learned community has formed around game studies, with the shared aim to evolve knowledge on games. Such institutionalization is also advanced by the associations, conferences and journals which have been created in this field. At a certain point, disciplines also become realized in the form of education offered in academic degree programmes, and even if game studies at the time of writing (in 2006) has not yet reached this stage in many universities, there are already a few such degrees in existence, and hundreds of courses and minor degrees turning up, as the wide interest of both teachers and students is expanding the field.

There are many reasons why game studies is expanding in popularity. One of them is obvious: the popularity of games themselves. With the rise of digital media and information technologies, millions of people have found games as one of the most fascinating uses for these new interactive devices. As new hardware and software are being produced, games continue to be the most challenging and popular application for all those advanced features of new technology. Games push the envelope in various areas of media technology and have been a major factor in information technologies entering homes in the first place. Today, digital games[1] are a significant cultural force, which has a prominent role in the lives particularly of those people who are living in industrialized countries. The commercial success of the games industry also cannot be ignored; even if it is a volatile and risky industry, games development and publishing nevertheless has grown into a global creative powerhouse, with a global market value regularly cited as exceeding 30 billion dollars annually. There is now also an entire generation of academics entering the faculty who grew up surrounded by arcade and home video game consoles and personal computers, and who have dedicated plenty of time both in their youth and adult life into playing games. Thus, the two key factors were there for a new wave of game studies to emerge: an important and challenging, and largely yet under-researched phenomena, plus a fair number of young researchers with the expertise and enthusiasm necessary for embarking upon study on this field.

A (very) short history of game studies

Game studies is faced with the double challenge of creating its own identity, while at the same time maintaining an active dialogue with the other disciplines. As long as there are only a few institutions dedicated solely to the study of games, the majority of game studies will continue to be practised by individuals who are nominally situated in some other field: in literary, film or media studies, or in departments of communication research, sociology, psychology, computer science, or in some other of the numerous fields where game studies is currently exercised. In a lucky case, they will find it easy to apply the traditions of their native fields into the study of games without compromising their real interests either in terms of games as their central subject of study or without conflicting with the core identity of their discipline. In many cases, the road is not so easy, and students focusing on games may find it hard to get the advice, support and understanding they need while engaging in the academic study of games. In career terms, specializing in game studies has been a difficult choice, as there have been very few job opportunities for games researchers in most universities (See Box 1.1).

Box 1.1 GAME STUDIES RESOURCES ONLINE

Digital Games Research Association – DiGRA: *www.digra.org*
DiGRA conferences: *www.gamesconference.org*
International Simulation & Gaming Association – ISAGA: *www.isaga.info*
Game Studies Journal: www.gamestudies.org
Games and Culture Journal: www.gamesandculture.com
Journal of Game Development: www.jogd.com
Digiplay Initiative: *www.digiplay.org.uk*
Game Research website: *www.game-research.com*

For more online sources, see the companion website *www.gamestudiesbook.net*

The situation is changing, and in the future the issue is likely to be put the opposite way – why should there *not* be game studies represented in a modern university? Failure to address games in academic education may also lead into research lagging behind more generally. The international academic community is directing their energies into understanding games not only because of their personal enthusiasm for them, but also in order to learn important lessons about the forms social life and creative practices are taking in late modern societies. After all, games are the most successful example of information and communication technologies becoming *domesticated,* which means that they evidence being integrated into the everyday life and practices of groups of people. Study of games and our near-universal fascination with them can also teach about the human nature and about our attraction to *interactivity.* Games are interactive by heart, to the degree that it is tautology to use the expression 'interactive games'. The makers of software and new technology in general can study games to learn about ways to make interactivity an enjoyable experience. To a certain degree this has already happened: there is a change in the ways technology is discussed by experts, and some have started to speak about *design of experiences* rather than features or applications. Games may even have important effects on the ways, particularly, the younger 'gamer generations' think and operate and to the direction our societies are developing. It is easy to come up with several answers for the question 'Why study games?'

Giving a clear-cut definition for game studies is much harder. On a general level it is simple: *game studies is a multidisciplinary field of study and learning with games and related phenomena as its subject matter.* It is only when one starts to organize this diversity into a collection of theories and methodologies or forms it into a single body of knowledge to be communicated in teaching and publication, that things get complicated. It is impossible to include all theories and approaches from every possible academic discipline even if they could *potentially* be useful also for a researcher of games; a 'science of everything' can just as easily lead into confusion and become a 'study of nothing'. Therefore we need to understand why and how game studies has emerged in a certain form and why some questions appear more central for the practitioners of the field than do others.

When we define something, we trace out the boundaries and state what is included and what excluded. Sociologists of science point out that disciplines are actually social formations, developing their own language, shared perceptions of the world and even ritualistic conventions. The identity of game studies is also a historical process, and it is evolving in time. There has been academic study of games actually for a rather long time already, particularly within such disciplines as history and ethnography. To point towards two of the classics of the field, ethnographer Stewart Culin's *Games of The North American Indians* was published in 1907, and a *History of Chess* by an Englishman, Harold James Ruthven Murray in 1913, both of them still useful and impressive works of learning. Various games have also had an active role in the private and social lives of university students as well as academics, for a long history spanning several centuries. During these years, when professional and personal interests collided, research work sometimes sprang up, but there was no institutional support or discipline to encourage such activities.

Looking at the early disciplinary formations, it should be noted that games have a close relation to simulation (imitation of operations of a large system by other simplified system) and in this subfield the roots of the academic attention to games reach long into history. There exists a rich tradition of using various kinds of simulations for learning purposes – learning by playing may even be called the oldest learning method there is. After all, even animals learn by imitation, and play behaviour that is simulating hiding or fighting is familiar to anyone observing small kittens or puppies learning skills necessary for later life. History of research into the systematic design of games for learning purposes can be traced back to certain tactical and strategic writings from eighteenth-century Germany. Helwig, a master of pages at the court of the Duke of Brunswick, adapted chess into an early war game in 1780; he also wrote about his goal to design a game to create an 'agreeable recreation' for young pages, which would render 'sensible, not to say palpable, a few principles and rules of the military art'. (Avedon and Sutton-Smith, 1971: 272.) Later, different varieties of war games were developed and discussed, both in military and increasingly in leisure contexts. A group of American war gamers formed in the 1950s the East Coast War Games Council, an organization which arranged a series of symposia and also published proceedings, including presentations from these meetings in the 1960s. Following a later expansion, the name of the group was first changed to the National Gaming Council, but since the society was compared largely of educators interested in using particularly simulation games to enhance learning, a new name – the North American Simulation and Gaming Association (NASAGA) – was adopted. In other countries, similar developments were taking place, and the simulation and gaming research community expanded into an international network of national associations. An umbrella organization, International Simulation and Gaming Association (ISAGA), was established in 1970 and has organized over thirty annual conferences since then, bringing together researchers focusing on games and simulations and their use for various applied purposes. An academic journal, *Simulation & Gaming*, has been published since 1970, making it the oldest regular publication in the field. (Duke, 2003; Knuth, 1994.)

Another group of North American scholars gathered together in Minneapolis for the first time in 1973 and soon formed an association focused on the study of play in 1974. Changing its name to The Association for the Study of Play (TASP) in 1987, the group has been publishing proceedings of its annual meetings from early on. (The original name of the group was 'Cultural Anthropology of Play Reprint Society'.) A series of journals produced by the association has also been an important venue for developing and publishing play research: *Play and Culture* (1988–1992), *Journal of Play Theory and Research* (1993–1997), and most recently, *Play and Culture Studies* (1998–) (Myers, 2006; TASP, n.d.). There probably exists other similar early groups around the world, within different disciplinary contexts.

There are several other routes for game studies as well, most importantly in the fields of play behaviour research, the offshoots of computer science studying graphics, simulations and artificial intelligence, and the humanities computing field. It was particularly from the last of these where the contemporary wave of game studies started to emerge. Many of the people working within this paradigm approached computers as a potential new medium. Early thinkers such as Vannevar Bush had already in the 1940s discussed their ideas concerning a tool or device that would operate in an associative manner like the human mind, rather than in a strict linear or category-based fashion. Theodore Nelson provided the name 'hypertext' for such a way of interconnecting written or pictorial material that 'could not be conveniently presented or represented in paper' (Nelson, 1965/2003: 144). The advances in human–computer interaction and the increasing availability of computers in public and private use played a role as artists and humanistic scholars embarked on examining the potentials and implications of these new technologies. For the literary scholars, digital media appeared, opening new interesting directions particularly in the experiments of hypertext fiction, and interactive fiction in general. In 1997, the Norwegian scholar Espen Aarseth published *Cybertext: Perspectives on Ergodic Literature*, suggesting that hypertexts, adventure games and MUDs (Multi-User Dungeons, see Chapter 7) provided a fresh perspective to a form of textuality that requires 'non-trivial effort' from their readers to traverse the text. The same year also saw the publication of *Hamlet on the Holodeck: The Future of Narrative in Cyberspace*, by Janet Murray, an influential work discussing the future possibilities for interactive drama and narrative. Together, these two works also function as symbols for the two alternative approaches which collided in the first major debate animating the young game studies community a few years later.

Debates can be useful in making even slight differences of opinion stand out more clearly. That is also true of so-called 'ludology-narratology debate'. Ludology is a term suggested by the Uruguay-born games researcher Gonzalo Frasca in an article published originally in 1999; taking its model from narratology, which was a concept 'invented to unify the works that scholars from different disciplines were doing about narrative', Frasca proposed the term 'ludology' to refer to the 'yet non-existent "discipline that studies game and play activities"' (Frasca, 1999). However, 'ludology' appears to have already been in occasional use before this. Also in 1999, the young Danish scholar Jesper Juul completed his Masters Thesis 'A Clash Between Game and Narrative', which is one of the clearest statements of the 'ludologist' position in its early form. In contrast to some other researchers working in the field, who had set realizing interactive fiction as their goal, Juul considered interactive fiction as a utopia (even if an interesting one), because of the fundamental conflicts between the player-controlled interactivity happening in present time, which is at the heart of games, and narrator-organized representation of events, at the heart of narratives. Juul not only claimed that 'you can have a computer game without any narrative elements', but he even concluded that 'it is then the *strength* of the computer game that it doesn't tell stories' (Juul, 1999/2001: 7, 86). Several researchers were nevertheless willing to continue pushing games exactly into that direction, developing the potentials of games for interactive drama and as a storytelling medium in general (see Box 1.2).

A student of this part of intellectual history of game studies should pay attention to the fact that many of the 'ludologists' are actually coming from the field of literary studies and narratological research, and perhaps precisely for this reason are particularly sensitive to the limitations of those approaches. Nevertheless, games are clearly different from any traditional narrative, and the counter-narratology reaction arising from the early literary studies–based ludology has helped to make those differences more distinguishable. Ludology as

---

Box 1.2 ON HYPERTEXT, CYBERTEXT, AND INTERACTIVE FICTION

Well, by 'hypertext' I mean *non-sequential writing* – text that branches and allows choices to the reader, best read at an interactive screen.

As popularly conceived, this is a series of text chunks connected by links which offer the reader different pathways. (Nelson, 1980/1990: 0/2.)

In ergodic literature, nontrivial effort is required to traverse the text. [...] A cybertext is a machine for the production of variety of expression. [...] Cybertext is a *perspective* on all forms of textuality, a way to expand the scope of literary studies to include phenomena that today are perceived as an outside of, or marginalised by, the field of literature – or even in opposition to it, for (as I make clear later) purely extraneous reasons. (Aarseth, 1997: 1, 3, 18.)

Not everyone will immediately agree with the assertion that a work with aspects of a game, and with a history so involved with the entertainment software market, should be thought of in literary terms. Isn't the pleasure of the text adventure purely a ludic pleasure or a pleasure related to mastery – one that comes from overcoming mental challenges formed as the verbal equivalent of jigsaw puzzles, with only one set of solution? There are in fact other aspects of interactive fiction that prevent an easy affirmative answer to this question.

For one thing, the puzzles in a work of interactive fiction function to control the revelation of the narrative; they are part of an interactive process that generates narrative. (Montfort, 2003: 2–3.)

---

a novel concept also helped to highlight how games, when considered in their own terms as forms of art and culture, were in some sense unique, and in need of their own theories and methodologies of research. This was an important realization, and at the turn of the millennium an energetic phase of theorization and research had started. An important venue for this was opened by the establishment of a new online, peer-reviewed journal, *Game Studies*, which was first published in 2001 and saluted as 'Computer Game Studies, Year One' by the Editor-in-Chief Espen Aarseth. The formation of the journal coincided with a series of mostly European games research conferences and then with the formation of the academic society to support the research community – Digital Games Research Association (DiGRA). The years 2003, 2005 and 2007 saw the first three world conferences organized by DiGRA, and a proliferation of research papers, reflecting intensive academic work, which soon also surfaced in book-length publications, as academic publishing houses started to provide room for the work of games scholars.

Despite the differences of approach, there are no real 'schools of game studies' in existence, not at least in any more substantial sense, and researchers are continuing discussions about the fundamental concepts and methodological issues across disciplinary boundaries. Even the 'ludology-narratology debate' has turned into discussion whether it ever really happened in the first place (see e.g. Frasca, 2003a; Pearce, 2005). No one actually seems to be willing to reduce games either into stories, or claim that they are only interaction, or gameplay, pure and simple, without any potential for storytelling. But the different emphases and foci for the study of games remain, and that is the single most valuable contribution of this debate for game studies: games can be several different things, depending on how one approaches them. Looking for narratives, one can find (or construct) them, and it is equally possible to search and find the essence of games in their interactive character – in their gameplay. Applying this lesson in practice, the different chapters in this book will each introduce concepts relevant for study of games and play through discussions of certain influential games. A rather general overall framework will be developed during these discussions, but no single 'master theory' will be provided to contain all conceptual aspects, since the reality of games and play does not fit in any narrow model. Games, players and their interactions are too complex and interesting in their diversity to allow for all-powerful simplifications.

Looking at the history of game studies from a geographical perspective, it is apparent that the international scope of this research has been broad from the start, but the majority of the internationally available academic activity has centred on Europe, North America, and Australia – an obvious effect of language barriers. However, broadening of the field and increasing interaction is taking place also in this respect; currently, particularly the East Asian countries, like Japan, South Korea and China are entering the research community, contributing research based on their rich native gaming cultures.

South America, India, Africa and other parts of the world will probably be following the lead at some point. There is no country or society where games would not be played and enjoyed.

Summary and conclusions

- Game studies is a new academic field and interdisciplinary field of learning, which focuses on games, playing and related phenomena. Its recent rise is linked with the emergence of digital games as a cultural force, but it is not restricted to any technology or medium.
- There are several disciplines and approaches which have contributed to the study of games, ranging from history and anthropology to psychology, sociology, educational sciences, computer sciences, and lately, particularly literary and art studies. It has been suggested that the study of games and play activities should form a scholarly approach of its own, called *ludology*.
- Recent years have meant growth for the international game research community, as research publications, books, seminars, conferences, journals and associations have been created in the field of game studies. The history of games research, however, extends far in several fields of learning.

Suggested further reading

Johan Huizinga, 'Nature and Significance of Play as a Cultural Phenomenon'. In: Katie Salen and Eric Zimmerman (eds), *The Game Design Reader*. Cambridge (MA): The MIT Press, 2006, pp. 96–120.

Orientation assignment: Personal game history

This is an introductory assignment, designed to start you off into the appreciation of games and play cultures; and as it has been said, the foundation of all true knowledge is self-understanding. It was already known as the first piece of advice provided by the Oracle of Delphi for those seeking wisdom: 'Know Thyself'. For a researcher of qualitative phenomena such as games and playing them, self-understanding has an important double role: on the one hand, understanding the tilt produced by one's personal history and background is paramount for any informed self-critique. Researchers or professional experts are rarely 'typical' or average representatives of wider demographics, and it is good to know where one stands, as compared with various other groups with different backgrounds. (This is something we will discuss later, in Chapter 8.)

On the other hand, in order to really understand the fascination of immersive gameplay, or to be able to make qualitative distinctions between games with very different look and feel, we need to experience games and play ourselves. Understanding what are the strengths and possible weaknesses of ourselves as a research instrument are important steps in making us better in evaluating, researching and developing games.

Start by making some notes or a map on a large piece of paper on your personal games history – just freely try to jot down names and titles of games you have played. It might help if you engage in some small-scale archaeology and look into the boxes in the attic or in a cupboard for some traces of games and play sessions of years passed. Have you remembered to put also down childhood street-plays and board games played at home? How about card games, poker, or a lottery? Some of the multiple forms of games can easily escape our attention.

Write a text where you describe your personal relation to games and playing. It might be impossible to fit all the key moments, highlights and phases into a short account, but try to focus on creating an accessible summary, where you reflect on the kind of gamer you represent – or, alternatively, explain why games have not played such a major role in your life personally. Have you noticed that age correlates with interest in certain kinds of games? Have you been similar to, or different from other people you know in terms of your game playing? Do you have some particular field of expertise or certain favourites among games?

This is suitable as a joint orientation assignment for the entire course and will also work as an introduction which helps students, tutors and teachers get to learn to know each other. Everybody is encouraged to actively discuss and comment on each others' histories, pointing out both similarities and differences between them. To summarize jointly your findings, do you consider yourselves a typical sample in terms of your generation and cultural background?

(Associated research methods: qualitative methods of social sciences, biographical methods, memoir, group discussion.)

Notes

1. Note on terminology: this book uses the expression 'digital games' to refer to all kinds of contemporary games utilizing computing technologies within its operation. This includes, but is not limited to, the video games played with home console systems, arcade video games, computer games played with mainframe or personal computers, mobile games for mobile phones and various new digital devices. In some contexts and countries 'computer games' or 'video games' are used as similar umbrella categories, but 'digital games' is here being adopted into use as the most neutral of the available terms.

2

GAME CULTURE: MEANING IN GAMES

Games as cultural systems

The first of the key concepts for game studies introduced here is that of *game culture*. Contemporary game studies differ from the earlier traditions of studying games within such disciplines as history, ethnography, military simulation or educational sciences principally for the emphasis on games as a particular form of culture. This change in perception is partially due to games becoming such a noticeable part of popular culture during the last decades. Games are not only cluttering the children's rooms and arcade game parlours, but are conquering the living rooms and stepping out from the computer screen to various multifunctional devices, such as interactive televisions and mobile phones. On the other hand, the field of science has also undergone changes. It has become customary to speak about a 'cultural turn', which relates to the increasing role of linguistics and meaning for academic study. This development has often been linked philosophically to *social constructionism*, the view that our perceptions of reality are socially and culturally produced, rather than independent and objective facts. Even if its strong forms easily evoke accusations of relativism, the basic thesis of social construction theories, that our social existence affects what kind of meanings we are able to associate with phenomena, continues to gain popularity.

For the purposes of this book, culture is here understood rather generally as *a system of meaning*. One might claim that this is just passing on the problem, since 'meaning' is an equally slippery concept, which multiple traditions of thought have been addressing. In the context of game studies, it is just as important to think about meaning that is related to actions, or images, as it is to find meanings in words. The linguistic theories of meaning have often focused on the role of convention in sounds or symbols. When a community of language users establishes a convention to link certain expressions with phenomena, it can be said that these sounds or symbols start to carry meaning. The fixed convention as a vehicle of meaning, however, is not the complete truth. Language users do not wait until they master the established conventions of grammar and vocabulary of a language completely before they start to communicate. If a language system was the sole vehicle for meaning, we would not be able to understand or communicate with very small children, and also incremental language learning would be equally impossible. Yet, even without words, we can engage with simple games, or playing behaviours with babies, like young animals do among themselves. (See e.g. Piaget, 1966/2000; Smith, 1984; Vygotsky, 1934/1986, 1980.) In a fundamental sense, playing *is* a form of understanding. We can decode messages that carry information in unconventional forms by simple trial-and-error behaviours, as the feedback we derive from our interaction tells us whether we have understood each other or not. And in many cases it is even not so crucial that we are receiving and decoding messages exactly as they were originally intended; playing is fundamentally a form of *contact by interaction*, and while playing, it is most important that we keep the interplay going, and derive its predictable or surprising outcomes. A concept of games culture can help to bring into light the mostly unspoken backdrop against which games make sense for their players.

Meaning is also intimately tied to the concept of communication, which a dictionary defines as 'a process by which information is exchanged between individuals through a common system of symbols, signs, or behaviour' (*Merriam-Webster*). Meanings that are shared or produced in explicit acts of communication are nevertheless only a particular case of meaning-making. Much of the meaning or significance that is produced in human activities remains silent and, even at its best, is only implicitly or indirectly apparent for an external observer from the behaviours a particular individual is engaged in. In many cases, game playing appears permeated by this sort of 'silent significance'. An immersed player can be engaged with the game for hours on end, and yet it is hard to tell precisely what the actual meaning of game is for this player. Hands may be locked to the game controls, there are movements and maybe sometimes (conscious or involuntary) sounds, but even when interviewed, a player is rarely able to verbalize very well the exact quality of gameplay experience. The internal experience can be rich and multidimensional, and yet hard to communicate precisely (cf. Ermi and Mäyrä, 2005).

Much of the scholarship within game studies has been dedicated for understanding the similarities and differences of games to literature, cinema or other forms of storytelling. This is helpful to a certain degree, as it can help us to situate games in the ways narratives are redefined or challenged by the interactive character of games. While storylines, characters, milieu and other similar narrative elements often dominate discussions of games, there are actually many reasons why one should look for similarities also in such areas as *music* or *dance* while aiming to understand the ways in which games produce meaning. The musical experience has been characterized as 'non-linguistic' because music (at least in its instrumental form) does not use words to convey its meaning, yet it regularly succeeds in evoking feelings and sometimes also in conveying more precise ideas. The basic character of playing music, or dancing to its rhythm or melody is *performance*, as is also in the case of playing games. There are actually not very many extended discussions of a particular gameplay experience, but David Sudnow has attempted to describe the performance of playing the arcade game *Breakout* (Atari, 1976) in his book *Pilgrim in the Microworld* (1983):

I'm rising up with the shot then, the volume turned up high now, filling the room with bleeps, and I'm putting the shoulders and head into the action, singing a song with this ten-second sequence. I'll make up for the lack of heft in this knob by enveloping the frictionless calibrations in an encompassing style of undulating. Hum the sixteen-note melody created by the bleeps when the ball hits paddle, bricks, and side wall. *Bleep*, the serve ... *bloop*, the return ... *blapbleeb* ... a quick brick bounce off the side wall back down to ... *bloop*, the next return after the beat, and then up, down, off the side back up, *bleep* back down, up down, off the side down up. Throw yourself into the unfolding melody, carry the hand smoothly from one point to the next, ride with the ball through the whole five places. [...] (Sudnow, 1983: 133.)

Removed from its context of an Atari video game, which is structured around breaking down a virtual brick wall with a paddle and a bouncing ball (see Figure 2.1), the description of Sudnow's experiences becomes almost a nonsensical flow of actions, movements and sounds. Yet, playing *Breakout* or a similar seemingly simple game can be an intensely engaging experience, with the player's skills being constantly challenged and risen to a new level by the need for precisely directed and timed interaction with a computer-controlled environment. It appears that our language for describing gameplay performance is still rather limited. Sudnow's text is aiming to convey the *phenomenology* of gameplay, its internal sense and feeling for a game player. This text also reflects

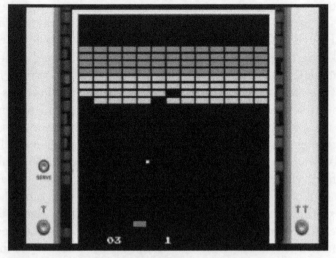

Figure 2.1 Screenshot from *Breakout* (Atari, 1976). [Image credit: *www.thocp.net*, Ted Stahl and The History of Computing Foundation.]

GAME CULTURE

Box 2.1 WHAT IS GAMEPLAY?

Gameplay is what doesn't change when you change the surface: the rules. In board games this is clear: the sundry local editions of Monopoly all have identical gameplay despite the different names of the streets. In videogames this is rather more delicate, as virtually everything is gameplay, and a slight change of a single parameter (say, speeding up a character, or making a weapon stronger) may radically change the effective strategies that emerge from the game.

The gameplay isn't the entire experience of a game, but it's what makes it a game, what makes it *this* game. (Nils von Barth, in Newman and Simons, 2004: 67.)

Gameplay is what you do. It's not the interface (thus, saving your game is not gameplay), it's not the graphics and it's not the story. It's the part of the game that absolutely requires the player's participation.

Gameplay embodies the rules of the game. For example, in a game like chess, each playing piece has its own rules, and along the playing field, the chess board, these rules interact to create gameplay.

The most interesting gameplay arises from rules that have both positive and negative consequences. This means that the player must make decisions that are not always clear and automatic. Good gameplay, in effect, arises when choices are non-obvious, and the player must explore different tactics to see what the trade-offs are for each decision. (Scott Miller, in Newman and Simons, 2004: 76.)

its author's particular mindset as a jazz pianist and social scientist trained in phenomenology – a rather unique combination has left its traces to the way Sudnow approaches and describes gameplay experience.

Semiotics, or the study and science of signs and meaning-making, has traditionally mostly focused on linguistic signs and the way signification is created through the use of images. However, words, text or representational images like spaceships do not operate in the same way in games as they usually work in non-interactive medium which is primarily used for carrying messages. David Myers, a semiotician who has focused on signification in games and play, has claimed that when a space war game starts, signs like the moving images representing spaceships are still symbols of physical objects moving through space. But when the player continues to play the game, the game itself starts to impose its own rules, making the actual rules of nature governing real physical objects effectively less important. A spaceship in a game now principally stands only as a symbol of value it has inside the game and for the gameplay. Myers calls this specific phenomenon 'aesthetics of play', where the elements of game derive their significance from the performance of gameplay; spaceships or other such game elements attain their value within the contexts players themselves construct during play. (Myers, 1990, 2003, 2004, 2005.) Similarly, the aesthetic qualities of dance or music are available for those who perform them even if it is probably impossible to translate the richness of associated, physical or performance-based meanings completely into verbal language. These kinds of meanings essentially remain embodied in their performance or action. There also remains nevertheless representational aspects in meaning-making associated with games, a topic which we will discuss shortly.

In order to make further sense of the many dimensions related to digital games, we first need to make some conceptual and structural characterizations. One of the key foci of game studies is analysis of games, which involves capacity to make meaningful distinctions within and among games, and between different factors related to playing them. In this book, games are approached as many-dimensional objects of study, additionally complicated by the fact that the full range of significance of games as objects are available only through the activities of various players. Thus, the multiple subjects and contexts of playful interaction further add to the complexity of signification, which therefore needs to be recognized as an irreducible and essential part of games and their study.

There appears to be a seemingly endless richness of uses and meanings provided by creative player–game interactions, but games also have certain structural features which make it easier to distinguish between different forms of this meaning-making. To start analysing this, a primary distinction is made here to differentiate the two elementary senses or 'layers' in the concept of game: (1) core, or game as gameplay, and (2) shell, or game as representation and sign system. Sometimes when the concept of 'game' is used in discussion, it remains unclear which dimension is actually addressed, and misunderstandings ensue. While the core, or the gameplay layer concerns everything a player can do while playing the game, and also game rules that govern these actions, the shell includes all the semiotic richness modifying, containing and adding significance to that basic interaction. For example, game board or game world, game pieces or characters all might be 'extraneous' to the core gameplay, but they belong to game as parts of the semiotic shell, where they modify the overall gameplay experience. This division is further illustrated in Figure 2.2.

Core and shell, or gameplay and representation, both form the structural key elements of a game, but they are different kinds of structures. It is important to understand that at the level of core gameplay one can find something abstract and transferable: the actual rule structure of a game. For instance, a game of chess or poker can be played with many different kinds of boards, pieces or cards, and yet it will still be the 'same game' in this most abstract sense. The identity of a game in this narrow sense is based on its rules. However, somewhat like the material used for manufacturing the chess pieces has some effect on the actual experience of playing a game of chess, the identity of a digital game is inseparably tangled with many other factors, including the audiovisual design of its game world and its objects and inhabitants. Various details in the programming code, and even the hardware and controls used to play a digital game, have an effect on how it is experienced. Player attitudes and competences also affect how the game will be realized during gameplay.

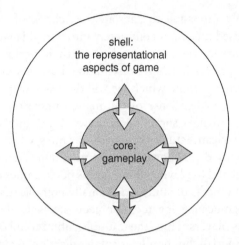

Figure 2.2 The dialectic of core and shell, or gameplay and representation in the basic structure of games.

While playing, some gamers concentrate more on the rule system and play the game to win or finish it, without much regard for the game world or its backstory, for example; but it is likely that all players are to some degree influenced also by the representational parts of the game, such as the quality of graphics or audio. Some derive intense pleasure exactly from this kind of 'secondary' element in the digital games they play, even if the 'game itself' (meaning the actual game rules, defining the gameplay at its core) would not be so original or even interesting.

As when compared with the discontinuous history of game studies, the study of music and musical meanings has been the subject of relatively sustained academic attention. Leonard B. Meyer, an American musicologist, separates in his *Emotion and Meaning in Music* (1956) absolute and referential meanings in music; in the former, the meaning of music is seen as being essentially intramusical (non-referential), whereas in the latter case we would look at music as communication of some referential content. Even if referential meanings are not excluded, as they include the entire field of music as 'language' utilizing its own means and symbolisms to express concepts, emotions or moral qualities, the majority of music scholars' efforts have focused on intramusical meanings. But even such 'absolute' meanings are not completely self-sustained. Meyer acknowledges the relational nature of meanings: there needs to be (1) an object or stimulus, (2) that to which the stimulus points, and (3) the conscious observer for meaning to be produced (Meyer, 1956: 1–3, 34). In reality, the structure of this meaningful linking is more complex than a simple chain of stimuli evoking reactions. Inside a musical system, notes in a composition, such as Beethoven's *Fifth Symphony* or Madonna's hit song *Material Girl*, receive their meaning by their ability to connect to the earlier musical history and experience the listener has. Also, the musical system appears in different form to a listener and to a person playing music or making his or her own compositions. Meyer talks about individuals in different cultures learning to understand the styles of music practised within them – music is in this sense a 'habit', which is also capable of evoking effective experiences, partially arising from the internal organisation of a particular piece of music, partially related to the various connotations this music has derived due to its private or collective association with various events, persons or experiences (ibid.: 61, 256–8).

Games constitute similarly interactive cultural systems, with a specific emphasis on *meaning-making through playful action* (*ludosis*), as contrasted with meaning-making as decoding of messages or media representations (*semiosis*), typical for such cultural systems as television shows or contemporary poetry. Understanding and appreciation of a game like chess is based on pleasures derived from the actions and events taking place during game playing, but there are also many other dimensions of the game. There are various social values and norms that do not belong to the actual written game rules but nevertheless regulate game playing. While learning a game, a player simultaneously adopts the explicit rules and also various implicit guidelines of chess that not only tell which pieces to move and how, but also tell what it means to play chess, in the first place. This, of course, can be many different things, depending on where you learn to play chess. In their book *Rules of Play*, Katie Salen and Eric Zimmerman separate three kinds of rules: operational, constitutive and implicit. The operational rules are those basic guidelines that players require in order to play ('rules of play'), the constitutive rules are the mathematical and logical structures underlying the rules presented to players, whereas implicit rules concern proper game behaviour. A child might be allowed to 'take back' a foolish move, whereas in a contest match the same rule would not apply (Salen and Zimmerman, 2004: 130). From a cultural perspective, the implicit layers of a game extend far and wide, informing the basic sense of game – what it is all about and what is the nature and aims underlying the activity of playing it, within this particular sociocultural context.

In most cases it is not reasonable to speak about the meaning of a disconnected game element, and even an entire game gains its significance only when experienced by a player in a cultural context. James Paul Gee (2003: 24–6) has argued that it makes no sense to talk about such things as thinking, learning or reading 'in general': all these things are always situated within a material, social and cultural world. The same goes for games. The phenomena this book calls 'game culture' are built upon layers of learning and experience among all the previous games that the particular group of individuals sharing this culture have interacted with before. Thus, it is similar to the 'habit' Leonard B. Meyer spoke about in the context of music: a shared frame of behaviour and understanding. Originally phrased by philosopher Bertrand Russell, this view of culture emphasizes the playful and game-like, or ludic qualities of our understanding: 'Understanding language is ... like understanding cricket: it is a matter of habit acquired in oneself and rightly presumed in others' (Meyer, 1956: 39).

Cricket may be a particularly British game (and thereby, maybe, a particularly civilized one), but all games require a similar shared cultural frame to make sense. In his work *Homo Ludens* (1938/1971) the Dutch cultural historian Johan Huizinga, one of the key theorists of game culture, lists the free and voluntary nature of play activities, along with a particular separation from the rules of everyday reality (what he calls the 'magic circle') as its main characteristics, but he also notes how central a 'play community' is for play behaviours to become fixed into cultural forms and be preserved as 'games'. Huizinga also emphasizes that play itself is older than culture, since animals like to play just like men do. He calls 'higher forms of play' the social manifestations that this play impulse takes within human societies, including arts, sports and rituals (Huizinga, 1938/1971: 1–12).

There are many ways of using playfully systems of various kinds. As different word games prove, a language system can offer the basis for gameplay, as do the rules and game pieces of a board game, or the programmed objects and functions in a digital game. General systems theory, mathematical game theory and cybernetics are fields that have focused on the behaviours associated with complex systems. For our intentions, the concept of *dynamics* is useful while approaching games. Dynamics is here used generally to signify 'forces or motions that characterize a system', while within the actual study of dynamic systems, it is important to distinguish between various dynamics of change and the unchanging dynamical principles needed to analyse that change (Morrison, 1991: 2). In game theory, games are considered dynamic when players do not make their moves simultaneously, but on the basis of knowledge they have about earlier actions in a game. From a game studies perspective, structures which underlie the dynamism of a game system are often based on a conflict between players, or between the goals of players and the obstacles and challenges provided by the game environment. This book discusses games in terms of multiple different dynamics, including dynamics of conflict or challenge, as well as spatial and temporal dynamics. There are also games with more extensive player populations and spatio-temporal reach, which highlight the importance of discussing social dynamics, or even economical dynamics of a game (see Chapter 7).

Within the study of culture, relations as complex as those underlying gameplay in real-world contexts are rarely formulated into mathematically precise logic. For the work in contemporary game studies most typical are the qualitative approaches. An important influence for this tradition is Roger Caillois, a French philosopher and writer, who took it up to process the broad-ranging cultural play theory of Johan Huizinga into a more defined study of games. One of the key steps into this kind of deeper and more detailed cultural understanding is the ability to separate and name the studied phenomena and to make meaningful distinctions within it. Caillois suggested categorizing games into four main types, and also named two attitudes of play that create variety within each of them. Based on the dominant role that competition (*agôn*), chance (*alea*), simulation (*mimicry*) or vertigo (*ilinx*) have in each of them, the games within each category appear to provide distinctly different experiences for their players. In styles of play, the attitude of carefree improvisation or 'uncontrolled fantasy' is named as *paidia* by Caillois and separated from *ludus*, which stands for a tendency to bind play within the arbitrary, imperative and 'purposely tedious conventions' (Caillois, 1958/2001: 3–13). Later, Gonzalo Frasca has argued that the most useful way to conceptualize the *ludus/paidia* distinction is to consider the ludus to refer to the attitude associated with games with binding social rules, whereas *paidia* is a more 'playful' or loosely formalized form of play. *Paidia* also has its own logic or rules, but no clear-cut winning conditions as laid down by the rules of *ludus*-oriented games (Frasca, 1999, 2003a).

Nevertheless, all games have their uses, and only when situated within such contexts of play do they derive their meaning. In the scale of societies, Caillois even suggests that it would not be absurd 'to try diagnosing a civilization in the terms of the games that are especially popular there' (ibid.: 83). More modestly, one can certainly say that the games played within a particular game culture have an important role for the lives of the individuals sharing that culture. The study of games is important for understanding the game culture, and vice versa, by learning to understand better the actions and conventions of thought constituting this particular culture, we will be better positioned to understand games, the meanings they hold for their players and the reasons why people play them.

Game cultures as subcultures

As noted above, the concept of culture is wide and complex, and it plays an important role in many different research traditions and disciplines. This is partly owing to the centrality of culture for the lives of each of us; it can be said that culture is an inextricable part of our existence. For a long tradition of humanists, culture is what humans have and do, in contrast to other animals. Consequently, culture is not a neutral term, but rather one loaded with significance that is related to the values, carrying even political implications. One way to exemplify this is to look at the way concepts 'art' and 'culture' are often connected. This use is historically determined: the word 'culture' was originally used for the rearing of plants and cultivation or improvement in other concrete and figurative senses. Thus, the evaluative use signifying 'the training, development, and refinement of mind, tastes, and manners' of a civilized person is older than the more value-neutral usage standing for the customs, artistic achievements and so on of a certain people (see the *Oxford English Dictionary*).

Taken in this context, discussion about 'game culture' easily becomes debate about the cultural value and merits of games. In opposition to discourse which positions digital games as harmful, industrially produced rubbish, there are many proponents of games who would like to get games placed within the 'art and culture' discourse. According to this view, it is meaningful today to speak about games being culture because of their high – or at least rising – artistic qualities. Games can offer their players experiences that range from the aesthetic pleasures of impressive graphics, music, storylines and (sometimes) even well-scripted dialogue. Many games also provide players with active experiences that are more akin to the tests of skill, strategy, strength or endurance that are typical of some sports. There are also several games where the central focus is on the building and creating activities that people in non-digital contexts have enjoyed while being engaged in arts and crafts, or in hobbies such as building miniature models. The long tradition of non-digital play and games includes a rich accumulation of various kinds of puzzles, hopscotch style of street-play, dice, card and board games; and these all hold a major influence on digital games, but whose extensive traditions are typically not included in discussions of art and culture. Music, literature and painting have a long tradition of being regarded as art, and consequently related aspects of games are relatively easy to associate with the concept of 'culture' too. In contrast, sport activities, such as children playing in the streets, or people building dolls' houses or miniature railways as a hobby have not necessarily been perceived as similarly artistic or cultural in this sense of the word.

The above view is linked to and defined by the concept of 'high culture'. Traditional art criticism often either explicitly or implicitly favours this version, and within it, the aim can be set to identify truly artistic and significant works from those which do not merit being included in the concept of culture. Classic formulation of this view is captured by the poet and literary critic Matthew Arnold when he defined culture as 'contact with the best which has been thought and said in the world' (*Culture and Anarchy*, 1869/1909). Adopting this view, a critic of game culture might approach current digital games looking particularly for aspirations or aesthetic qualities which show in some of them success or failure in becoming art, and thus a part of high culture. Such art criticism of games should also be able to discuss the basis of its criteria and standards, and thereby engage with the formation of game culture as a critical and evaluative 'meta-discourse' for game-cultural forms. The fields of normative or evaluative cultural criticism are contested, and no doubt many friends of contemporary high culture consider digital games as plain rubbish, or the opposite of culture in its 'genuine' form. An opposite example is the Italian *Ludologica: Videogames d'autore* book series, which is designed to 'honour the most significant video games of the last 40 years'. Featuring prominent game designers in their covers, these book-length studies of single games openly aim to contribute into similar high-culture aura for the masterworks of digital games, as has been the case of classics of visual arts, literature and more recently, cinema (see: *www.ludologica.com*).

An alternative view on the concept of 'culture' to that of art criticism has been developed within the academic traditions of humanities and social sciences since the nineteenth century. As broadly encompassing and descriptive, rather than prescriptive in its approach, it can more easily accommodate such human activities as hopscotch, sports and building dolls' houses as forms of 'culture'. This view implies that such activities will be approached from a particular angle, as organized parts of a larger constellation of social and symbolic meaning-making.

An important discipline for the development of this approach on culture has been anthropology. A broad-ranging field of scholarship, it holds several sub-disciplines, with cultural anthropology being close to sociology terms of its approach and subject of study. A holistic inquiry, involved with all humanity and all its dimensions, cultural anthropology has evolved the concept of culture into a veritable umbrella of human life and thought. A typical definition of 'culture' within the field of cultural anthropology is:

> The system of shared beliefs, values, customs, behaviours, and artefacts that the members of society use to cope with their world and with one another, and that are transmitted from generation to generation through learning (Bates and Fratkin, 2002: 7).

If the concept of culture is taken in this broad and general sense, and applied as such directly into game studies, this can lead into a rather heavy-handed way to conceptualize 'game culture'. Could games be meaningfully related to 'shared beliefs', and are game playing practices 'transmitted from generation to generation'? Even if the form and rules of many children's games are inherited from previous generations, and considering the fact that there are so-called hardcore gamers who dedicate large parts of their lives to digital games, there are many more people who simply regard them as a hobby or an occasional leisure time activity in their lives. One could also certainly argue that games do not define our existence or place in a society in a way that belonging to a traditional ethnic culture, say Bantu or Inuit culture, defines the way of life and identity for those people. But games and game playing practices do have some significance for those people who are actively engaged with games. The public visibility of digital games, as well as the numbers of people playing them, has also increased strongly for several decades. It is questionable to rely heavily on information coming from commercial interest groups, but the sales and survey figures published by the Entertainment Software Association are nevertheless often quoted. According to them, 69 per cent of American heads of households play computer and video games, the average age of a game player is 33 years, and 38 per cent of game players are women (ESA, 2006). There are only a few academic studies that survey larger populations about their relationship to games, but some studies already appear to confirm that at least among younger demographics games do play a central part in life (see, e.g. BBC, 2005; Ermi, Heliö and Mäyrä, 2004; Fromme, 2003; Jones *et al.*, 2003; Kallio, Kaipainen and Mäyrä, 2007). To venture some characterisations at this point, it seems that particularly if card and board games as well as more physical games and sports are taken into account, games in general have a rather wide appeal for different audiences. On the other hand, enthusiasm to intensive playing and studying of digital games seems more typical for certain specific groups that include stronger representation of younger generations. Particularly among these latter groups the cultural role of digital games can even be compared to that of cinema or rock music. However, more large-scale and also more detailed studies of game playing are required before we can define the cultural roles of different games and styles of playing more precisely.

The cultural studies movement is another broad discipline, or interdisciplinary approach, which has played an important role in the contemporary conceptualization of 'culture' in academic contexts. The movement, born both in Britain and in the USA and then spreading throughout the world, attracted particularly British cultural studies scholars such as Raymond Williams and Stuart Hall, who were initially interested in providing critique of capitalist mass culture and exposing the power relations in areas like mass media and advertising. Elsewhere, especially in the USA, some critics started to pay particular attention to the ways consumption and appropriation of media could be seen as liberating and empowering. However, differences between the British and American strands of cultural studies have largely faded away. Just to give some examples of this wide field, Lawrence Grossberg (1992, 1997) has been influential in paying attention to how complex the affects and emotions related to rock music can be. From a feminist cultural studies perspective, Janice Radway (1984/1991) has pointed out the interesting ways how even the Harlequin romances can be empowering for their female readers, regardless of their 'patriarchal' content. It seems that people are very capable of creating multiple uses for things that cannot be directly deduced from their 'intrinsic' or formal qualities (such as the lyrics of a rock anthem, or narratives of the popular romances).

There appears to be a dialectic in more recent games related research, oscillating between work that focuses either only on games, or only on play behaviour or its various cultural contexts, whereas it would be very valuable to see how these two are interrelated. Contextual studies of players and their contexts, highlighting the purposes and uses for games, are nevertheless an important part of game studies. Like rock music, games are put into meaningful uses by their players, resulting in games and playing *making sense* for these individuals. Anyone who has spent a sleepless night in front of a glowing computer screen, trying to progress through a particularly challenging and immersive game, can bear witness to the powers of games and to the strength of motivation they are capable in eliciting in their players. But how can we find a 'game culture' behind such individual experiences, and how should we define it? For a non-gamer, games can appear just as isolated phenomena at the edges of modern life, devoid of cultural significance.

Under a closer look, games can in fact play many different roles in such overall, life-defining systems as cultures discussed by cultural anthropology, but in order to see them, the cultural analyst needs to be sensitive to the way identity is being negotiated and defined within late modern societies. The most notable way that game cultures can be interpreted to be working within this context is in their role as *subcultures*. Discussion of this concept here is influenced by branches of cultural studies focusing on forms of urban social life. Subcultures are groups of people who have some practices, values and interests in common and who form through their interaction a distinct group within a larger culture. Looking at the assortment of people living in a typical Western metropolis, we can discover how members of various religious and ethnic groups have their own subcultures even while they can simultaneously also share the schools, supermarkets, brand clothing or other outward signs of contemporary commercial 'mainstream culture'. In the streets of the same generic city, some youth groups like punks and skinheads show distinctly with the same double gesture both their difference from the 'crowd', and their belonging to the group of likeminded with their hairstyles and clothing. But also lifestyles within a workplace or profession sometimes display features of developing subcultures of their own. Contemporary studies of 'post-subcultures' have dedicated increasing attention to the fluidity and instability, which seems to characterize the late modern formations of taste and lifestyle (see e.g. Bennett and Kahn-Harris, 2004; Gelder and Thornton, 1997; Hall and Jefferson, 1975/2002; Hebdige, 1979; Muggleton and Weinzierl, 2004; Trice, 1993).

Members of game subcultures rarely carry distinctive outward signs as punks or skinheads do, but one only has to participate in a meeting of hardcore strategy gamers, visit a role-playing convention or take part in a *Quake* LAN party (a gathering of gamers with their networked-together PCs), when the features of the associated game cultures start becoming apparent. People seem to share the same *language*: they play the same games, after all, and have adopted terminologies that suit those purposes. All the above-mentioned player groups also have some *rituals*: they gather together to play games and are often also interested in the *artefacts* (like original packaged games, gaming devices, books, posters and such paraphernalia) that can also be used to mark one's room or keep as display tokens that are used to produce identity and verify one's membership in a game culture. These and other objects may work as *memorabilia* that carry some private or shared moments, or capture into symbolic forms the significance that precisely those games have for these people. These days, members of game cultures often subscribe to websites or discussion boards that are produced and maintained by active gamers in their free time and which stand as a virtual but identifiable *shared space*. This sense of a game culture comes close to fandom and fan activities, and such subcultures as have emerged within the fandom of science fiction, fantasy or horror often overlap to a certain degree with that of game cultures. Another interesting flexible cultural borderline of digital game cultures is the one that touches upon the 'techno subcultures' where the interest focuses on computers, electronic music, Internet and other digital media and technologies. From organizing games conventions to groups of people maintaining extensive websites focused on games, there is a wide and expanding range of interesting game-cultural activities, but the main 'symbolic centres' for members in game subcultures are nevertheless built around games and playing them.

Millions of digital gameplay sessions take place daily around the world, but not all of the people engaged with them fit within the afore-described subcultural framework. Most importantly, games have grown in popularity to reach significant parts of populations within a broad range of social background and in both sexes and in different age groups. A different phenomena from that of clearly identifiable gaming subcultures, these more diffuse gaming behaviours are often discussed in terms of so-called *casual gamers*. Rarely explicitly identifying themselves as 'gamers' or members of any games subculture, people falling into this vague category can nevertheless be considered to form the 'invisible majority' of digital game players (see also chapter 7). The casual gamer and her opposite, the *hardcore gamer*, are hard to define, for example, by their weekly playing hours alone. The concept is further complicated by some games being considered as 'casual games', which typically are easily approachable games, such as various puzzle or card games. Consequently, it might be that a

---

Box 2.2 ON SUBCULTURES

Subcultures, therefore, take shape around the distinctive activities and 'focal concerns' of groups. They can be loosely or tightly bounded. Some subcultures are merely loosely defined strands or 'milieux' within the parent culture: they possess no distinctive 'world' of their own. Others develop a clear, coherent identity and structure. When these tightly defined groups are also distinguished by age and generation, we call them 'youth subcultures.' (Clarke, Hall, Jefferson and Roberts, 1975; in Gelder and Thornton, 1997: 100.)

Two basic strategies have been evolved for dealing with this threat [of spectacular subcultures]. First, the Other can be trivialized, naturalized, domesticated. Here, the difference is simply denied. ('Otherness is reduced to sameness'.) Alternatively, the Other can be transformed into meaningless exotica, a 'pure object, a spectacle, a clown' (Barthes, 1972). In this case, the difference is consigned to be a place beyond analysis. Soccer hooligans, for example, are continually being placed beyond 'the bounds of common decency' and are classified as 'animals.' (Hebdige, 1979; in Gelder and Thornton, 1997: 133.)

'casual player' is used to refer to a person who actually invests rather heavily one's time into playing games, but is considered to be a 'casual' one because of one's preference of game style or genre (see Kuittinen *et al.*, 2007).

The crucial element here is to notice how such categorizations as 'casual' or 'hardcore' operate as cultural distinctions within a game culture. Identity is commonly produced through acts of separation as much as through a sense of belonging. I am what I am, because I feel similarity with my own group, and we can jointly define our identity through some significant difference of ours, when we are compared to others. The distinction between hardcore and casual players operates in this kind of way, providing means for people who are playing digital games to situate themselves as well as other people in terms of the intensity or 'seriousness' of their commitment into gaming. To adopt a concept from a literary scholar (Spivak, 1992), players are effective participants in 'identity talk' in their exchanges during and surrounding game playing, making visible their attitudes towards games and playing. Both words and performance of play operate in sensitive roles organizing the social nature of games; the particular extent of interest or passion governing the life of a hardcore gamer might be incomprehensible and alien for a less committed game player. Nevertheless, while playing games, both types of players infuse games with their own kinds of significance, to the degree that they utilize playing, discussing or other uses of games as vehicles for meaningful action.

While studying game cultures one should acknowledge their wide range and also look beyond those areas that are most manifest in popular gaming magazines or online forums of game fandom. There appears to be a mostly unquestioned 'hegemony' where certain kinds of games receive most of the attention in media (Dovey and Kennedy, 2006). Still largely unexamined, there also exists the 'invisible everyday' of digital game cultures in its many forms. A businessman playing *Tetris* with his mobile phone in the airport lounge, a young mother participating from her home with an online puzzle game in the Internet or a teenager developing an expensive habit with an SMS-operated cross-media game running in a television channel may all or may not move into the centre of our analysis, among those other individuals and groups engaged with games that are more familiar from the sales charts of PC or console game-oriented media. Lack of such visibility in popular media does not make those games and players insignificant if one is aiming to understand the larger picture of the digital games and play in contemporary life and society.

─────────── **Summary and conclusions** ───────────

- Meanings in games are created in playful interactions that take place within specific cultural contexts. Such meanings are related both to games conveying meaning in the manner of symbolic communication, and to the non-symbolic meanings inherent in the act of playing and in the overall gameplay experience.

- Cultures are structures of meaning, underlying the language, thought and action of people sharing them. Game cultures are often recognized as subcultures organized around games and playing, bringing together enthusiastic players who organize in their speech and behaviour the meanings attached to these play forms.
- A game subculture can be recognized and analysed by studying the language, rituals and artefacts, or the outward signs and material culture surrounding the activities, including memorabilia related to games. The physical and virtual sites of game playing and game community formation also contribute to the formation of game cultures, as do relation to other centres of signification, for example, family life, school, work or hobbies.
- Nevertheless, large parts of game cultures remain mostly invisible, as significant numbers of people playing digital games do not actively participate in any communities or fan activities created around such games. The distinction between casual and hardcore gamers is used to identify and discuss these kinds of differences. However, both concepts remain somewhat ambiguous as they can mean either perceived differences in terms of playing intensity or dedication to games as a hobby, or different preferences in games and playing styles between more simple or complex games. Particularly more casual gaming practices may easily escape the attention of students or researchers, as they have not been a popular focus of attention in games related media.

Suggested further reading

Henry Jenkins, "'Complete Freedom of Movement": Video Games as Gendered Play Spaces'. In: Henry Jenkins and Justine Cassell (eds.), *From Barbie to Mortal Kombat: Gender and Computer Games*. Cambridge: MIT Press, 1998. Also available online: *http://web.mit.edu/cms/People/henry3/complete.html*.

Assignment: Game culture survey

The aim of this assignment is to uncover and compare different game cultures, and in that way to become more aware of the cultural diversity surrounding games, reaching beyond one's own personal history as a game player.

Look around in your home, visit your friends and relatives and then explore wider at your neighbourhood or in a nearby city centre and try to find evidence of two game cultures, one that you think is of more 'hardcore' (intensive, dedicated, self-conscious) and other which you regard as more 'casual' (informal, relaxed, unselfconscious). You can also turn to the Internet as a source for information, but remember that it is often more useful to go in person to locations where games are played and get immersed in all the real-world details surrounding play activities.

Write a short essay where you organize your findings into categories of language, ritual, artefact and memorabilia, and how these objects and practices are used to create meaning and identity, or not, in your examples. Compare them and give grounds for why the other is 'hardcore' and the other 'casual'.

(Associated research methods: ethnographic field research, online ethnography.)

3

PLAY AND GAMES IN HISTORY

Writing for game history

Setting up the historical perspective for doing game studies, this chapter will play dual roles: first, it will present questions about game history and the prehistory of games, and second, it will introduce certain key theories of games and play. This division will also illustrate different dimensions of game studies as divided into more formal and aesthetic study of games and more cultural study of play and players. However, the argument here is that these two angles of research cannot be separated, that they often blend into each other in the research practice and that they actually can fruitfully combine to create a more comprehensive understanding of the phenomena. Interdisciplinarity is further discussed in Chapter 8.

Writing of a history for games is not a particularly easy undertaking. There are several reasons for that:

- Lack of archives and museums dedicated to the preservation and documentation of digital games, as well as devices suitable for playing early digital games.
- Lack of reliable professional research into history of games; timeline-style chronicles, anecdotal evidence and personal histories dominate, often linked with an industry-driven perspective.
- Main reason for the above is the public status of games as 'low culture' or commercially produced 'mass culture'.

The academic field of *digital game history* is not yet established in any systematic sense, a fact related to the state of game studies as a currently emergent discipline, as discussed above. However, it can be expected to be a growing subfield in the future: as games have established themselves as an important form of popular culture, it is important from critical educational and scientific, as well as from artistic and industry perspectives to learn to know the past.

There are many research directions or perspectives into games history that can be explored, some of them already actively practised and some just at their beginnings. Here is a schematic list:

- Art historical perspective.
- Software industry perspective.

- Technology history perspective.
- Social historical perspective.
- History of mentalities perspective.
- Games historiography, or meta-history.

Adopting any of the perspectives is related to the research questions and knowledge interest one is starting one's study from – an issue that is discussed further in Chapter 8. An *art historical* investigation into digital games will describe in formal and aesthetical terms the development of digital games, and detail what are the artistic and aesthetic criteria for games of both audiovisual and interaction design in different decades, and how the concept of a 'good' or original game has changed during the years. To date there is very little published academic research into this fundamental games history area.

Writing about the *software industry* aspect of games is something that has already been started in numerous articles and books. Research in this area can adopt a case study approach, and study some individual game companies, as David Sheff (1999) has done in his book *Game Over* that focuses on Nintendo. Alternatively, the character and role of games industry within the larger picture of software industry can be the focus of research, as in Martin Campbell-Kelly's work *From Airline Reservations to Sonic the Hedgehog* (2003). Critical examinations of the marketing and labour practices of the games industry can be based on this kind of historical evaluation and analysis, as in *Digital Play* by Kline *et al.* (2003). The biographical studies of certain industry luminaries like Nolan Bushnell, the founder of Atari, or Shigeru Miyamoto, the creator of Mario, often fall between the art historical and industry perspectives.

Technology history perspective in its popular form is well captured by the numerous webpages that eager fans set up for their favourite video game systems of the past. These try to trace the chronology of various gaming hardware and also provide images and technical specifications. History of technology in its more ambitious academic form would make an attempt to understand also the wider social and cultural dynamics hidden behind each individual piece of hardware. There are researchers working on the history of information technology and publishing in venues like the *IEEE Annals of the History of Computing*, established in 1979 by IEEE Computer Society, exploring the advent of computing in different countries and offering personal memoirs of computing pioneers. The agenda of the journal *Technology and Culture*, from the Society for the History of Technology, goes even further in its range of subjects; this publication is described as an 'international quarterly dedicated to the historical study of technology and its relations with politics, economics, labor, business, the environment, public policy, science, and the arts'.

The *social historical* perspective is at least equally important, as are the aforementioned areas. According to this view, technology should not be observed in isolation, but rather as related to the social history in general; for example, how the changes in the family or working life, or in the amount of leisure time and money available to people from different social backgrounds are related to the rise of a phenomenon like digital games. This research field can be further divided into several sub-areas: e.g. social history of science and technology, the social–technological developments in different countries, the alternative or subversive histories, where technologies are perceived as socially shaped or constructed, and issues like gender or age being linked to technology in ways that are relevant for the study of digital gaming.

Mentality is a complex concept that can loosely be defined as the 'collective consciousness' of a time. Popular among cultural historians, histories of mentalities try to make sense how certain kind of ideas or practices become prevalent in some contexts. This kind of cultural history can also be related to so-called *microhistories*. Microhistory is history that focuses on a very small scale; typically, a microhistorian might write about a period, mentality or other subject by focusing on a village, community or even an individual. To give an example, for the early history of computer games, the mentality of hackers was important, and Steven Levy's book *Hackers* (1984/1994) is an interesting popular study of the subject.

This short text is an example of an attempt of the last category, *games historiography*, or *meta-history*. This kind of text tries to make sense of how we write about the history of games, what kind of activity it actually is, and what are the narratives, interpretations or other 'discursive rules' that govern this kind of writing. In the future, as there will be more games history in its various forms, there will also be more need for reflection of its basic character.

Defining games

Any attempt to find the 'firsts' or the origins of innovations in the area of digital games will inevitably also end up in the hazy regions of prehistory or the time before actual digital games. But before any historical outline, some reflection is needed on defining the subject of study: what actually is a 'digital game'? Games of this kind can be related to both the emergence of digital technologies and the more general developments in games, toys and play as forms of leisure, culture and business. It is also worth considering where to put the actual emphasis of inquiry; for example, whether in terms of game studies the focus of attention should be on the design of computerized chess, or on the evolution of chess itself, as a game. Scholars working in the field known as media archaeology have aimed to uncover from the 'pre-digital era' various forms of toys and other devices that have opened up the road for the modern media and gaming devices to develop. Adopting a concept from Jay David Bolter and Richard Grusin (1999), it can be said that from this perspective digital games *remediate* activities or forms of representation that have originally appeared elsewhere. The boundaries defining the subject of study for game studies are permeable, forcing us to make a more thorough scrutiny of the basic starting points.

There are inherent challenges in preparing an all-inclusive definition of games or play, as the flexibility, ambiguity and diversity of the phenomena become easily oversimplified in the process. Thinking about definitions is nevertheless valuable, as we need to learn the practice of constantly defining and criticizing our concepts, so that they can evolve further as our learning and understanding develops. There are various attempts at precise definitions that try to capture both the *necessary* and *sufficient* features of games and play. Such careful formulations are particularly instrumental to any *formalist study* of games. In practice, formalism can mean many things as there is a range of different formalist branches of thought within disciplines such as literary studies or mathematics. In our context, the formal study of games focuses on the nature of game and play and aims to provide concepts, models and theories that accurately describe the essential and unique features in game form and its functions. In the context of art criticism, with a special reference to the Russian Formalist school of literary studies, formalism generally emphasizes form over 'content', meaning that the aim of formalist study is not to cover the reference or meaning for some individual, but rather to uncover the functions of the artistic form. A traditional element in such inquiry is to prepare a careful definition of the subject of study; this approach goes back to Aristotle, who argued in his *Posterior Analytics* that scientific knowledge should be based on a set of first principles that are necessarily true and directly knowable. Analogously, starting from faulty premises will just lead into further fallacies.

It is debatable whether any single definition of games will ever be so obviously true that it could not be refuted from some particular angle. This can be related to the cultural approach adopted here: within a cultural frame of thought, the reality of games appears not as something permanent and immutable, but rather as changing and gradually redefined in socio-cultural processes. Nevertheless, for purposes of analysis, the formally exact definitions of games and play help to articulate particular versions of what games are and what they mean; they participate in the evolution of language of game studies, shaping our understanding, and finally such definitions also have an effect on the roles games are granted in our culture. At some point such activity tends to establish *language-games* of its own, to borrow a concept from philosopher Ludwig Wittgenstein; the preparation of a game definition becomes a rule-governed activity which is based on simplification and generalization of the complex reality behind it. The powers and potentials of this kind of definition game can best be illustrated with examples, starting from Roger Caillois, according to whom game playing is:

an activity which is essentially: Free (voluntary), separate [in time and space], uncertain, unproductive, governed by rules, make-believe (Caillois, 1958/2001: 10–11).

The effect of adopting such definition of play is notable on widening the perspective of a games scholar to consider an extensive range of human activity. Pre-digital examples of games playing include the use of certain toys, including the war games played with miniature soldiers, the various sporty 'Cops and Robbers' or football-style street games played both by children and by adults, and the hundreds of different dice, card and board games played throughout the ages. All of them involve 'rules and make-believe' as defined by Caillois, and people play them typically freely in their 'unproductive' leisure time, excited and immersed in action to face the surprises provided by the uncertain outcome. The rules of play associated with toys are, however, not always very clear, and this is where Caillois' distinction between *ludus* and *paidia* (see Chapter 2) becomes useful. The *ludus* games are closer to the type which common language use currently recognizes as games. Caillois is willing to include playing with toys such as the kite or yo-yo into his categories of games, and his approach is therefore extending the conceptual field of game, being in that sense similar to the wide range of play behaviours (discussed below in the context of Sutton-Smith, 1997). It is important to recognize this full field of play phenomena, but a narrower definition of game is also needed for purposes of doing more focused analysis within the game studies and games criticism contexts. Another interesting definition for these purposes is provided by the game designer and researcher Greg Costikyan:

[Game is:] an interactive structure of endogenous meaning that requires players to struggle toward a goal (Costikyan, 2002: 16).

Costikyan's definition comes from an article that is recommendable reading in its entirety as it discusses in detail all steps that are involved in creating this definition. Thereby it provides a logical genealogy or birth history for this particular way of conceptualizing game. For example, the 'endogenous meaning' of this definition is related to the 'separation' of Caillois, and 'magic circle' in Johan Huizinga's *Homo Ludens*. Costikyan explains that the key thing to understand about games is that 'game's structure *creates its own meanings*. The meaning grows out of the structure; it is caused by the structure; it is endogenous to the structure' (ibid.).

The structural formalist definitions have already begun to converge, a number of authors agreeing on several key elements. Jesper Juul has provided a synthesis of game definitions in his study *Half-Real: Video Games between Real Rules and Fictional Worlds* (2005). As an outcome of detailed comparison and analysis of seven such definitions, Juul presents the 'classic game model' as follows:

A game is 1) a rule-based formal system; 2) with variable and quantifiable outcomes; 3) where different outcomes are assigned different values; 4) where the player exerts effort in order to influence the outcome; 5) the player feels emotionally attached to the outcome; 6) and the consequences of the activity are optional and negotiable (Juul, 2005: 6–7).

The earlier work Juul bases his formulation on includes studies by Johan Huizinga (1938/1971), Roger Caillois (1958/2001), Bernard Suits (1978), Elliott M. Avedon and Brian Sutton-Smith (1971), Chris Crawford (1982/1997), David Kelley (1988), and Katie Salen and Eric Zimmerman (2004). Juul's synthesis includes many features that previous authors agree upon while making an informed compromise between the extremes of generality and specificity. When applied to the wide field of contemporary games and game cultures, this model puts certain 'classic games' into the main focus, and certain other ludic forms become excluded by its criteria. As interesting 'borderline cases' Juul discusses phenomena like gambling, games of pure chance, open-ended simulations and pen-and-paper role-playing which share some characteristics with the 'core' phenomena accepted within the classic game model, but not all of them (ibid.: 44). One way of approaching the discrepancy between the definition and the cultural phenomena that is being defined is to point towards cultural and linguistic change. One could claim that modern games have 'evolved' outside the classic game model. Juul states that the history of digital games is partly about departing from the classic model of games, with new games either implementing its features in new ways, or breaking away from it altogether (ibid.: 7, 53–4).

There are even slightly paradoxical issues involved in this kind of attempt at defining a 'moving target'; it appears that some of the most popular and important contemporary forms of games, including open-ended simulations and role-playing games, are not games at all, or 'borderline cases', when classified through such formal definition. Juul's answer is that a definition makes it possible to talk about those things that games do have in common, and also to address the boundaries between games and what is not games. Juul also acknowledges that it has been a mistake of the early ludology not to take into better account the importance of the 'non-gamelike', or representational, fictional world elements that are actually rather central for a typical player experience in contemporary digital games. 'Nevertheless, fiction *matters* in games and it is important to remember the duality of the formal and the experiential perspectives on fiction in games' (ibid.: 199). This is why contemporary games should be described as 'half-real':

Half-Real refers to the fact that video games are two different things at the same time: video games are *real* in that they consist of real rules with which players actually interact, and in that winning or losing a game is a real event. However, when winning a game by slaying a dragon, the dragon is not a real dragon but a fictional one. To play a video game is therefore be interact with real rules while imagining a fictional world, a video game is a set of rules as well as a fictional world. (Ibid.: 1.)

At this point we should pay attention to how a formal definition and theory of games is starting to evolve into different kind of thought, where the internal features of game form are no longer sufficient to explain its basic character. In this manner, the formalist study of games often starts to gain features from cultural or psychological study of games, and vice versa. One of the basic reasons leading into such intermingling of research approaches is rooted in the difficulty of separating a game from its use; particularly, several contemporary digital games appear as rather flexible interactional frameworks which can be played in multiple different ways. Many structures or features of games emerge and make sense in gameplay only due to certain behaviours or certain players. One might speculate that 'pure formalism' might be possible at the level of programme code, but then it would have a rather limited utility for cultural study of digital games.

This book was started with the idea that games take place in a playful interaction, within various cultural contexts, relating both to games as well as players (see Figure 1.1 in Chapter 1). Also Salen and Zimmerman adopt a cultural perspective in their approach to games and playing them in their book *Rules of Play*. Their definition of game is a systems-oriented and formalist one: 'A game is a system in which players engage in an artificial conflict, defined by rules, that result in quantifiable outcome'. (Salen and Zimmerman, 2004: 80.)

From this formal core Salen and Zimmerman move on to embed and intertwine the formal nucleus of game together with the activity of playing, which, in turn, extends the core in a way that makes games capable of providing us with 'meaningful play'. This multi-layered process reveals games' character as deeply cultural constructs:

> *Meaningful play* in a game emerges from the relationship between player action and system outcome; it is the process by which a player takes action within the designed system of a game and the system responds to the action. The *meaning* of an action in a game resides in the relationship between action and outcome. (Salen and Zimmerman, 2004: 34.)

Salen and Zimmerman also define another use for 'meaningful play'; from game design perspective it can be used in evaluative sense as the goal for successful game design, which occurs when 'the relationships between actions and outcomes in a game are both *discernible* and *integrated* into the larger context of the game' (ibid.). Both uses emphasize how the sense of game and its playing rises from within the system and structure of the game itself; in that sense these are formalist definitions. Also in Salen and Zimmerman's model the emphasis put on game–player relationship underlines how the formal system of game is integrated and functional within experiential realms of real players, embedded in and constituted by their social and cultural realities and associated systems of meaning. Salen and Zimmerman call these overlapping circles of signification 'schemas', and point out that these are useful tools for analysis and design of games. There are three primary schemas in their model, *rules*, *play* and *culture* (see Figure 3.1).

The game design schemas are built around these primary schemas and conceptualized as ways of understanding games, 'a lens that we can apply to the analysis or creation of any game' (ibid.). The resulting structure is also useful as a system for understanding the layering of systems of meaning in games. There are more detailed ways in how the various intersecting layers of significance and experience can be presented, and we will return to this in Chapter 6, but at this point it is important to understand that each schema is required, as each of them contribute to games and play their interconnected but distinctive layers of meaning. Salen and Zimmerman argue that this kind of structure forms a conceptual *framework* that is necessary for the study of games, and that it is the role of a framework to organize how this study is carried out.

The aim here has been to point out how formal theories and definitions of games are necessary for understanding the fundamental nature of games, yet they also need to be linked with other – cultural, social, historical and psychological – theories of play, game players and game cultures to situate games and their theories within more comprehensive understanding provided by game studies.

Prehistory of games

Equipped with some conceptual tools for approaching the basic character of game, we can now start off into our path through the history of games and play. The lessons from cultural anthropology tell that the pre-digital history of games is long, indeed, and that games and playing appear to be *cultural universals* – they are found everywhere. The early anthropologists used to relate the birth of

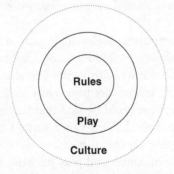

Figure 3.1   Primary Schemas. (Salen and Zimmerman, 2004: 102.)

games to the religious elements that they were interested in studying. Edward Tylor, who is called the founder of anthropology, suggested that dice games have their original roots in *divination*. Chance, represented by the random behaviours of falling stones or bones, reflects the fate or the will of the gods (Tylor, 1879/1971). Division between 'games of chance' and 'games of skill' was the first fundamental classifying distinction made in the study of games, presented by the American anthropologist Stewart Culin in his work *Games of the North American Indians* (1907/1992a; 1907/1992b).

The meanings and practices related to games as parts of the sacred *rituals* or as forms of entertainment were, however, not so far from each other in the non-Western or pre-modern cultures, where spheres of life such as art, religion or entertainment are not as separate from each other and institutionalized as they are in modern Western societies. Sacred and profane uses of games have existed side by side.

The continuous history of bans or restrictions on games playing is also something that tells us how the power of games has been recognized by different societies. There are stories of the madness created by dice in the ancient Indian *Rig Veda*. There were laws against gambling already in Roman times, and not only dice or card games were regulated or banned, but also the currently socially endorsed game of golf was banned at one time by the Scottish parliament (see Avedon and Sutton-Smith, 1971: 22). Current media violence debates and legislative attempts to ban or control digital games are part of a long debate that highlights the cultural ambivalence of games and playing in general.

The exact reasons for each case of games being banned or restricted are complex and individual ones, but it is clear that games are capable of capturing our attention and energy and holding it for extended periods of time. This immersion into games can be perceived as disruptive by the society, or it can be integrated and regulated to become something that a person in that society can do under certain conditions and to a certain extent. The holding power of games is one of the main research problems for any student of games. Why do we play? What are the general or universal elements that are shared by all games and gamers, and what are the particular ones that relate only to certain kind of games? Questions related to gameplay immersion will be discussed further in Chapter 6.

When the digital computing technology was still being invented and developed, there were already early intents and attempts to make games for these new machines. The affinity with games can also indirectly be perceived in the playful relation the innovators have with technology. Following Levy (1984) and other observers, it could be said that 'hacking' is a kind of playing in itself; a hacker enjoys the challenge represented by technology and gets a similar kind of free, self-purposeful pleasure from solving problems, as is generally true of the case of games and play behaviour. Some researchers see the core of playing and games in this kind of dialectic between challenge and reward that a solution or overcoming challenges provides for the player (see Loftus and Loftus, 1983).

As is recorded in the various computer chess histories, already in 1945 mathematician Alan Turing used chess-playing as an example of what a computer could do. The first functional chess program appears to be written in 1950. Chess-playing was early on related to the idea of an artificial intelligence (AI): since a complex set of skills such as playing the 'intellectual' chess game could be programmed into a computer, the expectations were high that computers could soon also be able to have real conversations and be indistinguishable from humans; this ability to carry human-like conversation is known as a 'Turing Test' for a real AI, after scientist Alan Turing.

The later developments in computing have shown that a game of chess with its 64 squares and limited set of movements is, despite its complexities for humans, a relatively easy challenge from a mathematical and computing perspective. In contrast, such basic human skills as understanding natural language or being able to recognize faces or navigate in real environments have appeared to involve such abilities that evolution has provided humans and even some animals, but that are very hard to replicate with even the most powerful of contemporary computers. For some time yet, naturalistic interactions with computers seem to remain merely at the level of toys, whereas the really varied and interesting challenges in social multiplayer situations are presented by other real human beings. As digital environments continue to sophisticate, and gather populations that are composed of humans mixing freely with computer-generated agents, play situations also continue to develop into increasingly complicated and fascinating forms.

In the 1950s the digital domains of today's digital games were still far ahead. Early computers were sometimes referred to as 'electronic brains' in the popular press, but those brains relied on fragile vacuum tubes and manual rewiring, and required the operation of switches to produce results to the mathematical challenges their operators presented them with. The first commercially produced computer UNIVAC (1951) had a construction cost close to one million dollars and was not likely to be used for game playing. Some of its earliest users were the US Census Bureau, the US Air Force and the US Army Map Service. Some electronic but non-digital games were, however, beginning to emerge in another front.

The cultural character and human responses evoked by technology are very much related to the form in which you face it. The early digital computers were hulking machines, confined to laboratories and operated only by specially trained technical personnel. Such technology could not form the foundation for 'media' in the sense of forums for meaningful human interaction, let alone for popular culture. When digital games finally became a cultural and economical phenomenon, they were already relying on a different industrial and technological infrastructure. But the 'prehistory' of that era includes some important innovations influencing or prefiguring the form this new form of entertainment would later take.

One of these early precedents is the first graphical computer game known to exist: a computer version of *Tic-Tac-Toe*, programmed already in 1952 by A. S. Douglas, a Ph.D. student at the University of Cambridge, England (see Figure 3.2). Another one is accredited to researcher Willy Higginbotham, who created a 'physics demonstration' known as *Tennis for Two* in 1958. Working at the Brookhaven National Laboratory, New York, Higginbotham aimed to create something that would capture the attention of laboratory's visitors and provide them with a 'hands-on' experience of the possibilities of the new technology. With his associates, Higginbotham created a simple tennis game, played on a five-inch oscilloscope screen. In contrast to many later digital versions of tennis, this game portrayed the game from a side view, the 'net' presented as a bar in the middle and the ball bouncing over it (or into the net). Based on an analogue computer and a non-programmable assemblage of electromechanical components, the game nevertheless provided players with the means to control the angle of the ball's return and the moment of the hit. It also modelled simple game physics, including gravity, wind speed and bounce, and was thus more advanced than some later digital tennis games (see Figure 3.3). The earliest history of electronic games is complex and, to a large degree, unrecorded. For example, the existence of an even earlier electronic game is known only through a patent application filed in January 1947, registering a 'cathode-ray amusement device' designed for game playing (Goldsmith *et al.*, 1948). This simple game simulated a missile being fired to a

Figure 3.2 *Tic-Tac-Toe*, created by A. S. Douglas, 1952. [Image credit: Martin Campbell-Kelly, Department of Computer Science, University of Warwick.]

Figure 3.3   *Tennis for Two* – a screenshot and a controller. [Image credit: *www.bnl.gov*, Brookhaven National Laboratory.]

target and several knobs were used to adjust the speed and curve of the point marking the missile.

The digital tennis, rather than the radar simulation, would later re-emerge as the first commercially successful video game. Long surrounded by patent disputes, the now accepted industry historical view is that engineer Ralph Baer first developed the concept and the working system for playing games on a television set in 1966–1969. Originally manufactured by Sanders Associates, and later licensed to Magnavox, the equipment became known as the Magnavox Odyssey 1 TL200 and arrived to the market late in 1971. The system came with twelve games, many of them relying on players to attach plastic overlays to the television screen; 'play money' and dice were also used in some Odyssey games, carrying such names as *Cat and Mouse, Football, Ski, Roulette*, and *Haunted House*. Perhaps the most basic of the games was *Table Tennis*, a ping-pong game that Nolan Bushnell, founder of Atari, saw in a demonstration in May 1972. Atari's own arcade ping-pong game, known as *Pong* (1972), became a huge success soon after release; Bushnell has said that a total of 38 000 Pong machines were installed and sold. Atari also had to pay a reported $700 000 to acquire the official licence from Baer and Magnavox for their digital table-tennis game (see Baer's own account in his book *Videogames: In the Beginning* [2005]).

It is important to note that neither of these games involved radically original gameplay concepts: both *Tic-Tac-Toe* and tennis were games that people were already familiar with from their non-digital versions and knew how to play. The situation with the third 'prehistorical' game example is slightly different.

Computer company Digital Equipment Corporation (DEC) had donated their PDP-1 mini-computer (a large mainframe by contemporary standards) to Massachusetts Institute of Technology with hopes that the MIT would come up with innovative new uses for their technology. Tech Model Railroad Club (TMRC), a group of students enthusiastic about playing with the possibilities of technology, got their hands on the PDP-1 and came up with a plan to make a game with it. Steve 'Slug' Russell, who did most of the game programming,

41

was a fan of science fiction and designed a game to be a duel of two spaceships. Two players would control either a needle- or wedge-shaped rocket and fire torpedoes while trying to avoid being shot. Later a background of stars and a central sun with gravity were added. Originally conceived in 1961 and made playable in 1962, *Spacewar!* took Russell reportedly more than 200 hours of work to complete, but remained also finally open for constant additions such as the 'hyperspace' function which made the spaceship suddenly vanish and reappear in a random position. This fast-paced computer game and the hacker culture creating, playing and constantly modifying it fitted well into the general countercultural developments in the 1960s and early 1970s (Brand, 1972).

Another important direction for studying the prehistory of digital games is the history of mechanical entertainment in general. The very early digital games were technical demonstrations that were created not with entertainment business use in mind, but the culture of pinball machines, sports and other play and game forms surrounded the early experimenter. Slug Russell, for example, says that it was only after making *Spacewar!* that he realized fundamental similarities with a pinball machine (Herz, 1997: 12; cf. Levy, 1984/1994: 65). Popular among the MIT staff and students, the game was never released to larger audiences. An early commercial adaptation, *Computer Space* (Nutting Associates, 1971) by Nolan Bushnell and Ted Dabney failed commercially, demonstrating the need to understand the differences between various groups of players and their game cultures. The game concept, challenge level and controls that were right for the MIT hackers were apparently too alien and complex for the customers of bars and early gaming arcades.

Apart from some publications from coin machine hobbyists and collectors, the history of pinball arcades and other sites for mechanical entertainment is a not very well researched area, possibly because of the seeming banality of this kind of low entertainment. (For an exception, see Huhtamo, 2005.) The classic coin-operated machines were sitting at the corner of a bar, or attracting passers-by in 'games arcades' next to other diversions like movie theatres or restaurants. Attractive to people of all ages, slot machines hold an ambiguous position. The classic slot machine, or 'one-armed bandit', was built by Charles Fey, a San Francisco car mechanic in 1895, and provided a simple and effective means for gambling. Even prior to that, there existed a long history of 'penny arcades', shooting galleries and other fairground attractions. The cultural history of fun fairs, on its part, goes back long into history, including the carnivals of the antiquity. Carnivals were and continue to be celebrations that inverse the usual order of things and offer their participants a 'semi-regulated' way to engage with some curious, frightening, titillating or other experiences uncommon or suppressed in our more regulated lives. A look into the cultural history of game arcades opens up many further directions for study, where one of the fundamental issues concerns the cultural character of play: what happens when we play, and why we do it in the first place?

As introduced by the previous chapters, play and games hold a particular place in human cultures and societies. Stepping aside from the history of individual games for a moment, in this subchapter the focus will be on games as play and on the emergence of digital technologies as particular kind of sites for these activities. As games have moved from streets and living room tables into various computer systems, the associated activity has also altered its character, or, at least, gained different dimensions. Engaging in a digital gameplay session also necessarily means *play with/in machine*. Therefore, game studies need take into account both the particular character of game playing, as well as the more general issues influencing human–computer relationship.

There is a long history of thought which honours play with a very special place in culture. Johan Huizinga and Roger Caillois, who have been mentioned in previous chapters, are parts of a tradition of thought reaching back into early romanticism and beyond. Influencing the French Revolution, Jean-Jacques Rousseau wrote about the idea of freedom and 'natural man' in his works *Social Contract* and *Emily: or, On Education* (both from the same year, 1762). The German poet and playwright Friedrich Schiller called attention to the link which connected play as free and deeply human behaviour to these revolutionary thoughts in his essay *On the Aesthetic Education of Man* (Schiller, 1795/1983: 107) – to quote:

> man only plays when he is in the fullest sense of the word a human being, and *he is only fully human being when he plays.* [Emphasis in the original.]

In the history of thought, Schiller was an influence to other theorists of play. Adopting a more natural sciences inspired approach, Herbert Spencer, a British philosopher, formulated in his work *The Principles of Psychology* (1880) a theory of play as 'surplus energy'. Influenced by theories of Darwin, according to this view it often happens in 'more evolved creatures' that there is an energy 'somewhat in excess of immediate needs', which produces a pressure to engage in otherwise 'superfluous and useless exercise of faculties' – that is, play (Burghardt, 1984: 16). The surplus energy theory holds that an instinct to play has risen to consume the extra resources, and it still has some support among scientists, albeit in modified forms. However, mostly surplus explanations are superseded by various practice theories, which consider learning as the root of playing or which hold that the main evolutionary benefit from play is that it enhances behavioural flexibility. (Burghardt, 1984; Byers, 1984.)

Brian Sutton-Smith, one of the leading modern scholars of play, has paid much attention to the deeply elusive fundamental character of play, and he has noted how play appears to refute any single theory, continuing to taunt generations of theorists. In his work *The Ambiguity of Play* (1997), Sutton-Smith connects this fundamental ambiguity firstly with the diversity of play itself; almost anything can occur within its boundaries. To illustrate this, he provides a long list of various play phenomena, organized from private to more public ones: mind *or* subjective play (e.g. daydreams, role-playing games), solitary play (e.g. hobbies, collections), playful behaviours (e.g. playing tricks, playing around), informal social play (e.g. joking, parties), vicarious audience play (e.g. television, rock music), performance play (e.g. playing music, being a play actor), celebrations and festivals (e.g. birthdays, carnivals), contests, games and sports (e.g. athletics, gambling), risky and deep play (e.g. caving, hang gliding) (Sutton-Smith, 1997: 4–5).

Rather than reducing the inherent differences and complexities of this wide field under a single totalizing theory, Sutton-Smith prefers to organize different play theories under seven distinct 'rhetorics' or ways of speaking about play. Starting here from the ancient discourses, Sutton-Smith discusses Play as Fate (including theories of luck, chance and gods controlling human life), Play as Power (which emphasizes the links of play to warfare, athletics and contests), Play as Identity (here nature of play is seen as ways of confirming the communal identity in festivals and celebrations) and Play as Frivolity (which emphasizes the subversive and carnivalesque potentials of play). Sutton-Smith moves into the modern discourses while discussing Play as Progress (play is seen as something intimately connected with growth and evolution of children and animals), Play as the Imaginary (play as art, or as having its own separate reality) and Play as the Self (play is considered principally as fun and relaxing activity where individuals aim for balance of their skills and challenges) (ibid.: *passim*).

For game studies, Sutton-Smith's studies are valuable in pointing out the multiplicity of playing, and how those contemporary forms of culture that we recognize as games are only a subset of much larger phenomena and field of research. It is necessary for a scholar of games to be aware of the history of play scholarship, because of the intimate relationship between these two key concepts. Simultaneously, aiming to understand the specific forms into which digital games and their playing have evolved during the last decades will require more particular theories about contemporary games. As discussed above, Jesper Juul has argued that many contemporary video games differ from what he calls a 'classic game model' in that they take place in a fictional world, whereas most traditional games are abstract, including most classic board and card games and sports. Similarly, it is possible to argue that the different types of play behaviours as discussed by Sutton-Smith can all take place within contemporary digital games. For example, in online virtual game worlds (see Chapter 7) it is possible to meet virtual or mediated versions of most of Sutton-Smith's categories, ranging from in-game celebrations and festivities, different forms of performance play and virtual-world–embedded versions of contests and sports as well. The seven play rhetorics can be applied to the discussion and study of these virtual play phenomena, but with that cautious note that virtual distance and separation from face-to-face interaction with other players has its own consequences for the interpretation of the phenomena.

As performance, play of games can also be situated within the larger field of human actions that is explored within the performance studies. A scholar and experimental theatre director, Richard Schechner, has helped establishing the field with his several books and as the editor of *TDR: The Journal of Performance Studies*. Pioneered by the approach developed by Erving Goffman, a Canadian sociologist, in his *The Presentation of Self in Everyday Life* (1959), performance studies look at the full range of human actions in social situations and point out how our actions are structured according to certain socially sanctioned models. Providing a social interactionist perspective, Goffman defines performance as 'all the activity of a given participant on a given occasion which serves to influence in any way of the other participants' (ibid.: 15). This also involves games and is not limited to the study of so-called role-playing games, even if Goffman's work has become a particularly important influence within this subfield of game studies (see Chapter 5). Even those games that are played alone, like many single-player computer or console games, can be interpreted as a performance within social interactionist framework, because of the fundamentally social character of our self. Playing a certain game affects not only the way other persons perceive the individual in question, but also the way she perceives herself. In an extreme case, game playing might even be something a person tries to deny from herself, because it is incompatible with her self-image, or something to keep hidden and silent. Thus, a person can consider game playing to be something belonging only to her private self, or, on the contrary, celebrate it as a visible part of her 'front', or public interpersonal self in Goffman's terminology. Performances serve a wide variety of human needs, and to illustrate this, Richard Schechner has organized the functions of performance into seven interlocking spheres (see Figure 3.4).

Such models emphasize that as performances games come into being, or take place, within the socio-cultural networks of human action and thought, they consequently provide their players (and also observing non-players) with opportunities to experience beauty and entertainment, or community feeling, and also to engage and deal with the learning experiences, persuasive messages, opportunities for identity construction or even personal healing or recovery. At their symbolical level some contemporary games quite often also deal with confronting the demonic or divine figures and themes. But these kinds of function are not necessarily visible from games as objects; a cultural function is a feature of play performance and thus something situational and optional. Only when a game is positioned and adopted for use within the lives of individuals or in particular subcultures do such functions start to have an effect. Thus, games that appear as *potential* sites for performative meaning-making, and related individual and social commitments into games, ranging from highly intensive to most casual, have an effect on what kind of significance becomes realized (see the previous chapter).

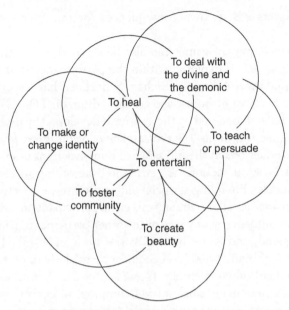

Figure 3.4   The seven interlocking spheres of performance. (Schechner, 2002: 39.)

There remains some indecisiveness regarding how exactly play and games are related within the wider field of performances. In his textbook of performance studies, Schechner makes two attempts in providing this kind of performance continuum; the first consists of a single continuum, forming the following range of phenomena:

play–games–sports–pop entertainments–performing arts–daily life–ritual.

The second modified model considers the continuum between *play* and *ritual* as a more general performative scale of their own, underlying and supporting the other human activities where games and daily life form the opposite poles. (ibid.: 42)

Similar to Caillois' model which positioned more 'playful' *paidia* together with more 'strictly structured' *ludus* as attitudes that can be applied to any of his game categories, the latter alternative of Schechner's model suggests that play and ritual are fruitfully conceived as fundamental attitudes that can be adopted across the full range of human performance. Revisiting Bertrand Russell's example of a game, cricket, Schechner points out that the 'same game' can be played in very different ways.

> Cricket at a test match is not the same as that played on a neighbourhood oval. And cricket in the Trobriand Islands, where it was changed into a ritual encounter

between towns, with the home team always winning, and where it features dancing as much as hitting and fielding, is something else again. (Ibid.: 42.)

But, as Schechner reminds us, certain generalizations can be made; within game studies, formal models and theories of games are also needed, addressing the internal organization of game form and facilitating comparisons between game types, thus leading into better understanding of game genres. Formal theories of games are necessary for complementing the cultural theories of play.

Huizinga introduced the scholarly community to the question of ritual and its cultural relation to play by making it a central issue in *Homo Ludens*. Observing contemporary computer game playing quickly reveals many surface similarities to rituals; such behaviours often take place in darkened rooms, remaining intensely focused on screens, and are thus circumscribed within the altar-like separation of game space from common reality. Also, the repeated, ritualistic character of endless jumping, climbing, fighting or navigating in labyrinths and other obscure quests that digital game players regularly take upon themselves to carry through hold structural similarities with ancient ritualistic behaviours. Nevertheless, game playing seems to belong to the domain of non-serious 'leisure activities', which appear to be the opposite of serious religious rituals. Actually it is perfectly possible to engage in 'game playing' in the honour of gods or spirits in several cultures; even the origin of the Olympic Games is a good example for this. It is not necessary to approach all games and all acts of playing them as rituals, or from a ritualistic perspective, but it is helpful to notice the similarities. As Huizinga asserts, the 'ritual act has all the formal and essential characteristics of play [...], particularly in so far as it transports the participants to another world' (Huizinga, 1938/1971: 18). Rather than considering gameplay as a subset and derivative of rituals or religious impulse, Huizinga is willing to place rituals and other forms of more 'serious' cultural activities as derived from the original play impulse and behaviour.

The cultural perspective on games is important while considering also the developmental aspects of game playing. Digital games and other play forms are situated within large and complex networks of various culturally inherited structures, including the structures of language, behaviour and thought that we are both aware and, perhaps even more importantly, not aware of. When we are children and start playing for the first time, we most probably have no conscious theories of what we are doing. Yet, this realm of activities reaching into un- or preconscious stages in our being is very central for our growing up into functional human beings. Vivian Gussin Paley, a recognized figure in study of play and child development, argues in her book *A Child's Work* (2004) for the importance of fantasy play. She observes kindergarten-age children playing almost obsessively 'Tom and Jerry' in different violent variations and refers back to Russian psychologist Lev Vygotsky to point out that in play a child 'stands taller than himself', above his age and ordinary behaviour.

> Pretending is the most open-ended of all activities, providing the opportunity to escape the limitations of established rituals. Pretending enables us to ask 'What if?' (Paley, 2004: 92.)

As we learn more about the important role that fantasy play holds in the life of children, we also need to examine more carefully the roles it has on adult life as well. Gerard Jones, an American author, has made keen observations of young people and contemporary digital games, arguing that those, often rather violent, game fantasies, are important vehicles for powerful and conflicting emotions these teenagers are already experiencing. According to this view such violently themed games provide opportunities to feel powerful and in control in a complex society which often limits the possibilities for those experiences not only for children and young people, but for individuals of any age (Jones, 2002). There are probably many such 'unconscious' uses of games, which further research will illustrate even better.

One of the most central structures in cultural processes was analysed by the French anthropologist Arnold van Gennep in his work *The Rites of Passage* (1908/2004). Rites of passage are rituals which many societies utilize during moments of important change in the life cycle of individuals. Such transitions as moving from the status of child to that of adult, from being single to being married or from alive to dead are points where rites of passage are customarily taking place in most societies. van Gennep pointed how these rituals follow a three-part structure, where the first phase is separation, the second transition and the final phase is incorporation to the new status and order of things. At the second phase, at the 'threshold' (Lat. *limen*) between two rather stable categories a period and area of ambiguity takes place, as neither the old nor the new structure of meaning applies. Researched further by such thinkers as Mary Douglas and Victor Turner, the 'liminal', as the associated category for the culturally ambiguous, in-between states, has proved to be important also for understanding the late modern societies and seemingly innocuous forms of entertainment such as games and play.

Victor Turner, who is the foremost proponent of liminality as a concept for cultural analysis, has pointed out that there are important differences in the social and cultural organization between tribal, pre-industrial and other 'total communities' as compared with the culturally complex and pluralistic life of late modernity. As Turner moved in his approach, which he called comparative symbology, into the study of complex societies, he also introduced the term 'liminoid' to denote the quasi-liminal character of modern cultural performances. According to Turner, liminality appears as ambiguously appealing because of the liberation it promises from normative constraints associated with social roles. Associated with 'communitas', the ideal experience of unity between people, liminality provides access to 'anti-structure' and the 'liberation of human capacities of cognition, affect, volition, creativity, etc.' it entails. (Turner, 1982: 44.)

Games and play are liminoid phenomena in Turner's analysis, and he links them to *flow* experience as analysed by psychologist Mihaly Csikszentmihalyi. Csikszentmihalyi has described the loss of sense of time and self, combined with a complete focus on the task at hand, often experienced during demanding exercise, artistic performance or within similar extreme undertakings. The key precondition for this immensely rewarding state appears to be suitable balance between the skills and challenges. If the challenge is too easy for our current skill level, we lose interest, and if it is too demanding, we become frustrated. This is something that good game designers regularly take into consideration. Reaching flow can have a powerful impact, and Csikszentmihalyi speaks about a sense of discovery, as flow state pushes the person to higher levels of performance and thereby even into inner transformation, or 'growth of self' (Csikszentmihalyi, 1991: 74). Turner recognizes the similarity of flow phenomenon with his 'communitas', but whereas flow is experienced within an individual, communitas is evident between or among individuals. From a Turnerian perspective, game playing then appears at least dual in character: games can be both conceptualized as settings or spaces for liminoid entertainment, and as a technique or attempt to reach a temporary communitas feeling and the associated liberation from pervasive socio-cultural structures (Turner, 1982: 55, 58).

Such themes as the anti-structure and the possible subversive or liberating potentials of games are important for more thorough cultural–psychological study of games in culture. More particularly, there are occasional public debates that focus on the representations of virtual violence, supernatural, occult or demonic imagery within certain popular digital games. An important theorist in this regard is the Russian philosopher Mikhail Bakhtin who has posited *carnivalesque* as a particular kind of cultural category, which stands in opposition to the official and serious life. He has examined its qualities in literature as well as in cultural history and states that obscenities, amoral laughter, debasing acts, wanton cruelty or grotesque imagery are all classic elements of the carnivalesque. Bakhtin's examples are from the antiquity and the Middle Ages, but some contemporary scholars have begun to pay attention also to the ways in which similar dynamic and controversial elements play a role in the modern 'low culture', explaining both some of its popularity and simultaneous rejection from the 'official' culture. The playful, ludic nature at the heart of games involves transporting us into a state where we are governed by rules other than our regular working days. But the liberation from everyday social norms and rules does not imply that the alternative digital worlds would be without a logic of their own. Bakhtin points out that within the carnival logic all hierarchical value opposites were reversed in parodies and comic crownings of fools. He also claims that during carnival time 'life is subject only to its laws,

PLAY AND GAMES IN HISTORY

that is, the laws of its own freedom' – thereby being very similar to the 'magic circle' of play as conceived by Johan Huizinga (Bakhtin, 1965/1984: 7, 11). Thus, digital games appear to offer fruitful opportunities for interpretation as practices and places with potentially subversive or carnivalesque potentials.

Summary and conclusions

- The way we organize and record the history of games affects the way we perceive the nature and significance of games, ranging from primarily technological or economical to artistic or social–historical understanding of games.
- Similar fundamental roles for game studies are occupied by the definitions of game and play. There are several formal game definitions introduced in this chapter, followed by the conclusion that they have to be combined to a more comprehensive framework of game, player and culture in order to profitably function in a game studies context.
- In the prehistory of games the sacred and profane uses were closely connected together and games served a wide range of purposes in social and individual life. The holding power of games is also evidenced in the long history of bans and restrictions set for game playing.
- The first generation of digital games appears to have been created as outcomes of self-purposeful play with the challenges presented by electronics, and as demonstrations of the capabilities of new technology, but these experiments were soon followed by commercial enterprises. Early digital games also extended the play styles and game cultures born around earlier non-digital game devices like pinball machines.
- Theories and discourses of play are numerous, matching the diversity and scope of play phenomena. Situated within the continuum of human performances, game play holds a resemblance to ritual and can provide modern humans with 'liminoid' escapes from their social roles and related constraints.

Suggested further reading

James Newman, chapter 2, 'What Is a Videogame? Rules, Puzzles and Simulations. Defining the Object of Study'. In: James Newman (ed), *Videogames*. London: Routledge, 2004, pp. 9–28.

Assignment: Remediation of a non-digital game

Compare an existing, non-digital game with its digitalized version. The aim is to become more aware of the possible unique strengths or weaknesses that digital technology contributes to games.

Pick a game that exists both in a digital and non-digital version. Write a short analysis in which you compare the ways how such game elements as controls, game mechanics, visuals and possible social interaction are similarly or differently handled in the digital vs. non-digital version. Discuss the comparative strengths and weaknesses of digital games.

(Associated research methods: structural gameplay analysis, comparative game analysis.)

4

DUAL STRUCTURE AND THE ACTION GAMES
OF THE 1970s

Digital games as multi-layered meaning-making systems

In the previous chapter we discussed the multiple historical perspectives where digital games can be approached from. One key issue is how to understand the role of digital technology in the phenomenon we are interested in.

There are numerous aspects of digital games that are not unique to them. For example, if you think how popular such a simulated card game as *Solitaire* has been among the millions of Windows operating system users, it soon becomes clear that many of the digital games are in fact remediated, or 'disguised' versions of non-digital ones.

There is nevertheless an argument to be made for the specificity of digital games, too. The absolute majority of digital games is based on screens of various kinds; this dominance of audiovisual technology is reflected also in the terms of 'television games' or 'video games' sometimes being used as synonyms for digital games as a whole. Terminology also carries a particular kind of power with it: for instance, reading Ralph Baer's views on the 'invention of video game' (Baer, 1996, 2005), it is clear that he prefers to talk about 'video games', since video electronics technology, related to cathode ray tubes (CRT) and television sets, is that background context in which Baer started making games, as a television engineer.

Digital games have a close relationship with the advances of technology. The existence of consumer electronics as a whole is of course dependent on integrated circuits and the subsequent drop in prices. Early games such as *Tennis for Two* or *Spacewar!* were developed or used as demonstrations of the powers of new technology. Very few software applications are capable of delivering similar experience of genuine and rewarding interaction with the system as digital games do. It can be said that *interactivity* is what games are and what they do, at the very core of gameplay. Since those games which are capable of presenting us with images and audio are also live audiovisual presentations, they can be used as spectacles of novel technologies, enjoyable precisely because they show us something we have never seen before. Each subsequent generation of digital games has been visually different from the previous one. (The recent revival of 'previous generation' games in hand-held devices and in retro-gaming, in general, affirms rather than negates the rule.)

The game software and the game technology hardware can be separated, but only with some violence. Games are 'ported' to other gaming platforms, sometimes with success and sometimes not. Old games which were programmed to be run on old arcade machines or home consoles can be transferred to the screen of a contemporary personal computer, but the gameplay experience will not be the same. The controls, possible special cabinet, size of screen, quality of audio are all factors that contribute to the total gameplay experience, as well as do the surroundings where the game is played. Playing with a special arcade machine, in a noisy and crowded games arcade, surrounded by other gamers, is a different kind of experience from that of a solitary play session on the home PC.

Thus, even if it is important to understand that a game can be approached as something separate from the programming code or hardware used for its particular implementation, gamers face only particular, fully implemented digital games, not universal or abstract ones as defined only by their rule-sets. It is in those implementations that technologies play an important role. This is reflected in the way popular histories of digital games tend to present games as a succession of generations, identified on the basis of the hardware used. The advances or changes in the quality or character of core gameplay, in contrast, are not as clearly perceivable as the more surface-level changes that are related to the apparent themes of games or game visuals, where the more powerful processors, graphics chips or increasing memory of new game technologies are a background factor.

It is also important to realize the tight interconnection and interwoven character of gameplay and representation in games. The abstract rule-set of games can be implemented in various ways, but in digital games this actual implementation plays a major role. There is also player activity involved in both dimensions, at the core and shell. Markku Eskelinen (2001) has called these configurative and interpretative user functions, and sees configurative activity as the dominant one in games and the gaming situation as a 'combination of ends, means, rules, equipment, and manipulative action'. However, even if the interactive dimension of gameplay is a necessary condition for games to be games, there is always also interpretative activity involved: in the end, we cannot escape our human capacity to interpret meaning into sign systems and phenomena.

Particularly from historical perspective, the role of gaming hardware is relevant for understanding the quality of gameplay in digital games. Technological decisions influence how the game looks, sounds and feels, like using raster rather than vector graphics, having game sequences as digitized video playback rather than generating everything in real time, or having synthesized audio in contrast to digital samples. A student of games needs to be able to make distinctions both in terms of the core gameplay or rules of interaction, as well as in the multiple layers of audiovisual and tangible realities built on top of them.

Nolan Bushnell writes in his 1996 paper 'Relationship between Fun and the Computer Business' of the history of computing and the changes it has brought: in 1971 monitors were still rare with computers and typical interfaces were punched cards, paper tape or output from large line printers. Bushnell perhaps exaggerates in his claim that 'game industry invented user interfaces', but, nevertheless, he had learned from his own experience that non-specialist users do not read manuals: as mentioned above, his first coin-operated game *Computer Space* (1971) was based on the MIT hackers' classic *Spacewar!* However, a game that had been a success in the university context proved to be too complicated for the general audience of the time. Bushnell underlines that the games industry has pioneered the development of non-keyboard interfaces, immersive microworlds or digital 'alternative realities' and the use of anthropomorphic characters. Games have also provided a model how to optimize the learning curve so that the user's skills are gradually tested and balanced with increasing challenges.

The later symbiosis between games and hardware industry is clearly visible in the advertisements and sponsorship that many processor or graphics card manufacturers place in games-related events and media. The utility programs like spreadsheets or word processors do not necessarily demand that kind of computing power which is the contemporary standard, so much of the pressure has for decades been coming from games, competing for attention by offering ever more spectacular graphics, physics modelling and booming multi-channel audio. These, in turn, require more memory, faster processors and better graphics cards. When these kinds of systems are on the market, it is possible for the operating system manufacturer to provide more aesthetic and enjoyable experiences for the office machine user, too. Thus, influences and relationships through and around gaming technologies fork into multiple directions.

'Moore's Law', the doubling of computer power every eighteen months, has long maintained its role as the cornerstone of the constant progression of hardware technologies. However, the technological focus is increasingly challenged by the content and user-centred approaches, both in business and in academic sector. A superior technology does not equal to a superior game. Even in graphics-intensive areas as in photorealistic character animation, some experts are saying that technology itself is no longer giving significant competitive advances. Advanced technology might even be holding games development down, if the demands (and economical risks) to hire and train teams of dozens, even hundreds of professionals to implement a single games project decrease experimentation and artistic creativity. The focus of a game historian should therefore be neither on the 'latest and greatest' products, nor on the one-dimensional perception where the history of games is built only on technological progress.

The dictionary definitions of the word 'classic' refer to its etymology in French or Latin: originally borrowed from the French *classique*, which is derived from Latin *classicus* meaning of the highest class of Roman citizens, of the first rank, from the root 'classis' (*Merriam-Webster*). The key meanings of the use of a term like 'classic' are related to the need for a 'standard of excellence' which we refer to when we carry on discussions that compare, contextualize and, in general, make sense of the object or topic in question. Some of the key meanings of a 'classic' are that it is something of 'recognized value', 'enduring' and 'historically memorable.' The last use of 'classic' is related to its meaning as something that is authentic or typical representative of a period or development.

The talk about classic games is closely linked with another concept: 'canon'. Particularly in art and literary history, canon is the body of 'great works' that a civilized person is expected to be familiar with while engaged in discussions about art. The origins of this use are in Latin and religious history, where 'canon' is an authoritative list of books accepted as Holy Scripture. This origin of the concept also helps to understand why there is often controversy around any construction of canon: it is a normative concept (Guillory, 1993).

This chapter will provide some historical examples of digital games that can be considered representative, influential and popular during their period and/or later, thereby making them 'classic games'. Whenever this kind of selection is done, it will for practical reasons be small, omitting representatives from entire genres and subgenres that are certainly important and 'classic' for many gamers. It is probably also biased, in the normative sense typical for canon formation: it is an attempt to find historically significant games, thereby passing over thousands of games that could probably better represent the tastes of some gamer demographics. As every selection is necessarily biased, the reader is invited to challenge and question the version of games history represented here. The suggested assignment at the end of this chapter is offered to encourage explorations of 'non-canonical' games, and creation of alternative games histories.

There are many sources of game history that offer much more thorough treatments, some mentioned in the attached information box.

Box 4.1 ON THE HISTORY OF DIGITAL GAMES

The Ultimate History of Video Games: From Pong to Pokémon – The Story Behind the Craze That Touched Our Lives and Changed the World, by Steven L. Kent (2001)

Supercade: A Visual History of the Videogame Age 1971–1984, by Van Burnham (2001)

Box 4.1   cont'd

Arcade Fever – The Fan's Guide to The Golden Age of Video Games, by John Sellers (2001)

Power-Up: How Japanese Video Games Gave the World an Extra Life, by Chris Kohler (2005)

High Score! The Illustrated History of Electronic Games, Second Edition, by Rusel DeMaria and Johnny L. Wilson (2004)

Game Over – Press Start to Continue: How Nintendo Conquered the World, by David Sheff and Andy Eddy (1999)

Joystick Nation: How Video Games Gobbled Our Money, Won Our Hearts, and Rewired Our Minds, by J. C. Herz (1997)

Trigger Happy: The Inner Life of Video Games, by Steven Poole (2000).

Three decades of digital games: The rise of modern information society

In this textbook we are dealing principally with phenomena taking place in three decades: the 1970s, 1980s and 1990s, including some developments from the early years of the new millennium. This narrowing of scope is based on the 1960s and preceding decades being here classified as the 'prehistory' of digital games, and on the other hand the first decade of the new millennium is still continuing and being too close for historical summaries.

There are various conceptions of how significant each of these decades has been for the development of digital games and game cultures. It can be considered as symptomatic of the current early stage in games historiography, that various authors do not agree on the exact years of the periods in games history they discuss. The expression of the 'golden age' of video games can refer to the years 1978–1981 (Herman *et al.*, 2002), 1978–1985 (Sellers, 2001: 10), 1971–1983 (Stahl, 2005) or 1971–1984 (Burnham, 2001). One feature that is shared by these early game histories is, nevertheless, that they put much emphasis on the 1970s and early 1980s, while paying lessening attention towards the late 1980s and the 1990s. If these accounts are to be followed, it appears that most of the historically significant games were published in the first one or two decades of digital game design, after which creativity started to decline. This may, of course, also be a perspective error, remedied by later research that will better perceive what is the unique identity and contribution of each period in the evolution of this history.

In her book *Supercade* (2001: 23), Van Burnham writes how she sees this 'golden age of videogames' as the transition point when society shifted from analogue to digital culture. She makes the point on how the 'future of technology' was made accessible – and fun – to a whole generation through the rise of video games.

In social historical terms, a popular digital game is rooted in the rise of affluence and free time in the late industrial societies. The increasing role of leisure and hobbies has been rising to the focus of research, too. For example, *Hobbies: Leisure and the Culture of Work in America* by Steven M. Gelber (1999) points out how 'hobbies' are activities that reflect and reproduce the values and activities typical to the working place even while presenting themselves as a break from work. Typically, hobbies such as collecting or engaging with various home crafts imitate the operation of the marketplace and bring utilitarian rationality into homes. On the other hand, a sociologist like Anthony Giddens pays attention to the self-centred character of late modernity; in his *Modernity and Self-Identity: Self and Society in the Late Modern Age* (1991), Giddens argues that modernity is characterized by the 'reflexive project of the self'. Politics becomes 'life politics' and life decisions or lifestyle choices like hobbies and other leisure activities central parts in realizing this project. Games can be interpreted to play their own role in this transformation of the late modern society, as they take their place as popular leisure activities.

One way to conceptualize this change is to look at the role information technologies, in general, play in our lives. The favourite name for this development has been 'information society' (as discussed by, e.g. Yoneji Masuda, Alvin Toffler and Manuel Castells, who uses the term 'informational society'). The key idea in this line of thinking is that industrialized countries are transforming into 'post-industrial societies' where traditional industry work will no longer be the main source of income. Instead, our work and lives are inextricably linked with knowledge and information in its various forms.

A digital game is immaterial information – software code – at its heart; therefore, the rise of the games industry is an interesting example of the information economy in action. The obvious volatility of the games business is also symptomatic of the challenges to this 'new economy'. Games business has repeatedly rapidly expanded and dramatically collapsed, most notably in 1977 and 1983 in the USA, and thereby foreshadowing the 'dot-com crash' of 2000–2002. These highly publicized downfalls (based on the unrealistic future expectations and poor-quality products) hide behind them the slower but undeniable growth in the role of digital technologies in everyday life. Digital games have been increasing in presence and spread from laboratories to arcades, homes and the pockets in the forms of mobile games. While the US arcade revenues reached the 5 billion dollar point during the pre-crash year 1981 (Kent, 2001: xiii), in 2004 various estimations of the size of the global market for leisure software were reaching figures around 20–30 billion dollars.

There is the larger debate whether 'information society' is a correct concept at all to describe the world we live in. Large parts of the world still live without food and water, not to mention telephones or other emblems of technological lifestyle. In those countries where information and communication technologies do have a larger role, the utility software sales are generally dwarfed in comparison with the interest in games. (Microsoft operating system upgrades as the possible exception.) In the Internet, too, the services that people are actually willing to pay for are dominated by online games. There are some researchers who say that rather than 'information society', we have entered the time of either 'media society' or 'experience society' where the real currency is the value of the experience people derive from the activities they engage in.

Games in the 1970s: Learning the lexicon

The political and social climate of the 1970s was characterized by the tensions between East and West, South and North, at the same time when economical affluence and technological advances were radically changing the lifestyles of a few million people, leaving others aside. Cold War, moon trips, Watergate, rise of pop and rock cultures and the images from famines and catastrophes sent to the Western television screens are just some features of the news landscape surrounding the birth of video games as popular culture.

It is easy to see references to the surrounding world already in the earliest digital games, thereby making their traditional role as escapist diversion a bit more complicated. The spaceships in the MIT hackers' *Spacewar!* (introduced in Chapter 3) hark back to the conquest of space as the final frontier ruling the scientific(tional) imaginations of the twentieth century. It is also possible to see echoes of the Cold War in the quiet battle of two different spaceships, struggling over the annihilation of the other party and the survival of one's own. The iconic video game of the 1970s, however, did derive its inspiration from more peaceful sources.

Pong (1972): Introducing enjoyable core gameplay

The stories surrounding the creation of *Pong* are well covered both in the Internet fan sites and in literature (like *Videogames: In the Beginning* by Ralph H. Baer [2005] and the website *www.pong-story.com*). The perspective is usually one of industry histories, focusing on the debate (and eventual legal battles) on who 'invented' *Pong*, and was therefore entitled to the royalties, as well as the place in history. The game itself is often cast aside in these presentations. It is, nevertheless, curious that Willy Higginbotham created a tennis game as the first electronic (demonstration) game in his *Tennis for Two*, and both Ralph Baer (creator of the first video game system, Odyssey) and Nolan Bushnell (founder of Atari) ended up with the same basic game idea, apparently without knowledge of Higginbotham's demonstration.

Despite its simplicity, *Pong* deserves careful attention in a game studies context. Part of the legal troubles surrounding *Pong* is related to how the fundamental character of a ping-pong game like it holds in the birth of interactive entertainment and how it exemplifies the early spatial dynamics of digital games, in addition to the basic dynamics of competitive conflict. Three key success factors can be analysed in its core gameplay: (1) easy-to-learn controls, (2) familiar game mechanics and (3) the infinite variety generated by multiplayer interaction.

Steven L. Kent describes *Pong*'s core gameplay thus:

> *Pong* played more like squash than ping-pong. Thanks to Alcorn's segmented paddle, it had become a game of angles, in which banking shots against walls was an important strategy. Players controlled inch-long white lines that represented racquets, which they used to bat the small white square that represented the ball. The background was black. (Kent, 2001: 42.)

It was Al Acorn, the Atari engineer who actually designed the game, by a clever combination of digital electronic components (transistor–transistor logic, TTL) – *Pong* was not originally created as a computer program. Acorn had two key innovations which contributed to the improved gameplay. One was dividing the paddle into eight segments, so that hitting the ball with the paddle's centre part would return the 'ball' straight back, while the outer edges would create 45-degree angle shots. The challenges of controlling the ball in relation to space, and in relation to counter strikes provided by the other player, charge the simple rectangular space of *Pong* with surprisingly complex dynamics. Another Acorn's innovation was making the ball accelerate during extended matches. From gameplay experience perspective, both design decisions can be seen as intuitively reasonable. On one hand, the possibility of differently angled shots created both surprises and variety and (when the player learned to master the effect) contributed to opening up various strategic options. On the other hand, accelerating movement of the ball built up excitement as the challenges increased and the control gradually became more difficult. In contrast, Odyssey console's original tennis game did not include this kind of ball control, and it did not even display scores on the screen – players were required to do their own book-keeping with a pencil and piece of paper. (Kent, 2001: 41; Kohler, 2005: 14.)

From the perspective of the typical player at the time, *Pong* was yet another coin-operated machine at the corner of a local bar. It was excitingly futuristic with its electronics technology and television screen, but the basic test of hand–eye coordination was firmly in the tradition of pinball machines. The control of ball was based on simple physics where bounces, defences and cleverly surprising (or just lucky) shots tempted competitive players to use yet another quarter. The fact that *Pong* was a multiplayer game cannot be ignored as a key

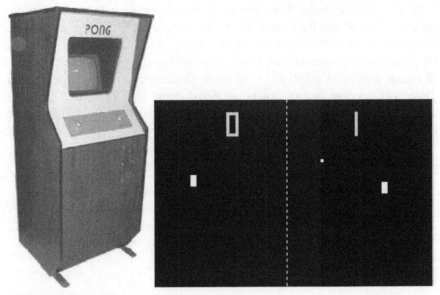

Figure 4.1 *Pong* cabinet and an in-game screenshot. [Image credits: *KLOV.com* and The International Arcade Museum.]

factor in the context of social leisure (see Figure 4.1 for an early two-player *Pong* cabinet and a screenshot).

The story of *Pong* is, of course, not limited to the arcade console version. The game was repackaged into the Atari home *Pong* console (1975) and has reappeared in innumerable imitations from various manufacturers ever since.

Even if Atari and Nolan Bushnell settled out of court and agreed to pay royalties to Sanders Associates (Ralph Baer's company) for the rights to produce *Pong*, one could make the claim that the idea of the game itself was so strongly derivative of tennis, ping-pong, squash and other physical ball games, that the core game design was a part of the heritage of sports, not an original invention. The technological leap required to make this kind of interactive electronics was, of course, very important. In 1975, General Instruments (GI) already manufactured an integrated circuit which had six games in one chip: four *Pong* variants and two shooting games, available to any manufacturer. The early 1970s were the years when a video game industry was born, and *Pong* played a seminal role in it. The 1970s was also the decade when the fundamentals of 'gameplay lexicon' were created. The subsequent years would add more expressions and digital gaming conventions that could be likened to 'grammatical structures' (e.g. ways to combine interaction mechanisms, scoring systems, gameplay modes, etc.) into this basis, but the core of a digital sports game or a shooter did exist already in the early 1970s.

The 1970s presented both the casual and the growing mass of hardcore game players, with an accumulating stream of games both for the arcades and into home machines. An important development was, of course, the birth of the programmable home computer, even if that line of development came to full fruition only later in the 1980s when IBM PC clones grew into a 'standard' environment, displacing the first generation of home computers, including machines such as Apple II, Commodore PET, VIC-20 and 64, Amiga, Sinclair ZX81 and Spectrum, and many others.

Atari dominated the popular perception of video games, as well as the US markets. While the Americans were enjoying a steady stream of variously innovative or derivative games with titles like *Asteroids, Battlezone, Breakout, Centipede, Missile Command* and *Tempest* (all Atari titles, 1976–1980), there were many parts of the world which were still waiting for their first electronic game to appear. More often than not, this first contact came via a home video game system with its graphically scaled-down version of the game, rather than in the form of the original arcade game version. Moderately priced, and rather underpowered if compared with the arcade consoles, these 'television games' continued the life cycle of arcade hits in downgraded home versions. The first home console Magnavox Odyssey (1972) was followed by Atari VCS/2600 (1977), which – in its turn – led to the success stories of the 1980s, including Intellivision (1980), Colecovision (1982) and Nintendo Entertainment System (NES; 1985).

Later, in the 1990s, the key gaming devices were SNES (Super Nintendo Entertainment System, SNES, 1990), PlayStation (1994; known later also as 'PSX' and 'PSOne') and Nintendo's Game Boy line of hand-held consoles (1989–). A new generation of game platforms was released at the turn of the century with Sony PS2 (PlayStation 2; 2000), Nintendo GameCube (2001) and Microsoft Xbox (2001). At the time of this writing, yet another generation of consoles is being rolled to the market by the same three companies: Microsoft Xbox 360 (2005), Nintendo Wii (2006) and Sony PS3 (PlayStation 3; 2006). The direction has been one of increased audiovisual realism, three-dimensional graphics and stereo sounds replacing the original relatively crude pixels and beeps of the 1970s systems. Historically, most successful products have been the original PlayStation, which was the first digital game console to cross the 100 million sold units line, and Nintendo's Game Boy series, with its reported 120 million sold units in 2006. These and many other less-known products of plastic and silicon have mediated and captured the attention of millions of digital game players, occasionally leading to passionate debates and 'system wars' about the comparative merits of various devices and related gaming technologies. Games technologies will be discussed in more detail later in Chapter 6.

Box 4.2 ON THE HISTORY OF GAME CONTROLLERS

Of the [Nintendo] Famicom's many innovations, the most important was the controller. The [Atari] VCS was initially designed to play sophisticated versions of *Pong* and *Tank* and came with both paddles and joysticks, but most of its games used a joystick. That turned out to be a weakness. VCS joysticks were versatile for their time but were uncomfortable to hold. To use them, most players had to grip the square base with one hand and move the stick with the other. People often complained that their hands cramped or their fingers locked around the base after long stretches of game playing. Also, the stick, not designed to withstand the kind of stress players often placed on it, often broke. [...]

For the Famicom, Nintendo designed a new kind of controller that was derived from the +– shaped direction pad that its lead engineer, Gumpei Yokoi, developed in the late 1970s for the Game & Watch LCD games. Somewhat similar in concept to the disk on the [Mattel] Intellivision controller, the Famicom controller allowed players to maneuver characters by pressing on the + pad with their left thumb. (Kent, 2001: 278–9.)

Space Invaders (1978) and the playability of a shooter

The Atari-led dominance of American companies and game products in the market was not seriously challenged until the Japanese entered the video game business. Nintendo, the future global game giant, had actually been formed already in 1889 as a company that manufactured Japanese playing cards. Another company, Taito, was established in 1953, but it moved into making electronic games only in 1973, when their first game appeared in the Japanese market. The third important player Sega was born as an amusement and jukebox company in a merger in 1964.

Space Invaders by Taito gradually grew into a huge success in Japan as the arcade game came out in 1978. There are even stories being told of a national coin shortage as more than 100 000 manufactured *Space Invaders* arcade machines were serving a steady stream of players. When manufactured and distributed in the US by Midway, an American game company, *Space Invaders*, made a similar impact and generated revenue in hundreds of millions of dollars within the first year of its American release.

Compared to *Pong*, *Space Invaders* had both similarities and clear differences that can be interpreted as advances in the art of digital game design. The ease of learning was also true in the case of *Space Invaders* even if the game and its playing instructions had started to become more complex. One can see how the learning curves for 'state-of-the-art' games have been rising higher as the game cultures have grown older. *Pong* had only a two-line

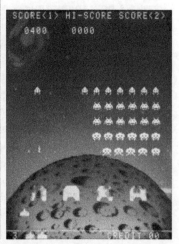

Figure 4.2 *Space Invaders* arcade console, set of instructions, and a screenshot with overlay colour effects. (Taito, 1978.) [Image credits: *KLOV.com* and The International Arcade Museum.]

'manual': 'DEPOSIT QUARTER' and 'AVOID MISSING BALL FOR HIGH SCORE'. In comparison, six years later *Space Invaders* dared to confront its potential players with much more instruction (see Figure 4.2).

The easily comprehended game concept can also be identified as one of the success factors in the case of *Space Invaders*. Some historians have claimed that *Space Invaders* was the first game to break away from the principle of making digital copies (or remediations) of older games and would thereby represent truly original innovation. However, one of the standard fairground attractions has long been the shooting gallery, and *Space Invaders* certainly relied on that same concept. But what Toshihiro Nishikado, the Taito engineer who designed the game, had achieved was important in itself: at the level of shell, or representation, the sharp-shooting competition was newly thematized into a battle of laser defence against invading space aliens, which effectively recreated the simple core concept into a new kind of experience. The shell of *Space Invaders* was that of a science fiction adventure, or, as John Sellers writes about the illustrations of the cabin, *Space Invaders* presented itself as 'a sort of mixture between a 1950s pinball game and a Marvel comic' (Sellers, 2001: 37).

The core gameplay in *Space Invaders* consists of moving the laser turret left or right, while trying to dodge enemy fire and shooting down the rhythmically descending aliens and occasional bigger UFOs. You start with three 'lives' (or laser turrets) and try to stop the alien invasion: the game will end if any of the alien will land to the bottom of the screen. The three laser cannons are an interesting element of the game, as the convention of 'multiple lives' would hold on to become a major part of digital games lexicon. Basically a 'life' in a video game context means a 'try' or 'take', indicating the unit that measures how many times you can fail before your game is over. The non-serious nature of the fictional battles of digital games is underlined by this iterative approach in game design, and this feature also holds relevance to the contemporary discussions about game violence.

The key invention of *Space Invaders* was the combination of (1) an endlessly accelerating and aggravating game tempo and challenge, and (2) a numerical record of the high score. The first element illustrates the importance of game, displaying variety in the dynamics of challenge or conflict; it is even possible to analyse a game by drawing a 'conflict tension curve' that estimates the intensity of gameplay as a function of time (Friedl, 2003: 243). As to the high score, this simple invention had important consequences for the social uses and significance of a video game. You could not only track your own progress in the game but also compare it with the previous top records achieved by other players. This probably contributed to the game's exceptionally strong holding power; a claimed record non-stop *Space Invaders* play session lasted 38 hours and 30 minutes and accumulated 1 114 020 points (reportedly achieved by 12-year-old Eric Furrer).

A high-score list can also be seen as an example of 'social playability' of the game. Playability is a concept that is related to 'usability', which is in turn defined in international engineering standards and by various human–computer interaction experts to relate to attributes like learnability, memorability and effectivity of use (see, e.g. Jakob Nielsen, *Usability Engineering* [1993]). Playability is often seen in this same line of thinking as an extension of usability in the area of 'fun', but is sometimes also equated with the entire gameplay quality of game, including such aspects like the quality of graphics and sound or intensity of interaction. One model of playability analysis divides it into four main components: functional playability (which roughly equates to the usability of the game software and its controls), structural (how enjoyable and well balanced are the game rules and challenges they create), audiovisual (how the implementation of sound and graphics affect the gameplay experience) and social playability. This last category is related to what kind of social practices the game in question is suitable for. (Järvinen, Heliö and Mäyrä, 2002: 28–38.) A high-score list is a sort of communication, even if it only conveys the basic message of who is playing this game and how successfully. In contemporary digital games the ways for communicating and interacting with other players are much more sophisticated.

There were also some important audiovisual advances worth noticing in *Space Invaders*. The hypnotic, accelerating soundtrack was one element. Despite being based on monochrome video technology, *Space Invaders* cabinets projected the game image from below on the top of a coloured lunar landscape, thereby creating depth to the otherwise two-dimensional screen. The simple alien figures also had crude animations, thereby gaining the notoriety as the first animated arcade characters.

Moreover, *Space Invaders* was one of the first recorded incidents of a games-related 'media panic' (called also 'moral panic'), as the residents of Mesquite, Texas, took their case all the way to the US Supreme Court in trying to get the game banned from their town. (An earlier arcade game, *Death Race*, published by Exidy in 1976 had also created controversy in the United States.) There is a history of moral panics, directed against various youth cultures, subcultures and popular media such as rock music, comic books, television and videos, featuring particularly prominently in the United States. The term 'moral panic' was introduced by Stanley Cohen in his book *Folk Devils and Moral Panics* (1972/2002). Without belittling such concerns for media influences, it should be noted that there was also much concern on the dangers of reading, when novels and reading of fiction were 'new' media (Aliaga-Buchenau, 2003). New cultural practices are always under suspicion, and various social problems will easily find their culprit among them. New practices are a threat to the established order of things and may also present novel, socially unsanctioned ways for self-expression or empowerment and thereby be potentially disruptive towards the existing power structures.

Space Invaders was also important for a whole category of games, known as 'shooters'. Shooting is a test of accuracy and hand–eye coordination skills, and has long been a popular attraction in fun fairs or carnivals. As digital games remediate earlier forms of activity or representation, shooting was one of the earliest conventions to be established. The MIT hackers' *Spacewar!* was already a rather complex shooting game, as it included navigation into multiple directions while engaged in space battle. As more games were designed that relied on similar aiming and shooting style of interaction, it became established as its own category and it started to make sense to talk about 'shooters' as a genre with its own established conventions. (For more discussion of the concept of 'genre', see the next chapter.)

Summary and conclusions

- This chapter started by introducing the special role digital technology holds for digital games and discussed how interactivity relates to this technology. Interactive game technologies particularly contribute to the construction of the multiple aspects involved in gameplay experience. Gameplay is here defined as a particular 'ludic' form of interaction that takes place between game and player during the play.
- In theoretical terms, a key distinction was made between the 'core gameplay' as an abstract set of rules as separated from 'shell' as a particular instantiation and concrete form of these abstract principles in various forms and representations. The core of game is embodied in the level of player actions, while the shell of game modifies how these actions are experienced in important ways. In contrast to literature or cinema, the world, theme, characters or other elements of game design are open for both player

DUAL STRUCTURE AND THE ACTION GAMES

interpretation and for player manipulation, and thus the analysis of games should involve elements from both these two main dimensions.

- The chapter also discusses the relationship between the history of computing and games' history, particularly in terms of the concepts of 'classic' and 'canon' within the relatively short history of digital games and related games cultures. Games are situated within the broader contexts of digital culture and information society, where they have established games business as an important part of the global economics, and also play a part in the construction of such post-industrial social and conceptual structures as 'media society' and 'experience society'.

- The case of *Pong* was presented to introduce the typical features of an early arcade game, and such core game elements for game studies as 'controls', 'game mechanics', 'multiplayer interaction' and 'strategy' were highlighted as constituent parts in its core gameplay. Within the history of game technology, the distinction between 'video game console' and 'home computer' was made. *Pong* also illustrates the role easily approach-able 'game instructions' and the 'learning curve' of games can have on their popularity.

- As a somewhat different example, the arcade game *Space Invaders* was brought in to emphasize the importance of theme (and thematization) of a game, and thus how the 'shell' level of representation cannot be totally separated from gameplay. *Space Invaders* is also an example of how innovations in game design such as aggravating game tempo and high-score list can change the experience of gameplay. The high-score list is also related to the concept of 'social playability', which is one important part of the multidimensional playability of the game. *Space Invaders* also introduced the ambiguous cultural status of digital games, as it is an early example of 'media panic' or 'moral panic' being evoked against it. This game also introduces 'shooters' (shooting games) as an early digital games genre. Genres are important for the emerging 'lexicon of gameplay' where such elements as game controls, game mechanics or interface design become established as conventions that both game designers and players rely on.

Suggested further reading

Steven L. Kent, 'The "Next" Generation (Part 2)'. In: Steven L. Kent (ed), *The Ultimate History of Video Games: From Pong to Pokémon and Beyond – The Story Behind the Graze That Touched Our Lives and Changed the World*. New York: Three Rivers, 2001, pp. 499–525.

Assignments on early digital games

Alternative Games History

Collect and document your own version of a 'canon' for the history of digital games. In your paper, give reasons for including these games rather than those included and discussed in this book.

Pick up a small number of games (three to five is probably enough) so that you can describe the games for those who have never played them. Try and think *how* you can describe a game so that you convey a sense of its unique gameplay and/or the other holding power factors. Why do you think this game deserves a place in the history?

Gameplay Experience of a 'Classic Game'

What kind of gameplay experiences do so-called classic games (early popular digital games) provide for a modern player? Is an old digital game worthy of attention only for historical reasons, or does it still fascinate or have holding power? How to account for the possible nostalgia and the effect of one's personal memories? This assignment demands taking a closer look at how the old games actually play when approached both critically and with appreciation.

Select an old game (preferably from the 1970s) that you can play in original format, or in a format as close to original as possible, for a minimum period of 2 hours. Base your presentation on your notes and observations, acquired during this analytical test-playing session. Try answering some of the questions above.

(*Associated research methods: games historiography, historical gameplay analysis, analytical game playing as a research method.*)

5

ADVENTURES AND OTHER FICTION IN THE 1980s' GAMES

Games and culture in the 1980s

The 1980s are remembered by what some call its 'culture of selfishness'. It was the era of Reagan and Thatcher, yuppies and suits with shoulder padding. Punk and rock were superseded by the popular culture industry represented by the likes of Michael Jackson and MTV. Like any age, it carried its contradictions; the decade that brought prosperity and computers to people's homes was also the decade of Chernobyl and AIDS.

From 1970 to 1980, the total recreation expenditures in the United States more than doubled, even if it is questionable that the available leisure time actually increased at all: there are signs that people were actually working more, even if they were also spending more in their leisure. The entertainment industry had expanded into multiple forms in different media, toys, sports and other attractions, and began to have a very strong presence and influence in both economical and cultural terms in people's lives (Vogel, 2004: 7, 20, 31). Digital games were one growing element in this increasingly media–technology naturated landscape. Conceptually, this chapter will introduce character and adventure as key digital game elements and draw focus on the expansion of digital games into exploration-inviting 'story-worlds' with increased expressive potential and thematic depth.

Pac-Man (1980) and digital game as pop culture

In many histories of the field, *Pac-Man* often carries the honour of being the 'most successful video game of all time'. There are digital games that can certainly compete (most notably, *Tetris* and *Super Mario* series games), but *Pac-Man* was the first game to reach out from the arcades and attain an iconic status; there were *Pac-Man* toys, cereal, lunchboxes and even a hit song made after it. Partly, this reflected the increasing brand awareness and inter-medial efficiency of the industry; the commercialization of intellectual property has since then continued its march, so that it is now typical business strategy to launch in one concerted effort an interlinked series of licence products, targeting particularly children and young people, including games, toys, books and movies, all linked to the same strong brand. There are multiple critical traditions, ranging from mass culture theories to contemporary critiques of multinational brand capitalism, which can be applied into study of games industry practices and related power relationships from this perspective. (See, e.g. Kline *et al.* 2003; McAllister, 2004; Strinati, 1995; Klein, 2000.)

When approached more narrowly from gameplay angle, there were many reasons why *Pac-Man* was able to reach such a wide audience. First of all, it had a recognizable main character that made identification and emotional attachment more directly possible than some more abstract implementation of its gameplay structures would have. It should be noted that many earlier arcade games had differently shaped graphical game objects that could be claimed to have 'character' of their own. But the figure of *Pac-Man* was not representing a vehicle or weapon (like the spaceships or laser turrets in some earlier games) but rather a creature that one could have an affectionate relationship with. Its neutral, family oriented theme was also important: while being based on the dynamics of conflict, it nevertheless did not include the obvious references to war and killing that *Space Invaders*, *Tank* or *Missile Command*, for example, displayed. *Pac-Man*'s designer, Toru Iwatani, from Namco explains his goals in an interview:

> At that time, as you will recall, there were many games associated with killing creatures from outer space.
>
> I was interested in developing a game for the female game enthusiast. Rather than developing the character first, I started out with the concept of eating and focused on the Japanese word 'taberu', which means 'to eat'.
>
> The actual figure of *Pac-Man* came about as I was having pizza for lunch. I took one wedge and there it was, the figure of Pac-Man. (Kent, 2001: 141.[1])

Iwatani himself was a confessed pinball enthusiast and the simplicity of controls and overall game concept (that we have also identified above in the cases of *Pong* and *Space Invaders*) is one important success factor, too. *Pac-Man* was easy to control and comprehend, but presented clear challenges and gameplay excitement as well. Keeping the Pac-Man character alive, busily collecting dots and other game objects, while navigating a maze and being simultaneously hunted by four ghosts, was not a trivial task.

For the history of digital games, *Pac-Man* was particularly important as an influential precursor for the genres of platform and puzzle games. The concept of 'genre' is not immediately clear while we are discussing games. Genre in literature can be, for example, that of a detective story, and a genre in cinema can be, for example, that of a western. These are established genres of narrative arts, based on the typical characters, milieu and stylistic conventions and perhaps most importantly, on similar storylines shared by those works that belong to a particular genre. A detective story is centred on a crime, the detective and the process whereby the detective uncovers 'who done it'.

ADVENTURES AND OTHER FICTION

A typical western is located in the mythical Wild West, has various 'cowboy' characters and often presents some kind of conflict between the 'good' and the 'bad' guys. (See, e.g. Altman, 1999; Frow, 2005; Todorov, 1990.)

A game genre is in principle a similar system of conventions: when we buy a game that is marketed or identified in reviews as a 'shooter' or 'strategy', we roughly know what kind of a game to expect. Mark J. P. Wolf, who has discussed game genres in his book *The Medium of the Video Game* (2001), warns against iconography as the basis of classifying games into genres. Rather than looking at what kind of visual elements (be they spaceships, tanks or intelligent mushrooms) are present in the game, in many games (at least action oriented) these could be changed into others, with the core game still remaining the same. The genre classification according to Wolf should be based on the nature of interactivity rather than iconography. Wolf then continues by presenting a list of forty-two different game genres, including categories like Abstract, Adaptation, Adventure, Artificial Life, etc. (Wolf, 2001: 114–17).

In this textbook such an extensive genre scheme is not followed, most importantly because genre terminology is like a language. Its practical value is dependent on the genre concepts being recognized, known and being adopted in use by the player communities and in game cultures in general; typically, genre system is also in a constant flux, as new games of influence present a certain combination of features that create pressures for a new genre to be established. Moreover, the needs of casual players, hardcore fans, popular games journalism or academic games research do not necessarily coincide. But the least we can do as students of games is to reflect on one's use of genre terminology.

If the case of *Pac-Man* is discussed with the principle that gameplay should be the decisive factor in naming a genre, then it should represent 'eating games' since that is what the player does, through the 'player character' of Pac-Man. Removing or consuming game resources by 'eating' such typical game objects as pills, power pills, fruits, mushroom or even opposing characters is certainly what is going on in *Pac-Man*, as well as in numerous other platform and puzzle games after it. The game mechanic itself predates digital games: many board games (chess, for example) are based on 'eating' other player's pieces by replacing them with one's own on the board.

Another important feature of *Pac-Man* is that it is a maze game. Mazes are a particular kind of puzzle: you are challenged to navigate successfully in the maze, either finding your way through it, escaping it or – as in *Pac-Man* – succeeding in your struggle to survive while navigating the maze. The maze of *Pac-Man* is not particularly complex, but the challenge is increased by the player having to do multiple tasks simultaneously: collecting or eating the pills, and special bonuses, avoiding the ghosts while collecting the power pills (or 'powerups') at strategically right moments in order to successfully surprise the ghosts. The four ghosts had different 'personalities' and their images and nicknames were shown during the 'attract mode' that the arcade machine displayed when no one was playing. Learning to anticipate the movement of ghosts was an important element in the learning curve while trying to master the game. (The direction of the ghosts' eyes provided the player with clues too.) For examples of the visuals, see Figure 5.1.

The level design of *Pac-Man* was also important: there were 256 screens of mazes to clear before the player eventually (if ever) reached the final level. The speed of the ghosts' movement and the length of time they remained blue and vulnerable after *Pac-Man* ate the power pill were the main factors by which the challenge increased. As in *Space Invaders*, the player started with three 'lives' or tries.

A traditional puzzle requires the use of one's acumen to unravel a riddle of some sort. Typically, it is not so much of a challenge to one's speed or coordination skills as to intellect. A video game puzzle like *Pac-Man* (or later, famously, *Tetris*) links the traditional puzzle with programmed movement, effectively producing a different kind of 'living puzzle'. Some puzzles are static in their character, making it questionable if they can be called games at all – think, for example, of jigsaw puzzles. In one of the classic works on game design, *The Art of Computer Game Design* (1982/1997), Chris Crawford builds his definition of games[2] on the comparisons between games and neighbouring cultural forms, including puzzles, stories and toys. According to Crawford, the essential distinction between proper games and static puzzles is in the quality and degree of interactivity: a puzzle does not actively respond to the moves made by the human. One can, however, quite easily create games out of puzzles, as successful examples like *Pac-Man* or *Tetris* prove. Even a jigsaw puzzle can easily be made into a computer game; for instance, the players visiting to play the puzzles in the *www.JigZone.com* website can compete against the record or average times recorded at the site; these jigsaw puzzles do thereby

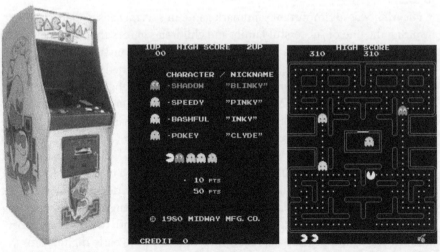

Figure 5.1   *Pac-Man* arcade console and screenshots. [Image credits: *KLOV.com* and The International Arcade Museum.]

ADVENTURES AND OTHER FICTION

respond to players' actions, simply by recording and giving feedback of the time needed for solving them.

In addition to interactivity, one key element in Crawford's discussion of games is conflict. In *Pong*, there are two players in competitive conflict with each other: only one player can achieve the highest score and win. Furthermore, the winning of the other player is based on the other player losing. These kinds of games are called *zero-sum games*. Zero-sum games are games where the amount of winnable resources is fixed, and it is possible to win only at the expense of others. There are also other kinds of games, where both players can win or benefit simultaneously. In addition to conflict, this kind of non–zero-sum games can encourage players to adopt various collaborative strategies, like forming temporary or long-term alliances. The conflict structures of the original *Pac-Man* are clear and simple enough when played against a human opponent. It also became common to play a game like *Pong* against a computer opponent, which is more predictable than a real human player. Thus even then *Pong* encourages the development of skills of coordination and pacing also in extended single-player sessions. In the anecdotal history of gaming 'records', the first recorded 'perfect game' of *Pac-Man* in 3 July 1999 reportedly took Billy Mitchell over 6 hours of non-stop play, preceded by 17 years of practice; he achieved the score of 3 333 360 points, without losing a single *Pac-Man*. Billy Mitchell was one of the earliest celebrated expert players, reaching top scores also in games like *Centipede* and *Donkey Kong*. Even during the latest years, there has been some developments of *Pac-Man* franchise that are of interest here, including a multiplayer version *Pac-Man Vs.* developed by Namco for Nintendo's GameCube console. In this version, released in 2003, three other players control the ghosts on a television screen, while the fourth, lead player, controlling *Pac-Man* on a hand-held device (Game Boy Advance) tries to escape them.

Pac-Man was an important landmark game in several senses, particularly in inspiring the line of successful family and children's games that dominated the home video game consoles market of the 1980s. Its non-threatening theme, yet challenging and exciting, high-speed gameplay provided a model for future home video games. *Pac-Man* as an identifiable character became the precursor for later gaming icons like Mario, Sonic the Hedgehog and Lara Croft. Some studies highlight the characters and storylines as the main reason behind the success of Japanese video games in general. Chris Kohler (2005: 16–24) points out that by the early 1980s, the strong Japanese visual culture had created the *shikaku sedai*, the 'visual generation' living immersed in *anime* and *manga*, Japanese animations and cartoons. The Japanese game designers were quick to realize how the gameplay experience could be strengthened by creating recognizable characters, exploration-inviting places and rudimentary story-lines, which would provide character motivations in the early digital games.

Finally, there are ways for critical player to read Pac-Man's compulsive eating in more symbolic terms and to see it as (perhaps non-intentional) irony or critique of the consumption-oriented decade, for example. British sociologist Stuart Hall has argued that this kind of 'oppositional' reading is always available for us, since messages of mass media do not determine how they will be interpreted (Hall, 1980). The relation between analyses and interpretations of games based solely with in-game values, and those emphasizing interpretative frames outside of actual gameplay are discussed further in Chapter 6. There is an ongoing debate about appropriate ways to analyse games, but in general, there is surely also room and need for critical, ideology-focused 'counter-readings' among the products of the digital games industry.

Donkey Kong (1981), the rise of interactive story-worlds

Pac-Man's ghosts illustrates how simple digital characters can have a look and feel that creates a sense of personality for the player. In terms of story or space, *Pac-Man* was nevertheless a rather limited creation. It was a series of successful games by another Japanese company Nintendo, which introduced how important these dimensions in digital games were to become for the game culture.

Another successful early 1980s video game *Donkey Kong*, by Nintendo, was influential in many ways, one of them being the introduction of Mario as the 'Jumpman' character which the player controlled. The top-down puzzle of *Pac-Man* is here replaced by a sideways view to a set of construction platforms – a setting that cemented the 'platformer' as a particular kind of genre, consisting of the combination of navigation (running, jumping and climbing) on platforms and ladders while making avoiding and attacking actions. While the controls of *Pac-Man* had consisted only of a joystick, *Donkey Kong* set the direction for future arcade action games by adding a jump button. As button presses and joystick movements were combined, this paved the way that eventually led into sophisticated and demanding 'combo' action configurations in the future games in the 1980s and 1990s. It is interesting to note that navigation in a platform-based game environment has in this case been recognized as the gameplay focus of 'platform game' genre; several popular platform games actually involve jumping, hitting or even shooting activities. The difference is mostly a matter of degree; in a 'shooter' genre (see above, *Space Invaders*) the gameplay focus is predominantly on the aiming and shooting activity.

As was pointed out in Chapter 1, the relationship between stories and games is a complex and often debated one. The question of cultural status is one that has an effect here; even nowadays it appears sometimes preferable to avoid the term 'game' and to speak about 'interactive fiction' or narratives instead. The 'ludological' counter-argument has highlighted the fundamental differences between games and narrative arts (cf., e.g. Frasca, 2003a). Nevertheless, *Donkey Kong* is an example of a game which makes it necessary to discuss its narrative characteristics and particularly its 'back story' as one of the key features that has an impact on player's experience with the game.

Shigeru Miyamoto, the artist who designed the game, was a fan of toys, cartoons and movies, as well as video games, and he started the game design from a story that would structure and make sense of the action. There was a stubborn gorilla (hence the name, 'Donkey Kong') who would run away from its owner, a carpenter, and steal his girlfriend to boot. In a storyline setting reminiscent of the *King Kong* movies, it is up to the player (in the role of the Jumpman/Mario) to get to the ape and save the girl. But the antagonism was playful rather than serious, and in future sequels like *Donkey Kong Junior* (1982) a player would ally with the ape instead. The scenery was cartoonish, reminding about the role manga and anime played in forming the sensibilities of Japanese game players and designers like Shigeru Miyamoto (see Figure 5.2).

From gameplay perspective, both the motivation and the reward are set out very clearly in *Donkey Kong*. The game design also utilizes 'cut scenes' or non-interactive animations to advance its storyline. When the game starts, you can see the ape climbing up with Pauline, the girlfriend that you can see also depicted in the arcade cabin art. Ape jumps up and down, making the building platforms twist into slopes, thereby creating a perfect setting for the barrels to roll down towards the advancing Mario. When the actual gameplay is about to start, there is a start screen with only one line of instruction, or challenge for the player: HOW HIGH CAN YOU GET? As the first platform screen is displayed, Mario's girlfriend is displayed on the top, screaming for help. The core gameplay consists of reaction and accuracy tests, as the jump button presses have to be precisely timed in order for Mario to successfully pass or break the approaching obstacles, and the player needs to do this while navigating the maze-like, multiple-level structures of platforms. This simple core interaction provides the player with a rich base for their game experience and has been the basis for the more expansive platform games that have

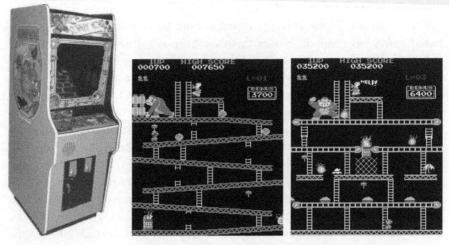

Figure 5.2 *Donkey Kong* console and screenshots. (Nintendo, 1981.) [Image credits: *KLOV.com* and The International Arcade Museum.]

followed it. The most notable among them is the *Super Mario Bros.* (1985), where Mario tries to rescue a princess who has been captured by Bowser (the evil antagonist central to the later Mario games). Both the core gameplay (sideways-depicted platform jumping game) and the story setting (advancing through fictional landscape to rescue a captured lady) of *Super Mario Bros.* was already apparent in *Donkey Kong*. The guiding principle was to incorporate the storyline into the playable structures of interactive game levels, thereby creating a unified, highly playable story-world.

Donkey Kong became very successful and it was followed by several arcade sequels, as well as versions produced for home consoles and in the popular Game & Watch hand-held electronic game devices. As digital games entered from the arcades into homes and the domain of the personal and private use, Game & Watch devices were particularly influential, prefiguring the later popularity of programmable hand-held consoles by two decades. In terms of game cultures, Shigeru Miyamoto has virtually become an institute in himself, gaining the status as the most successful game designer of all time. He has supervised the production of all Mario games since *Donkey Kong*, as well as the popular role-playing game (RPG) *Legend of Zelda* series (1986–). By year 2005, nearly 200 million units of games in the Mario series had been sold worldwide. As already evidenced in *Donkey Kong*, Mario games have been recognized as carefully designed and enjoyably colourful 'all-family-games' with a clear, story-driven line of progression that guides the player and provides motivations for in-game actions. An important element is also the style of interaction design in Mario games; the button-presses are organically linked with immediate visual and audio feedback that makes even the simple actions like jumping immediately rewarding for the player.

The reasons why the Mario games could become and remain so popular have received ample discussion. Successful production and marketing strategies are one obvious source for explanation, but apart from that, one cannot overlook how the actual game design quality of Mario games relates to their continuity of popularity. In his book *Game Over – How Nintendo Conquered the World* (1999) David Sheff derives much of this popular charm from Miyamoto's vision and sensitivity to what is universally appealing to adults as well as children.

They [adults] respond, Miyamoto feels, because the games bring them back to their childhoods. 'It is a trigger to again become primitive, primal, as a way of thinking and remembering', Miyamoto says. [...]

Miyamoto borrowed freely from folklore, literature, and pop culture – warp zones from *Star Trek*, empowering mushrooms from *Alice in Wonderland* – but his most captivating ideas came from his unique way of experiencing the world and from his memories. When Mario jumps up in space at certain locations, nothing ought to happen because nothing is there, but Mario finds secret, powerful mushrooms and invisible doorways to new worlds. 'I exaggerate what I experience and what I see', Miyamoto says. (Sheff, 1999: 50–1.)

Every digital game can be interpreted to create worlds, but while the 'world' of *Pong* was the rudimentary simulation of a playing field, it made increasingly more sense to talk about digital worlds as the content in these games continued to expand and diversify. In gameplay terms, a game that presented a player with the sense of a world was capable of evoking a particular kind of response: the desire to explore.

The 'world' of *Donkey Kong* was still simple enough, but it offered more variety than most arcade games before it. Miyamoto's classic design of the *Donkey Kong* world was divided into four screens, which together formed one game level; from *Super Mario Bros.* onwards, it was typical to have 'side-scrolling' screens that extend the gameplay space, but space in *Donkey Kong* was still emphatically discontinuous. After one screen was solved, a new screen of challenges would be loaded, with a cut-scene animation providing a moment of relief in between. In the first screen, Mario would run on sloping platforms, jumping and climbing ladders while *Donkey Kong* threw barrels from the top floor ('Ramps'). The second screen contained cement pans moving on conveyor belts (known also as 'Pie Factory'), the third screen involved the use of elevators ('Elevators') while avoiding bouncing weights and the fourth involved knocking eight rivets out of the construction to make *Donkey Kong* fall ('Girders'). In the following levels, the challenges of the screens become increasingly difficult, as the obstacles are moving faster and in new ways. The player can gain a sense of advancement as points are awarded from actions such as successfully jumping over obstacles, finishing a screen and by collecting objects such as purses, umbrellas or hats. A new action is revealed to the player when a hammer power-up is collected, useful for destroying obstacles. Thus, *Donkey Kong* was able to keep even the advanced players' attention by including several different game boards with a seemingly infinite number of challenges and actions in one game. Simultaneously, the playful logic, the visuals and musical score (composed also by Miyamoto) contributed to a sense of wonder and the need to explore further into this 'magical realm' of colourful toy characters, treasures and devious challenges.

Nintendo's powerful marketing strategies proved to be successful and, for the first time, digital games had become a major (and inescapable) cultural and social element in the lives of an entire generation. Nintendo characters broke from games into television cartoon shows, records, magazines, books, videos, cereals, notebooks, drinking mugs, T-shirts and bed sheets. David Sheff, documenting this 'cultural invasion' from the Japanese game company, notes that in 1990 'Super Mario' was a better recognized character by American children than Mickey Mouse (Sheff, 1999: 9). Nintendo was also phenomenally efficient commercially:

Fujitsu, with profits similar to Nintendo's, had 50,000 employees. Nintendo had 850. Nintendo, in 1991, earned about $1.5 million per employee. [...] In the entertainment business, Nintendo had become a force that could not be ignored. In early 1992, the company profited more than *all the American movie studios* combined and the three television networks combined. (Sheff, 1999: 5. Emphasis in the original.)

It is difficult to obtain reliable, global figures of the sales of digital games, but the list in Table 5.1 is at least indicative of the significance of Nintendo games for game history. Among the top ten best-selling games of all times are six Mario games.

Chris Kohler quotes an interesting survey among the editors of *Electronic Gaming Monthly*, a popular US gaming magazine, in their January 2002 issue, where editors' 100 favourite games of all times were voted for, and in the games listed:

86 had recognizable, distinct characters,
78 had a full story or story elements,
38 were role-playing games built entirely around a story progression,
93 were Japanese in origin. (Kohler, 2005: 8.)

The game design decisions in Nintendo games and the related Japanese visual culture and sensibility have obviously had major international impact on game culture in general. The position of Nintendo as the single dominating presence

Table 5.1 All-time top twenty games by sales.

1.	Super Mario Bros. for NES: 40 Million Units
2.	Tetris for Gameboy: 33 Million Units
3.	Super Mario Bros. 3 for NES: 18 Million Units
4.	Super Mario World for SNES: 17 Million Units
5.	Super Mario Land for Gameboy: 14 Million Units
6.	Super Mario 64 for N64: 11 Million Units
7.	The Sims for PC: 10 Million Units
8.	Super Mario Bros. 2 for NES: 10 Million Units
9.	Grand Theft Auto: Vice City for PS2: 8.5 Million Units
10.	Harry Potter and the Sorcerer's Stone for PSX: 8 Million Units
11.	GoldenEye for N64: 8 Million Units
12.	Donkey Kong Country for SNES: 8 Million Units
13.	Super Mario Kart for SNES: 8 Million Units
14.	Pokémon Red/Blue for Gameboy: 8 Million Units
15.	Half-Life for PC: 8 Million Units
16.	Tomb Raider II for PSX: 8 Million Units
17.	Final Fantasy VII for PSX: 7.8 Million Units
18.	Myst for PC: 7 Million Units
19.	Gran Turismo 3 for PS2: 7 Million Units
20.	Dragon Warrior VII for PS2: 6 Million Units

Source: gameState magazine, Summer 2003; via *Owtn.com.*

in the digital games industry was challenged later in the 1990s, but especially the games created under Shigeru Miyamoto's supervision continue to hold a particular place in games history. They are successful examples of how existing conventions, derived from multiple sources, and novelty can be combined and presented in a carefully fine-tuned and play-tested balance.

Text adventures and the evolution of computer role-playing games

Role-playing games (RPGs) had first entered into popular attention with the publishing of *Dungeons & Dragons* (D&D) table-top (or 'paper-and-pencil') role-playing game by Gary Gygax and Dave Arneson (TSR, Inc.) in 1974. Derived from such diverse sources as miniature war games and fantasy literature, the key innovation in traditional role-playing games was the emphasis on engrossment. Rather than just playing to 'win' the game, in role-playing games you were expected to become immersed in an alternative fantasy reality as characters living their lives in it. In *D&D*, a typical play session is run by the 'Dungeon Master' (DM) who describes the fantasy world to the players, plays the roles of the monsters and other 'non-player characters' (NPCs) and also arbitrates in tasks that involve the game mechanics. The players, in their turns, adopt the roles and describe the intended actions of the 'player characters' (PCs) which they have jointly created with the DM. To conclude, at the heart of a traditional RPG is a hybrid form of leisure that combines features from strategy games and interactive storytelling (more on RPGs: Fine, 1983; Mackay, 2001; Williams *et al.*, 2006).

There exists a long development history of games designed and programmed for multipurpose computers with interface and gameplay features that were distinctly different from the arcade video games described so far. The early ADVENT, or *Colossal Cave Adventure* for the mainframe computers was programmed by Will Growther and Don Woods in 1975–1976. The interface of these early adventure games was completely based on text, as, typically, that was the only thing a terminal could display. The player would read descriptions from the screen and type in commands like 'go north' or 'take dagger'. A specific program (called parser) would interpret the text input and the game would respond accordingly, with new text output.

Text adventures are an almost extinct species now, but in the early personal computers era (late 1970s to early 1980s) they used to be the most popular choice. Not particularly suited for (or even capable of) graphics, and hence any video game style action, computers with keyboards suited very well in text-based interaction. Most successful in this area was Infocom, a company started by Marc Blank and Dave Lebling that created the original *Zork* (1977, published in 1980) text adventure at MIT's Laboratory of Computer Science. Infocom used their advanced parser in numerous games, including the popular

The Hitchhiker's Guide to the Galaxy (1984) by Steve Meretzky and the author Douglas Adams. (For an analysis of text adventure games, see Montfort, 2003.)

The diversity of the early home computer market was reflected by the multitude of hardware platforms a company like Infocom had to support, including the Apple II family, Atari 800, IBM PC and compatibles, Commodore 64, Commodore 128, Apple Macintosh, Atari ST and the Commodore Amiga, all requiring different versions of the game. Contemporary game productions rarely support more than two or three of the most popular gaming platforms.

A different kind of step in the evolution of computer RPGs came with the 'roguelike' games which provided simple graphical interface by means of a top-down map of rooms and corridors, all still executed with ASCII characters only (Figure 5.3). The roguelike games also featured randomly generated dungeon levels which resulted in a high replay value, ensuring their continued popularity among enthusiasts. Classics of this (sub)genre include *Angband*, *Hack* (still developed during recent years as *NetHack*), *Moria* and *Rogue*, which gave this class of games its name. But it is worthy of consideration that even a 1990s highly graphical best-seller game as *Diablo* (Blizzard, 1996) can be considered to be close to this genre, on the basis of its roguelike core gameplay. Significant differences also exist; most notably, the roguelike games reliance on top-down, ASCII tile interface and turn-based action translate into distinctively different gameplay experience from that of later, real-time 'Action RPGs'.

The original roguelike games were mostly turn based, meaning that the monsters waited until the player had decided what to do next. This made the

```
 ------
|....|        ###########      #   Unlit hallway
|....|        #         #      .   Lit area
|.$..+########         #      $   Some quantity of gold
|....|        #     ---+---    +   A door
 ------        #    |.....|
              #    |.!...|     !   A magic potion
              #    |.....|
              #    |..@..|     @   The adventurer
 ----         #    |.....|
|..|         #######+..D..|    D   A dragon
|<.+###       #    |.....|     <   Stairs to the previous level
 ---- #       #    |.?...|     ?   A magic scroll
      ######        -------
```

Figure 5.3   Sample screen elements from Roguelike games. [Image credit: *www.wikipedia.org*.]

gameplay deliberative and more appealing to those who approached it with the chess-style preferences of strategy game players. It provides a distinctly different core gameplay experience from that which is offered by the fast-paced running, jumping and reflex-testing challenges of the typical arcade and home video games. The narrative consistency, or the logic that traditional RPG or 'interactive fiction' audiences expected, was not a central feature of roguelike games. Instead, they were strong in generating entertainingly random 'dungeon crawls' with random monsters and treasures, which, in later real-time, Action RPG versions, were especially suitable for 'hack-and-slash' type of gameplay, as *Diablo* and its followers proved. This distinction between four early game categories can be simplified into that: a matrix shown in Table 5.2.

This fourfold table is a simplification: however, particularly the degree of randomness and its relation to the pre-scripted parts of the game can be debated. Rather than absolute, the table aims to illustrate how two such elements as temporality of interaction and randomness of game world relate to gameplay experience. A game that presents the player with challenges that need to be solved in real time easily results in play sessions with more intense tempo than the more deliberative style that a turn-based game allows its players to adopt. Also, the difference that mostly randomly generated game levels and opponents create, in contrast to dominantly pre-scripted ones, is significant from gameplay experience perspective. Leaving a game level and re-entering it may lead the player facing either the same or most likely quite different environment and a combination of challenges in the case of randomly generated game environments. The continuity and logic of the storyline, on the other hand, is easier to establish in a dominantly pre-scripted environment. The success and influence of intense arcade-style gameplay is notable also for the evolution of computer games, and it is possible to consider an Action RPG like *Diablo* to be a crossbreed between roguelike games with Nintendo-style fast-paced movement while collecting various 'power-ups'. Contemporary commercial adventure games are almost all 'Action Adventures', which means that they require real-time interaction and coordination skills similar to classic platform and arcade games, while the structure of interlinking puzzles or tasks belongs to the legacy going back to the early text adventure games. The role-playing or character creation aspects of these games are generally lesser developed.

Table 5.2 Four game categories as a matrix between the temporality of interaction and the randomness of game world.

Game genre	Interaction temporality	Game world (mostly)
Action RPGs	Real time	Random
Interactive fiction	Turn based	Pre-scripted
Platform games	Real Time	Pre-scripted
Roguelike games	Turn based	Random

The core features of genuine role-playing games were long missing from digital games, but particularly MUDs (Multi-User Dungeons, discussed in more detail in Chapter 7) started to build upon the social interaction and storytelling between multiple players. Most early home computers, however, did not have modems or other means for establishing network connections. A 'computer role-playing game' (CRPG) became identified simply in the terms that it included characters with attributes like hit points, or experience levels, reminiscent of *D&D*-style RPGs.

Ultima IV: Quest of the Avatar (1985) and games' thematic depth

Richard Garriott's *Ultima IV: Quest of the Avatar* is an important game both on its own merit and as a central representative in an influential game series and popular game genre. It will also illustrate the growing ambitions within the game cultures to reach themes that had previously been solely in the domain of literature or cinema, and thereby reflects the maturing of digital games as an expressive medium.

Prior to the Ultima series, Garriott was a schoolboy with an interest in the triangle of fantasy literature, role-playing games and computers – an effective combination that would soon become increasingly widespread and typical among certain Western 'techno-gamer' youth subcultures. As recounted by Brad King and John Borland in their book *Dungeons and Dreamers: The Rise of Computer Game Culture from Geek to Chic* (2003), Garriott persuaded the principal of Houston's Clear Creek High School to allow him to program fantasy computer games as an independent study project with the school computer terminal. This project would conclude in the game Richard called *Akalabeth* (1979), published at first in Apple II floppy disks packed into Ziploc bags. Quoting King and Borland, '[e]ventually, the game went on to sell 30 000 copies, netting Richard $5 per copy, and bringing him a cool $150 000 – about three times what his astronaut father earned in a year. Not bad for a school project' (King and Borland, 2003: 43).

Ultima games grew into the form of game clusters: *Ultimas I–III* made up the first trilogy, *Ultimas IV–VI* the second one, and *Ultimas* from *VII* to *IX* the third trilogy (and the last one on which Richard Garriott worked). Several of these games were influential and memorable in different ways, including *Ultima III: Exodus* (1983) which can be credited with standardizing some of the key interface conventions for CRPGs. This time, the player controlled a whole party of adventurers and Garriott as the game designer relied on the players becoming conversant with a rather complicated system of PC keyboard–based controls, involving magic, battles and navigation, as well as dialogue options. The dungeons were integrated into the main theme and storyline rather than being presented as randomly generated or thematically disconnected series of obstacles. The total effect was that CRPGs had grown into a medium suitable for creation of original and cohesive works of fiction.

Ultima IV reaped the benefits of this opportunity. Garriott has commented on his starting points in an interview:

'I had already done three hack-and-slash kind of games and quite frankly, I was bored with that', he says. [...] At that point I had mastered the problem of making the game. Anything that I could imagine I now knew I could create. The hardest part of the problem was deciding what is the correct thing to imagine? I wanted to do something with more lasting meaning to it. (Herz, 1997: 157.)

The main contributions of *Ultima IV* to the history of digital games do not come from its audiovisual technology, CRPG mechanics or game controls. All that had mostly already been developed in earlier games (most notably in *Ultima III*). The major change was rather brought by the more serious attitude it introduced: *Ultima IV* was attempting to use gameplay as a means to build a story and a message with philosophical and ethical implications.

Admittedly, it was up to the player how to respond, and it is perfectly possible to play the game with a 'gamist' attitude, rather than with one of character immersion and ethical contemplation. 'Gamist' is a term of RPG lexicon, referring to the player attitude and style of action which focuses on the game challenges and the optimal strategies on how to overcome them. This is opposed with the 'dramatist' (or 'narrativist') and 'simulationist' attitudes or player styles and types; the overall system is called the 'Threefold Model'. The underlying insight that role-players made while developing the model[3] was based on recognizing how different players were looking for different things in their games and then also realizing how much freedom players actually had while interpreting these various game situations or designs. It is hard to impose a thing like 'emotional immersion into character' on players who have no such inclination. A pure challenge of dexterity or strategic skills is also something that appeals only to a certain part of the people who make up game cultures – albeit there exists players who are perfectly comfortable in chancing their play styles and strategies on occasion. The preferred style of play should not be considered as an essential or fixed part of person, but it is equally important to recognize the distinctive differences in temperament and fundamental disposition that also underlie play-style choices. The role of player psychology and gameplay experience research for game studies is discussed further in Chapter 7. The lesson nevertheless here is that even if certain games and playing them can superficially look the same to an outside observer, the qualitative experiences and the meanings attached to them can actually be very different for different persons.

Ultima IV sets the player into the role of Avatar, the generic hero-adventurer figure who is suddenly thrown into the fantasy realm of Britannia. Starting from the initial scene of answering the questions of a gypsy woman, the player is faced with ethical choices. Depending whether one prefers certain 'virtue' over the others, a character class and a starting town is selected during this process of character generation. As is typical in *D&D*-derived games, the different strengths and weaknesses of different characters are categorized into a system of 'character classes'. The combinations are represented in Table 5.3.

In terms of the complexity and extensiveness of the game world, *Ultima IV* is a far cry from *Pong* or even a console platform game classic such as *Donkey Kong*. Whereas the learning curve of an arcade game centres around the player gradually mastering the skills needed for increasingly complex coordination and faster paced challenges, the experience of playing a game like *Ultima IV* can be compared to entering a thick multi-volume work of fantasy in the tradition of J. R. R. Tolkien. This is, of course, where Richard Garriott, as well as numerous other RPG designers/authors, has explicitly drawn inspiration from. Battles and navigation in a computer game from this era do not make particular demands on dexterity or skills of hand–eye coordination. What they do test, however, is the attentiveness and perseverance of the player to explore an extensive world filled with potential friends and foes and the ability to comprehend and master the complex puzzle-like structure behind its façade of walking, fighting, magic and dialogue. See Figure 5.4 for the graphical style of *Ultima IV*.

A particular kind of derivative work known as the 'walkthrough' became important during the days of text adventures and continues to hold its value

Table 5.3 The *Ultima IV* virtues, character classes and starting towns.

Virtue	Class	Town
Compassion	Bard	Britain
Honesty	Mage	Moonglow
Honour	Paladin	Trinsic
Humility	Shepherd	New Magincia
Justice	Druid	Yew
Sacrifice	Tinker	Minoc
Spirituality	Ranger	Skara Brae
Valor	Fighter	Jhelom

Ultima IV FAQ/walkthrough; Simpson, 2005.

Figure 5.4 Screenshots from *Ultima IV*, taken from the Commodore 64 version. (Origin Systems, 1985.) [Image credits: *www.mobygames.com*, Electronic Arts.]

today for players of CRPGs and other game genres with adventure game structures. What these texts typically do is transform a non-linear (or multi-linear) software product into a linear storyline where challenges and their solutions are listed one after another until the player reaches the end scene. Considered as cheating by many, walkthroughs nevertheless play their own role in the service of the game communities. Players often use walkthroughs to control and manage their gameplay experience by setting up their own, player-created rules on what is 'fair use' of walkthroughs and when it should be considered cheating. For example, if the gameplay seems to be locked in an impasse for too long a time (to be decided by the player herself), it may be fair to consult walkthrough to solve this particular problem, but no more. Originally created by players either alone or collectively to be freely shared, there are now commercial 'game books' produced by the game industry itself as spin-off products and published alongside games that aim to provide similar help and other 'added value' for frustrated game players.

The storylines driving the gameplay in some successful games have even inspired the publication of full 'novelizations' of some games. These include, for example, novelizations, game-prequel or sequel novels centred on the events originally playable in *King's Quest*, *Gabriel Knight* (Sierra On-Line) and *The Myst* (Cyan Worlds) adventure game series, *Baldur's Gate* and *Planescape: Torment* role-playing games by BioWare, and the more recent series of books centred on popular *StarCraft*, *Warcraft* and *Diablo* series (by Blizzard Entertainment) and *Halo* games (by Microsoft Game Studios). Also several *Star Wars* games (LucasArts), *Resident Evil* series horror games (Capcom), as well as *Tomb Raider* games (Core Design) and *Tom Clancy's Splinter Cell* (Ubisoft) action game series have been at the centre of novel spin-off productions. The game novels are obviously a way for the game producers to expand and build upon the existing game world, characters and storylines and exploit their popularity in another medium, while game players seek to continue their experience with the fiction they enjoy. But there are also numerous fan-created, 'non-official' game novelizations that speak about the complex pleasures and significant investments of time and energy that participation in game cultures may involve.

When released in 1985, *Ultima IV* became the first game in the Ultima series to top the bestseller charts. Looking at the player response, the particular 'magic' of a game like *Ultima IV* relies on a careful balance where, to feel like an achievement, a major accomplishment must demand some hard work without actually becoming drudgery. The particular social contract surrounding all games – the game contract – is implicitly based on game playing being voluntary, self-motivated action and fun. Walkthroughs or game books are particular kinds of tools used for adjusting and balancing the challenge that players with different abilities and experience face in an extensive game like *Ultima IV*. For experienced CRPG players the interface, the game logic and quest structure would be obvious, while for newcomers the game might perhaps present too hard a challenge unassisted. The official and unofficial hint books and player guides have appeared to fill this demand.

Richard Garriott himself has regarded the quest structure of *Ultima IV* as rather simplistic.

> Ultima IV is, quite frankly, a pretty clunky game. There are eight virtues and eight quests that you have to go on for each of the eight virtues, and the quests are pretty much the same. You have to go learn what to do and what not to do, then reinforce the positive behavior to attain the virtue, and then you go to the next one. There were good guys and bad guys, but there wasn't much in between. It was a good first step but fairly uninvolved. (GameSpot, 1997.)

One can go much further and call *Ultima IV* as a significant turn from the trivial hack-and-slash into a slightly more 'adult'-oriented and artistically ambitious game design. The player no longer simply battled a series of monsters to reach the 'boss' monster to 'win' the game. The governing metaphor was one of self-improvement; the goal of the player character was to reach 'avatarhood' and conclude the quest. Multiple characters, situations and ethical concepts were introduced and interacted with. However, there remained the question of how much even an ambitious computer RPG could become of a 'moral simulation' and still retain its core identity as a computer *game*. The walkthrough authors were at least quick to translate Garriott's moral dilemmas into 'gamist' challenges and solutions. Looking from a walkthrough point of view, the entire saga can start to appear rather straightforward and trivial:

> The following can be done in any order you want. All you have to do to become an avatar is to go to each place and do good deeds (see the v. virtues section above). Talk to the Seer to find out when you have mastered a certain virtue (called Partial Avatarhood), then go to that shrine and meditate for 3 cycles. Master all 8 to become the Avatar. Don't forget to go to the shrines! They aren't listed in the walkthrough, but you must get to all 8 eventually!
>
> [Much later:]
>
> You will now be at the final destination in your quest. You will now be asked a series of questions, the answers are:
>
> [Answers deleted.]
>
> Wow, what a great Avatar you are! You won Ultima IV!
>
> (Ultima IV FAQ/walkthrough; Simpson 2005.)

The moral dilemmas thus become translated into just another puzzle to be solved if approached from a purely gamist angle. It is an inescapable consequence of *Ultima IV* being after all a game, with a rule-based challenge set at its gameplay core, which leaves it open for approach where the moral themes are irrelevant for the goal of 'solving the game'. David Myers (2003) has claimed that this is exactly what happens dominantly while playing *Ultima IV*: the gamist values constructed during game play, more often than not, 'trump' the values implied within the game backstory and its ethical message.

On the other hand, the experience of playing *Ultima IV* has been recognized by many to have been transformative in their personal gaming histories. There appears to be a mixed reception, where some players are more likely to immerse themselves with the fiction and some with the gameplay rules. The direction of increasingly serious subject matters and moral themes was adopted later in several other games, one famous example being *I Have No Mouth, and I Must Scream* (Cyberdreams, 1995), a collaboration between science fiction author Harlan Ellison and game designer David Sears, which included adult themes such as holocaust, insanity and racism. But this kind of approach has not become the dominant direction for the evolution of game cultures so far.

It is one of the fundamental signs of the digital games truly becoming a malleable and multidimensional cultural form that an expression like 'you have won this RPG' can make perfect sense to others and no sense at all to other players. Winning and losing appears essential for some conceptions of games and playing and completely trivial for others. From mid-1980s onwards it became clear that there was no single game culture and that while many genres were constantly influencing and mixing with each other, there were also so many different groups of players with so many diverse expectations that were hard to combine in a single game.

Summary and conclusions

- This chapter has discussed the expansion that games as products and game culture more generally went through in the 1980s. The game industry was increasingly dealing with concepts like 'branding' and issues related with 'licence products', expanding the visibility and influence of games outside the gaming arcade. In the area of game design issues, identification with a recognizable game character was one of the important steps, as was also adoption of family oriented themes, leading into success of Japanese digital games, which replaced the 1970s Atari classics in the marketplace.
- The concept of game genre was discussed and primarily seen to be defined via the quality of environment or interaction rather than iconography or storyline within game culture, in contrast to how genre operates in other arts like literature and cinema. Such genres as puzzle games (*Pac-Man*), platform games (*Donkey Kong*) and role-playing games (*Ultima IV*) were introduced, but critical awareness of the unsystematic nature of such genre concepts was also pointed out. Maybe these examples should belong to such genres as 'eating games', 'jumping games' or 'character exploration games' instead?

- Interaction with a digital game creates an illusion of virtual space that is central for games as fiction and media, and an increasingly prominent part of digital games from the 1980s onwards, as the available computer memory was expanding, alongside the graphical and audio capabilities of games technology. The platform games of the 1980s advanced and expanded the use of separate game screens into entire side-scrolling game levels, where artful level design became a key element for reaching successful gameplay experiences. These more extensive games grew gradually into entire fictional worlds, which were capable of evoking a sense of wonder in their uniquely designed story-worlds and also pointed the way for increased thematic depth and more adult themes to emerge. Text adventure games, which are sometimes also known as 'interactive fiction', were also an important step in the cultural maturation of games as an expressive medium.
- At the heart of playing a game is 'game contract', which is the implicit social contract behind every play session; with it, the players commit themselves to the logic and rules of ludic ('let's-do-this-for-fun') attitude and motivation. Within this general starting point shared by all game players, there is however much room for variation. A model developed within the role-playing games culture was introduced, separating 'gamist', 'dramatist/narrativist' and 'simulationist' style of playing (known as the 'threefold model' of RPG player types). The increasingly self-aware diversification of game cultures also entailed varied responses and attitudes to such activities as using 'walkthrough' guides as a means to solve or 'win' games. Role-playing games were an important case in creating complexity to the entire aim of game playing, because as 'non zero-sum' games, the victory of one player was not necessarily a loss for another. Winning was no longer the necessary aim for playing a game.

Suggested further reading

Mark J. P. Wolf, 'Space in Video Game.' In: J. P. Wolf (ed), *The Medium of Video Game*. Austin: University of Texas Press, 2001, pp. 51–75.

Assignments on diversifying game cultures

The birth of a genre

How do game genres develop? Is it enough for a single original game to appear for there to be yet another new genre? How do we recognize and define and categorize games that we are using (consciously or unconsciously) while participating in game cultures? What uses a system like game genres serves for us?

Select a digital game (preferably from the 1980s) that you consider to have started a new genre. Give a short description of it and give your reasons for attributing it as the first in a particular game genre. Pay particular attention to the way you define the genre in question: is it defined functionally through its interaction styles, or with reference to a specific theme or iconography, through its unique difference from other genres, or simply with reference to marketing and/or fan discourse (the text on the back of the box, for example, or references at websites)?

Maps in games

Study the image of the cloth map of Britannia shipped with copies of *Ultima IV* (Figure 5.5). What purposes might its inclusion with the game package serve? Is it pure decoration and thus similar to the attached Ankh trinket, or is there some real value for the gameplay? Why would someone want to own a cloth map of a fantasy world, in contrast to having the map just printed in the game manual? How does this kind of example contrast with the various in-game maps that are accessible while playing the game?

Look for examples of the use of maps in games, describe and discuss them. You can either take a particular game and map or write about the role of maps in games in general. Consider what do these examples tell about the role of 'fantasy' or 'fictional world' for the players of these games, as well as of games as a particular, virtual-space–based medium.

(Associated research methods: genre analysis, cultural analysis of game products and game space.)

Figure 5.5 A cloth map of Britannia. [Image credits: *www.uo.com*, Electronic Arts.]

1. The story about inspiration from pizza may actually be mythical, but as Iwatani has later explained, as the story has 'already passed into legend, so I am going to stick with [it]' (Kohler, 2005: 22).
2. Crawford presents the following definition: 'a game is a closed formal system that subjectively represents a subset of reality' (Crawford, 1982/1997: 21).
3. The model was originally developed during discussions at the *rec.games.frp.advocacy* Usenet newsgroup during the summer 1997. It was documented by John H. Kim in the newsgroup FAQ file (see Kim, 1998–2006).

6

THREE-DIMENSIONALITY AND THE
EARLY 1990s

Debating games in the 1990s

Moving into the 1990s, global tensions had a moment of relief, as the Soviet Union collapsed in 1991. The Gulf War (started in 1990), as well as numerous other conflicts, nevertheless guaranteed that world peace would still be far in the future. The dot-com frenzy started with the IPO (Initial Public Offerings, selling of shares) of Netscape in 1995 and led to a heated entrepreneurial climate in the high-tech sector of the late 1990s (which finally resulted in the market crash of 2000–2002). Digital game companies generally did not experience similar escalation of stock price nor similar hits afterwards; with the 1970s and 1980s fluctuations behind it, the game industry was perceived as a 'mature business', with known risks and expectations, as compared with the sky-high expectations associated with the unknown possibilities of more exiting 'new economy' companies. The digital games continued to sell strongly, and later the stock price of such big game companies as Electronic Arts reached new record heights in the early 2000s.

All was not easy for the games cultures, however. The public perception of games continued to be often negative and dominated by the images of violence associated particularly with shooter and war games, on the one hand, and by the claimed alienating effects of game playing in general, on the other. A new phase in the history of moral panics with digital games started on 20 April 1999. This was when two teenage students, Eric Harris and Dylan Klebold, entered Columbine High School in Colorado with guns, finally leaving 15 people killed (including themselves) and 23 others wounded. Later, a similar shooting spree by Robert Steinhäuser, a former student at the Johannes Gutenberg School in Erfurt, Germany, in 2002 left 17 dead (also in this case the shooting student committed suicide in the end) and ten wounded. Digital games were blamed in both cases as the killers were known to be active gamers.

However, it has proved to be hard to demonstrate scientifically a clear cause–effect relationship between game playing and violent behaviour. Like other media effects, the claimed impact of violently themed games remains a debated and controversial issue. Many social scientists and scholars representing cultural or media studies criticize those searching for media effects from ignoring the actual social and psychological problems behind the violent or aberrant behaviour, and methodologically the media effects research for setting up artificial laboratory studies to prove the direct cause-and-effect impact of media. Cultural studies practitioners, on the other hand, tend to emphasize the capabilities of children as well as adults as critical and discerning media users, who actively construct meanings to media. These researchers remain dubious of perceiving any people as media victims, helplessly reacting to its stimuli. Somewhere in the middle ground, the focus of critical media usage research has started to move away from search of unmediated effects into looking at particular, mediated and modified influences and uses of media. These may be positive and constructive for individual and society, as well as sometimes detrimental. From this perspective, it is also possible that digital games with violent themes may often serve a purpose, while being not meant for everyone's eyes and hands. (See e.g.: Durkin, 1995; Goldstein 1998; Griffiths, 1999; Jenkins, 2000; Barker and Petley, 2001; Freedman, 2002; Jones, 2002; Carter and Weaver, 2003.)

The public controversy nevertheless continues around digital games, and several countries around the world have seen it necessary to restrict access to various games through legislation, in addition to the age-limit–based classification systems introduced by the game industry.

Meaningful audiovisual technology?

Some scholars have characterized the games history of the 1990s as the 'era of 3D' (see, e.g. Järvinen, 2002b). This is certainly true of the latter part of the decade, when almost all games that were published had three-dimensionally modelled characters and graphical worlds. In the early 1990s the situation was still somewhat different.

The rise of 3D, or polygon-based computer graphics in games, is related to the upheavals in digital technology. Images, and particularly detailed images, gobble large amounts of computer memory, which used to be very expensive. Game graphics also tend to be extremely demanding when it comes to computing power. *Myst* (Cyan Worlds, 1993), a 1990s game applauded for its complex story-world and impressive visuals, mostly relied on still images that were gradually replaced by new ones as the user navigated with mouse clicks and the computer loaded them, step by step, from the CD-ROM. A console or PC running a contemporary digital game based on real-time graphics needs to calculate millions of polygons (basic units for three-dimensional shapes) and then hide those elements that are not visible from the current point of view, render wire-frame shapes into solid objects with appropriate colours, surface textures, and apply any lighting, shadows, particles and other special effects that might be needed for the particular scene in the game.

Graphical advances are the most visible outcome from the evolution in digital technology and the one that has produced much of the drive towards ever more powerful systems. Generations of computing hardware are generally named after the bit width of the data bus, reflecting the general speed and efficiency of the processor. The first video game systems, like Magnavox Odyssey, were not much more than a few logic switches in computing hardware terms. The visual style of the era was characterized by black-and-white, blocky graphical elements. The '8-bit generation' was based on integrated 8-bit processors and was first introduced in the Sega Master System (1984), followed by the Nintendo Entertainment System (NES, 1985). A later popular hand-held device, Nintendo Game Boy, was also based on 8-bit technology. Typical for the early 1980s digital games technology were graphics based on static tiles and moving sprites, with the exception of Vectrex and some arcade games utilizing wire-frame–styled vector graphics. Of the home computer platforms, Commodore 64 also used a dedicated VIC-II graphics chip and a sound chip (SID) in addition to the 8-bit 6510 microprocessor. This relates to C64's lively colours and sounds and thereby to its relative strength as a games and music device when compared with other home computers of the era. The popular Apple II was predominantly based on 8-bit architecture, as well, but was not as strong in audiovisuals as C64. The relative significance of the various platforms is difficult to estimate, but Commodore 64 became the best-selling computer model of all time as an estimated 17–25 million units were distributed before the model was discontinued in 1993. As mentioned earlier in Chapter 4, the most popular console gaming platform in the history has been Nintendo's Game Boy, which has sold over 120 million units in various versions (see Figure 6.1).

In 1989 the computing giant NEC launched their PC-Engine – renamed for the American market as TurboGrafx-16 to underline its advanced 16-bit technology. In reality, the main processor of TurboGrafx-16 was still 8-bit, but the graphics processor was 16-bit, providing more details and colours. It was

Figure 6.1 Commodore 64 and Nintendo Gameboy. [Image credits: *www.wikipedia.org*, Bill Bertram.]

quickly followed by Sega Genesis and Nintendo Super Famicom (renamed Super NES, or SNES). While 'superior technology' has repeatedly failed in the marketplace, due to reasons such as the lack of good games or right marketing and distribution channels, Sega Genesis did very well indeed (spearheaded by such success hit games as *Sonic the Hedgehog*; Sega, 1991) and competed evenly in the 16-bit market with Nintendo SNES. The graphical advances over 8-bit systems were clearly visible in increased details, smoother animations and richer colours. From gameplay perspective, many of the popular 16-bit console games nevertheless remained as upgrades of 8-bit hit games.

When it comes to the computer platforms, IBM PC, released in 1981, was already based on the 16-bit Intel 8088 chip. Expensive and lacking in sounds and graphics, the original PC was clearly not meant to be a machine for playing games. Only the later 'clone' PCs, fitted with Intel's 286 processors (released in 1982), started making a wider impact. But development was slow until the Intel 386 processor (manufactured in 1986–2007), which represented a significant technological step forward. This processor was already 32-bit, even if the cheaper version 386SX used a 16-bit data bus. Intel processors were 'downwards compatible' (meaning that old PC software was supposed to run on the new processors) and the open PC architecture allowed third-party manufacturers to provide add-on cards, like sound and graphics cards, for consumers to plug into their machines. This revolutionized the personal computer as a gaming platform later in the 1990s.

Returning to the console platforms, the 32-bit era started with the release of Panasonic's 3DO Multiplayer console in 1993, but was mostly passed over by developers and consumers alike; 3DO was intended to become the new video game technology standard, backed up by several manufacturers. Atari, Nintendo and Sega, launching their 'next generation' machines later, profited from advances in chip design, and were able to exploit more affordable solutions (Kent, 2001: 485). As an intermediate step, Sega introduced a system upgrade called 32X, which enabled 16-bit Genesis to run a new set of 32-bit games. Of the two major 32-bit consoles, Sega Saturn and Sony PlayStation (both released in Japan in late 1994), PlayStation turned out to be more successful. With its lifestyle-oriented marketing strategy (reaching young adults interested in games for the first time), an extensive developer support (ultimately producing a portfolio of about 1000 games) and a 3D-focused processor capable of handling 360 000 polygons per second, PlayStation heralded a change in the fundamentals that digital games were created on. Both the range of audience and the subject matter (mostly though concerning only the representational aspect of games) were expanding. PlayStation was also the device that made the CD-ROM a popular media for the distribution of digital games, and opened ways for media convergence by bringing music, videos and games into closer contact.

Sega Dreamcast was the first of the new generation of 128-bit consoles, launched in November 1998. Even with some highly successful games like *Soul*

Calibur (an arcade fighting game, or 'beat-em-up' by Namco, 1995/1998), and the built-in modem for online play, Dreamcast would eventually fall as a result of Sony announcing the development of their next-generation console. The release of PlayStation 2 in 2000 presented yet another step in the pursuit of technology companies towards more 'photorealistic' virtual worlds. The intermedial influences between media forms were increasingly related with the convergence of underlying digital media technologies; it was becoming possible to use the same devices to play games, watch movies, surf the Internet and chat online, regardless if the device in question was called a game console, a personal computer or an advanced version of digital, interactive television. Henry Jenkins has pointed out that technological convergence is actually not the same as media convergence; since media is about exchange of ideas and production of significance, the most significant aspect of media convergence is that it represents a 'cultural shift as consumers are encouraged to seek out new information and make connections among dispersed media content'. Convergence as a concept relates to technological, industrial, cultural and social changes, and its use is dependent on who is speaking (Jenkins, 2006: 3).

At this time, at the end of 1990s, some concerned game designers like Chris Crawford and Richard Rouse III started to write about the 'movie envy' affecting the game industry: the pursuit of the cultural status of cinema can according to them result in non-original imitation of the look of cinema, thereby sacrificing the core identity of games as interactive art (Rouse, 2000). Certainly in the marketing of new generation of digital games the adjective 'cinematic' was used more and more, as the new gaming devices were marketed in terms of how many millions of polygons per second they could produce and on other technical merits such as ability to produce multi-channel digital stereo sound or connect to high-resolution display devices, thereby aiming for 'movie-quality' audiovisual experiences. In the beginning of 2000s, Xbox by Microsoft, GameCube by Nintendo and Sony PlayStation 2 were starting the race for the position of the 'media hub' at the centre of the home, soon followed by the next 'next generation' (Xbox 360, Nintendo Wii and PlayStation 3).

Also in the area of personal computer technology similar developments took place; advances in 3D graphics cards, sound cards, gaming peripherals and broadband networking constantly provided new opportunities for the developers and temptations for the consumers. Media convergence appeared to become more of a reality at the turn of the millennium when it became possible to watch movies, play music as well as games and connect to the Internet with both game consoles and PCs alike. For digital game design this meant that an increasing number of games were produced on licences from popular movies and novels. The consolidation of media ownership produced large international companies with assets in music, movie and game industry alike, Sony Corporation as a prime example. Most of the best-selling games nevertheless continued to be published by independent companies specializing only in games production, like Electronic Arts and Nintendo.

Game production is entangled in an increasingly global network that includes several 'cultures of production' for digital games. Aphra Kerr (2006: 75–101) has described how the production and distribution of games is currently negotiated in a network of exchanges between such marketplace players as platform manufacturers, licence holders, venture capitalists, game publishers, engine developers, localizers, distributors and retailers, in addition to game studios. There is nevertheless growing pressure for the industry to consolidate further, as response to the challenges of high production values and a growing marketplace.

The concept of 3D as the hallmark of a new era of digital games relates not only to a particular computer graphics technology, but also to a larger trend towards more realistic simulation in computing. The increasing power of computers is used here to recreate such features of reality as laws of physics, for example, in an interactive simulated environment. During the late 1980s, great expectations were put on 'virtual reality' (VR), which was seen as the ultimate future media technology. Inspired in part by the work of science fiction author William Gibson, cyberspace (as it was also called) would constitute a shared fantasy or hallucination of an alternative reality for millions of people in the future. Currently, the stereoscopic VR goggles and gloves with tactile feedback continue to have some utility for special purposes, but the mainstream development of digital simulations took another direction in the 1990s. The following examples provide some key examples of these directions, while discussing the consequences of this development for game studies.

Civilization (1991): Ideological simulation or just strategic play?

A paradigmatic PC game of the early 1990s, and one of the most highly regarded games in the computer game history, Sid Meier's *Civilization* (Microprose, 1991) was based on an already long tradition of strategy and simulation games of various kinds. Sid Meier is a game designer whose games such as *Pirates!* (Microprose, 1987) or *Railroad Tycoon* (Microprose, 1990) are famous for their strong emphasis on various kinds of strategic and simulation elements in gameplay. Meier himself has discussed the origin of *Civilization*:

> Civilization had many influences. SimCity in its turning the world away from destruction toward construction, the idea that it's just as much fun to build something as to destroy it. Empire, which had that 'uncover the map' quality. Railroad Tycoon with the idea of economics and building and all it had.
>
> One defining quality of Civilization is the concept of simple systems interacting to create complexity. On their own, the finances, military, and so forth are all easy to understand, but combined, they create complex experiences. (DeMaria and Wilson, 2004: 190.)

Civilization has its roots in the miniature and board strategy game genres. There was also a board game called *Civilization* by Avalon Hill (originally by a British board game designer Francis Tresham) which appears to have given Sid Meier some inspiration. It is a twist in game history that another company, Eagle Games, later released a board game version of Sid Meier's computer game, effectively completing a full circle of board-to-computer-to-board game development.

The core gameplay of a board-game–inspired computer strategy has a distinct quality that is different from most of the games we have discussed earlier. The movement of troop symbols and the overall turn-based game logic is similar to that in *Ultima IV* discussed in the previous chapter; both of these games are descendants of board games and particularly strategy war games. The goals and the main gameplay focus in *Civilization*, however, have evolved in a different direction from those of a role-playing game.

The player of *Civilization* starts with one or two settler units on a mostly hidden world map, with the double goal of building a great civilization and vanquishing the competing civilizations. Using keyboard and mouse the player moves her units on the map, uncovers more of the terrain, builds new cities, irrigates the land and develops new technologies, while also taking care of diplomacy and war with the other civilizations. During this, game time proceeds, starting from 4000 BC, and concluding either with the destruction of all the other civilizations, the success of being the first civilization to reach space, or at the ultimate year of 2050. In later versions of the game there is a larger variety of end conditions, or conditions for winning the game. David Myers (2003: 131–48; 2005) has paid attention to the ways the 'Wonders of the World' (such as the Pyramids, Copernicus' Observatory or the Apollo Program, accessible at different phases of game) transform the gameplay from time to time, leading into increasingly analytical awareness of strategies and meta-rules as well as increased replay value being cultivated for an experienced *Civilization* player.

With its combination of both micromanagement (the player personally taking care of all her units) and large-scale strategy, *Civilization* can be a very long game that typically spans over multiple play sessions. For an overview of the various screens and play modes in *Civilization*, see Figure 6.2. Originally a single-player game, played on a computer-generated map against computer-controlled opponents, *Civilization* has also spawned popular multiplayer versions. Given the level of detail and the scope of the game, a multiplayer game demands several dedicated and patient players, ready to gather together for multiple sessions. Later, the developers of the multiplayer version of *Civilization III* introduced a 'turnless' game logic (effectively a move towards real-time strategy, or RTS games) to speed up the game when other players need not wait for one of them to complete his moves (Morris, n.d). Multiplayer implementation for a game that can last more than ten hours nevertheless continues to have its practical and technical challenges. A game like *Civilization*

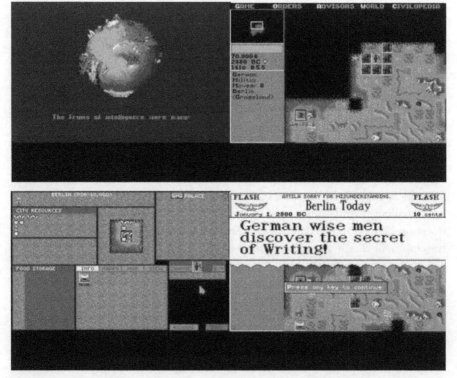

Figure 6.2 A collection of *Civilization* screenshots from different phrases of the game. (Microprose, 1991.) [Image credits: *www.mobygames.com*, 2K Games, Inc.]

also highlights the need to conceptually differentiate between 'game session' and 'play session'. One game session involves starting the game and playing it until some of the end conditions are met, and the game finishes. Play session, on the other hand, means a distinct period of time when the game is actually played (Björk and Holopainen, 2003). Thus one game session of *Civilization* can consist of one long or several shorter play sessions, with breaks in between.

The theme of *Civilization* makes it both an inviting and a controversial object of analysis for academic critics (see e.g. Douglas, 2002; Kapell, 2002; Poblocki, 2002; Lammes, 2003; Myers, 2003; Squire, 2004; Carr, 2005; and the collection of articles in Bittanti, 2005). While simulating the history of civilization as strategic battles for world dominance, the game refers to a complex network of discourses and representations that have much historical and political resonance. *Civilization* is a landmark in the general development of digital games into increasingly complex systems, capable of conveying and generating significance and interpretation that a simple game like *Pong* would not similarly provoke: you can disagree with the way *Civilization* is designed and programmed in a way that would not make sense in the case of *Pong*. At the same time, it is illustrative of the dangers involved in directly trying to interpret game in a way one would approach other, non-interactive media.

The entire world history, with emphasis on exploitation of nature, war and colonization, is at play in Sid Meier's creation. The player is placed in a position in which the only logical direction of action is to adopt an expansionistic strategy of world domination, exploit any scientific inquiry for economical and military advance, and finally colonize space. Furthermore, the rules of the simulation are built on a particular vision of history, crystallized by historian Arnold J. Toynbee in *A Study of History* (1934–1961, 12 volumes). According to this view, civilizations can be seen as units with life cycles, similar to those that organisms have (a view influenced by the German philosopher Oswald Spengler). In this line of thinking, a 'healthy civilization' encounters new challenges and adapts, while 'stagnation' is a sign of the civilization in question being about to die. In part, it is the simplicity of this organic birth-development-death model that has contributed to both the popularity of Toynbee's vision of history and its criticism. Following similar vision of history, *Civilization* as a game is open for similar criticism.

Other critical views have focused on the imperialist underpinnings in the game's operations. Kacper Pobłocki (2002) has pointed out that in order to succeed in the game, the player has to adopt principles of Western industrialized society to the degree that all successful civilizations in the end become images of the United States of America, the 'most perfect and most "civilized" state of all'. *Civilization* should be considered dangerous because it amplifies in an unselfconscious manner the hegemonic ideology of the West, with its ethnocentric views of non-Western cultures and their 'non-efficient' lifestyles, and thereby it has a hidden influence on its players. Other critics, such as Christopher Douglas (2002) and Sybille Lammes (2003), point out how *Civilization* acts out the American history and its colonial past, but Lammes also notices that the game modifies or 'reshuffles' this past, thereby creating possibilities for parodic play, while the player is coming to terms with the colonial aggression that the game represents. The main thrust of the critique is nevertheless that the game naturalizes the Western opposition between 'civilization' and 'savagery' and makes the related ideas of technological progress and exploit of nature appear inevitable and universal.

Putting this ideological criticism aside for a moment, a Toynbee-style view of history fits very well with the demands of gameplay, where the emphasis has to be on clearly operable and thereby rather simple rules. And it is also clear that with the publication of *Civilization*, the range and ambition of digital game design made a significant step – it was becoming obvious that almost anything could be made into a game. It was also becoming apparent that the game form carries with it some unique strengths as well as weaknesses. In a sense, *Civilization* was a 'toy version' of world history, the core game mechanic of which was mostly taken from a board strategy game, but it was the grand scale of global history of civilizations that added an important attraction factor to the game at the level of its representational shell. The representations and themes selected for gameplay, however, also inevitably carried with themselves the underlying history and largely unquestioned ideologies of an entertainment product from the 1990s United States.

Regardless of ideology, this caricatured adaptation of the world history was extremely successful. Such more recent critiques of *Civilization* as articles by David Myers and Diane Carr take the 'ludic' character of *Civilization* more into account in their analysis and try to reconcile it with the game's ideologically laden character as world history. David Myers (2005) claims that it is a mistake to approach *Civilization* as a historical simulation to start with; it may superficially appear to be a game 'about' world history, since it uses the signs and symbols found in conventional history texts, but at its heart *Civilization* is after all a game, which is an essentially different thing. According to Myers, only at the early steps of playing, and for a novice player only, *Civilization* may still carry the referential significance conventionally attached to its historical references, but during and after a repeated play, for an experienced (one might say 'hardcore') *Civilization* player the factories, fossil fuels and nuclear power plants no longer refer to their real-world referents. Instead, the 'aesthetics of play' will provide each element a new gameplay-related value that is completely independent of the history books that *Civilization* might ostensibly appear to be simulating.

Diane Carr (2006) has agreed that Myers' view has its basis on the actual experience of game players, but she also points that Myers is mostly only referring to the experience of expert players of *Civilization*, and thereby he has formed an exaggerated view where all real players operate with the 'representational equivalent of X-ray specs, cutting through the cosmetic wrapping of the game (such as the depicted landscape, or characterization)'. Carr quotes other more novice players (like Lammes, 2003) dominantly paying attention exactly to the 'irrelevant' representational aspects of the game, and concludes emphasizing that the meaning of a game like *Civilization* is neither universal nor static. There is no correct analysis of *Civilization*, but one can understand and appreciate the differences in meaning for different player groups and cultures. It is worth recalling here the dual structure of game introduced in Chapter 2 (Figure 2.2), with its multiple layers and dialogue between the ludic core gameplay, and the shell of representation with its interpretative significance. *Civilization* brings forth the core/shell differentiation in player reception very clearly.

In his book, *Trigger Happy* (2000), Steven Poole points towards two specific attractions of what he calls 'god games' – a category that includes history and city simulations like *Civilization* and *SimCity* (Maxis, 1989), competitive god games like *Populous* (Bullfrog, 1989) as well as various simulation strategies in the fields of global industry, railroad building or theme parks. The first one is the operation of the virtual city or other game world as a 'pet'; according to Poole, a player 'might form some sort of [an] emotional attachment to the gameworld' (ibid., 48). The other key attraction Poole identifies is the artificiality or playful nature of these simulations. One can, for example, fiddle with the speed of time, change the economic parameters of the simulation and derive enjoyment from seeing the results reflected immediately in this miniature universe (ibid., 48–9). In more general terms, these pleasures can be called building, collecting and controlling; the sense of power and control in a leisurely context and the feedback provided by the system seem to be particularly important to many people (cf. Ermi *et al.*, 2004). Myers (2005) states that within the experience of dedicated players of *Civilization*, the central place is occupied by the theme of opposition and conflict and by a systems-based approach (meaning recursive play, similar to the experimental methods of positivistic science) through which they aim to reach a control and understanding of game. Pleasures of power and control are important for understanding a game like *Civilization*.

Simulation theory is a large field of research in its own right. The very essence of simulation is in modelling the behaviour of a system – but not necessarily its detailed looks – with another interactive system. *SimAnt* (Maxis, 1991), for example, takes the behaviour of ants and simulates it by means of a computer program. In practice, simulation generally means simplification in which (the sometimes messy) reality is translated into something which is easier to understand and which perfectly follows pre-programmed rules (cf. Järvinen, 2003; Herz, 1997: 218–19). This effectively makes simulations potentially great tools for learning, which is something they have been used for from the times of the first flight simulators and beyond (Prensky, 2001; Gee, 2003; Squire, 2004). A good simulation game and a good learning simulation have slightly different goals, however, even if it is hard to make watertight distinctions between these categories. The main distinction is that a game is designed to be primarily entertaining; hence, designers tend to make more compromises on the accuracy of realistic details in games. It should also be noted that if only competitive games in which conflict and winning are central (the '*agôn*' category of Roger Caillois) are accepted as 'proper games', then several of the best-selling 'sim-games' are not games at all. Labelled 'software toys' by designer Will Wright and his company Maxis, they nevertheless occupy a very visible place within the digital game cultures (as well as in game product sales charts).

In philosophical terms, the reign of simulations in our late-modern lives has also been perceived as a problematic development. Most popular in this line of thinkers is French social theorist Jean Baudrillard, who in his book *Simulacra and Simulation* (1988/1994) argues that we live in a postmodern culture, which is predominantly a world of signs rather than of things. Relying on a long tradition of (leftist) critical thought, Baudrillard makes keen observations on the power of the media in shaping our consciousness and on the process in which a large segment of 'cultural industry' is increasingly blurring the boundaries between facts and information, information and entertainment, and between entertainment and politics. Games are entangled in this larger social and cultural development, and one can contrast current virtual game worlds with Baudrillard's descriptions of Disneyland as 'hyperreality', or simulation that is offered to consumers as 'better than the real thing'. It is easy to pass over such critique as exaggerated concern about something that is essentially just fun and games, meaning toys. However, following cultural critics like Pobłocki (2002), one might also claim that toys are all the more 'dangerous' in their seemingly neutral and simplistic manner of presenting their microworlds. As J. C. Herz puts it in her book *Joystick Nation*, 'you can build something that looks like Detroit without building in racial tension. [...] [I]f you are going to play these games – it is a good idea to know who's making up the rules' (Herz, 1997: 223).

Within game cultures, the influence of *Civilization* – both direct and indirect – is notable, both in thematically different renditions of the same turn-based ideas (as in the space conquest version *Alpha Centauri* [1999] by Sid Meier and Microprose) and in the rise of popular real-time strategy game series *Command and Conquer* (Westwood, 1994) and *Warcraft* (Blizzard, 1994).

Doom (1993): Controversy, immersion and player-created mod culture

Whereas *Civilization* occasionally both features as one of the rare positive examples of digital games in public discussions (due to its supposed possible educational benefits), but has also received ample critique from the academics, the next example is almost the total opposite. Abhorred by the non-playing media and public, the release of shooter game *Doom* in 1993 by id Software is heralded as a landmark event by most gamers and game historians. There were two main gameplay features which contributed to the unique character of this game: free movement in a 3D environment, and fast shooter-style action represented from a first-person perspective. On its loud, controversial representational level, *Doom* serves to illustrate how complex and probably even largely subconscious some of the pleasures related to digital games may be. When the *Doom* gameplay was combined with the distinctive way it was implemented, the ensuing totality would provide plenty of examples of player immersion that is one of the central concepts for analysing gameplay experience.

Both the freely navigable 3D environment and first-person perspective had existed in some adventure and action games before, notably for example in Atari's arcade tank game *Battlezone* (1980) and in the RPG adventure *Ultima Underworld* (Origin, 1992). But *Doom* and its immediate predecessor, *Wolfenstein 3D* (id Software, 1992) combined these features in a manner that helped to launch a new kind of game to dominate the mid- and late 1990s: 'first-person shooters' (FPS). *Doom* and the FPS genre were perceived at the time as a technologically advanced, revolutionary new form of digital games. This is certainly the view that id Sofware (n.d.) publicly maintains on its website: 'A technically stunning opus of heart-stopping action, unspeakable horror and

Box 6.1 ON UNDERSTANDING AND ANALYSING GAME SPACES

Effective game design can yield spaces that encourage our exploration, provide resources for our struggles for dominance, evoke powerful emotions and encourage playfulness and sociability. [...]

[Puzzle games] *Snood* and *Blix* use simple rules to offer players unlimited play within limited game spaces, whereas *Civilization*, *Unreal Tournament* or *Morrowind* use more elaborate spaces to stage conflicts. Other games, inspired by *Dungeons and Dragons*, offer exploratory spaces, where players complete quests, solve challenges or collect treasures. In exploration games, player mastery over a level, by besting an enemy, completing a puzzle or simply pushing through the obstacle course, is rewarded by allowing access to the next spectacular world. Reflecting this fascination with spatial exploration, the designers scatter these worlds with 'Easter eggs' (hidden treasures and secret areas not initially obvious to casual players). (Jenkins and Squire, 2002: 65–6.)

Spatial Structures in Video Games

1. No visual space; all text based
2. One screen, contained
3. One screen, contained, with wraparound
4. Scrolling on one axis
5. Scrolling on two axes
6. Adjacent spaces displayed one at a time
7. Layers of independently moving planes (multiple scrolling backgrounds)
8. Spaces allowing z-axis movement into and out of the frame
9. Multiple, non-adjacent spaces displayed on-screen simultaneously
10. Interactive three-dimensional environment
11. Represented or 'mapped' spaces. (Categories presented in Wolf, 2001: 53–67.)

pure gaming bliss, DOOM heralded a paradigm shift in video games'. For the graphical style of *Doom*, see Figure 6.3.

The popularity of *Doom* was partly related to the free distribution of the shareware version containing the initial levels of the game. For shareware to succeed, there needed to be both an audience and a distribution channel to reach them. According to statistics, the percentage of US households owning a personal computer increased from 15 to 35 per cent between 1990 and 1997; during the same time, the amount of money spent by the average household on computers and associated hardware more than tripled (US Department of Labor, 1999). Also during the 1990s, online data access begun

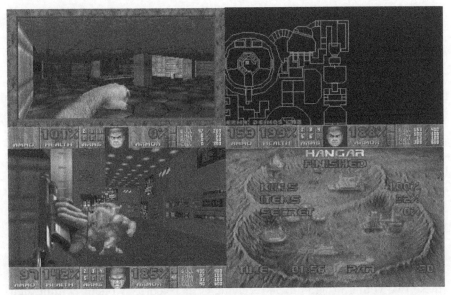

Figure 6.3 A collection of screenshots from *Doom*. (id Software, 1993.) [Image credits: *www.mobygames.com*.]

to gain popularity. One (indirect) measure of this is the number of server computers connected into the Internet; this figure was 313,000 in 1990, and in July 1999 the number was already 56,218,000 (Internet Systems Consortium, 2006). The popularity of earlier form of data communications, based on private computers with modems running BBS (Bulletin Board System) software, also reached its peak in the early 1990s. In other words, there was an increasing demand for content designed for PCs, and these computers were rapidly becoming interconnected into a global communications network. The release of the free *Doom* shareware version through the Internet and BBS systems benefited from both trends of development. id Software would make their profits from the full, retail version of the game which players were required to acquire if they wanted to play the game to completion.

There are distinct features of *Doom* that link it to the other products aimed at the youth culture of the time: game's stereoscopic sound effects were combined with a constant thumping of loud rock-and-roll music and the horror science-fiction theme, while its industrial environments and explosion-filled visuals can even be seen as remediations of films like those used in the *Terminator*, *Alien* and *Evil Dead* series. The reception of *Doom* should thus be seen emphatically in the context of popular culture and its role in society, not as an isolated incident in the history of digital games. The owners, and particularly active users of home computers in the mid-1990s included enough teenagers and young adult males to make the game by id Software an international hit phenomenon. Such scholars of popular culture as John Fiske (1989: 122) approach media studying the messages and uses it allows for its audiences; thus, for example a rock video by Madonna can be interpreted as an empowering text in the context of the socio-cultural needs of girls in the 1980s. *Doom* could be experienced as empowering by its players both at the level of its gameplay, and on its representation, which extended the expressive range of digital games from family entertainment to controversial, more adult-oriented pop culture. The FPS culture nevertheless remained overtly coded as masculine field, even with its share of female gamers, and even some all-female clans (Bryce and Rutter, 2003; Taylor, 2002).

The creation and the subsequent destinies of *Doom* and its makers are documented in David Kushner's novelistic book *Masters of Doom* (2003) as well as in several other sources. Existence of this kind of book also points towards the degree of general interest and cultural significance attached to digital games in the post-*Doom* era. The 'Two Johns' of id Software – John Carmack and John Romero – were the first true (Western) game designer celebrities. Their mainstream recognition and publicity value was still a far cry from that of movie or music megastars, but there is plenty of evidence of these two young programmers receiving clear celebrity worship within their specific game culture. *Doom* would also enter the vocabulary as a word which was evoked whenever videogame violence was debated. Particularly after it was found out that Eric Harris, one of the Littleton shooters, had been a *Doom* fan and a mod creator (building his own modified levels of the game), the public attitude towards *Doom* reached an all-time low in America.

The gameplay of *Doom* is at its core familiar from the early classics like *Space Invaders* (discussed earlier in Chapter 4); it presents the player with the clear and simple challenge of surviving while shooting everything that moves. The level design of *Doom*, however, appears quite different from these early shooters, due to the first-person view into a realistically modelled and textured 3D environment. The spatial representation of *Doom* has a major effect for the gameplay experience; like Aki Järvinen (2002a: 127) has noted, only in rather 'abstract' games can the essential defining quality be reduced to their interaction mechanisms (core gameplay, in our terminology). Particularly as conventions and audiovisual motifs start to move between different media, can entire genre be dominantly defined by its audiovisual style, as in the case of first-person-shooter games. For example, Järvinen (ibid.) writes, 'When audiovisual elements and styles, and interaction mechanisms, become fundamental aspects of a cultural form, they can together define a genre.'

Looking beyond the fascination of three-dimensional space reacting to game controls, a player will find several familiar gameplay mechanisms and game design conventions from *Doom*, familiar from even *Donkey Kong* or *Pac-Man*. For example, the player navigates her character inside a maze-like complex in a manner that is not fundamentally different from the challenge presented by *Pac-Man*'s maze. The *Doom* player character also climbs and descends (or is teleported) from one floor to another and finds various powerups, which mean more ammunition, more health or items like better armour or weapons – in core gameplay level thus much reminding the actions involved in playing Mario-style platform games. This is no surprise since as cultural processes, game design and gameplay tend to build on top of existing traditions and conventions. Even puzzle solving quests or exploration that was such a major part of 1980's adventure games has a large role for *Doom* gameplay, where the focus is on finding keys or remote door-opening switches that enable access to new areas on the non-linearly structured levels. And as in *Nethack* or other roguelike games, there are plenty of secret doors and areas with hidden powerups to find before the player reaches an exit room and can proceed to the next level.

A particular gamer subculture which is focused on the practice of 'speedruns', meaning high-speed rushing through a single level or the game as quickly as possible, got its start among *Doom* fans. One of the incentives for this form of competition was based on the *Doom* engine being capable of recording game events into a demo file and playing them back afterwards. Connected with Internet distribution, digital game playing had thus effectively become transformed into an audience sport, gamers being able to appreciate each other's gameplay achievements. In-game recording later also gave birth to 'machinima' or making of movies using game engines. Machinima series 'Red vs. Blue', a military science-fiction parody produced using the *Halo: Combat Evolved* (Bungie Studios, 2001) FPS game engine, is the first show within this low-cost production model estimated, achieving an audience reaching the one million mark with the means of its free Internet distribution (Delaney, 2004).

The *Doom* level structure consists of four episodes with nine levels in each; only the first episode, titled 'Knee-Deep in the Dead', was released as a free shareware version, the remaining three ('The Shores of Hell', 'Inferno' and 'Thy Flesh Consumed') were available only in the full commercial version. The shareware version is estimated to have been downloaded and played by 10–20 million people. The commercial version sold a total of 1.5 million copies. A sequel, *Doom II: Hell on Earth* (1994) sold more than 2 million copies. The *Doom* level design was iterated in many phases, which introduced several important changes in its challenge level and general dynamics, including changing the number and locations of monsters and powerups (see Figure 6.4).

The role of both the player character and the storyline is rudimentary in *Doom*. The character and story-driven 'Doom Bible', a design document originally written by Tom Hall, was abandoned during game development, leaving us only with the back story and the thematic frame of a science experiment gone wrong, and a base in Phobos, a moon of Mars, invaded by demonic monsters and Former Humans (zombie soldiers possessed by demons). As John Carmack's views were recounted in *Masters of Doom*:

> Doom didn't need a back story. It was a game about fight or flight. The player just needed to be scared all the time; he didn't need to know why. [...]

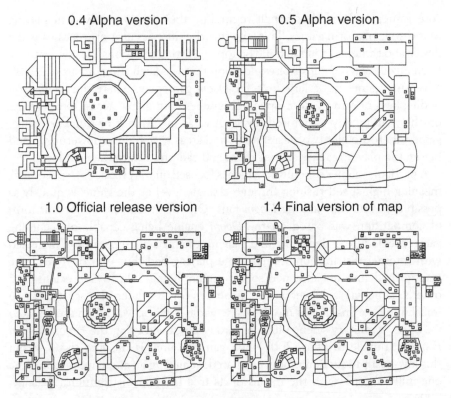

0.4 Alpha version   0.5 Alpha version

1.0 Official release version   1.4 Final version of map

Figure 6.4   Changes in the design of game level 'Episode 1, Map 4' from *Doom*. (id Software, 1993.) [Image credits: *www.wikipedia.org*.]

Romero agreed. Though he liked much of what Tom had put into the Doom Bible, a character driven story was clearly not going in the same direction as Carmack's technology. (Kushner, 2003: 132.)

The marginal or frame-like role of the space mariner character in *Doom* can be contrasted with that of Lara Croft in the popular *Tomb Raider* (Core Design, 1996) games. The latter are often categorized as 'third person shooters' because the virtual camera follows Lara, usually over the shoulder or from behind (see Figure 6.5). In the design of *Tomb Raider*, there are also clear influences from the popular adventure games of the 1980s, including the *King's Quest* series (by Sierra), and games by LucasArts like *Indiana Jones and the Last Crusade* (1989). In accordance with both representational and gameplay focus, player attention is typically centred more on the main character in third-person shooters than in the FPS. Third-person shooter's main characters are also generally given a name and some personal history, whereas in comparison, what we see of the player character in *Doom* is only the hand that holds a weapon, wobbling at the lower part of the screen, and the image of his face, with possible bruises reflecting the amount of damage taken.

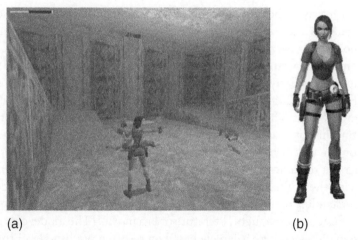

(a)   (b)

Figure 6.5   (a) Screenshot from the original *Tomb Raider game* (Core Design, 1996) and (b) image of Lara from *Tomb Raider: Legend* production (Crystal Dynamics, 2006). [Image credits: *www.tombraiderchronicles.com*, *www.wikipedia.org*.]

The quality of identification and immersion related to these two choices of perspective is distinctly different. When playing an FPS like *Doom*, the player gets a strong sense of 'being there' herself, as no mediating character is brought to the centre of attention. When there is need to look around a corner to check for possible ambushing monsters, the player needs to do the movement 'herself' – there is no alternative camera position that would give room to manoeuvre. The player can only see what the game protagonist can see. The quality of the identification and immersion in *Tomb Raider* is different, as it is not only 'ourselves' who are jumping, climbing and occasionally falling; but we are also guiding Lara, the player character, to do the fighting and the acrobatics. This duality – game player's in-game avatar as both a subject and an object – has received plenty of critical attention. Scholars such as Carr (2002), Kennedy (2002), Rehak (2003) as well as Dovey and Kennedy (2006: 89–93) argue that the quality of character has an impact on the gameplay experience and that in addition to manipulative action there is play of identification involved, as a *Tomb Raider* player is both 'playing as' Lara and 'identifying with' her while possibly also enjoying seeing her sexualized figure move and act. In contrast, Espen Aarseth (2004: 48) has claimed that the dimensions of Lara's body are irrelevant to him as a player: a different-looking body would not make him play any differently. 'When I play, I don't even see her body, but see through it and past it.' Again, a difference in gameplay focus and game culture emerges between the stance of those players who are more driven towards the fiction and representation of a game, in contrast to those players who claim to pay no attention to anything except the core gameplay and game mechanics. Regardless of approach, *Tomb Raider* is still fundamentally an action game, and the personality, inner thoughts and personal relations of Lara remain sketchy.

She is, in a way, a beautifully animated cursor for the player to use while solving puzzles and exploring the game world, while inevitably evoking also other thoughts or even fantasies.

Researchers of virtual reality and the sense of 'presence' related to it have held the lessons derived from *Doom* and other FPS games in high esteem. Alison McMahan (2003: 71), who has summarized this discussion in her article, refers to VR researchers who claim that the most transparent interface in computing history has been reached in *Doom*: the player is likely to focus totally on the task at hand. There are a number of dimensions or components of immersion to games, several of which are prominent in *Doom* and useful in introducing the multidimensional nature of immersion experiences, central to our understanding of not only gameplay experiences, but also to the experience of being immersed in thought, literature or in a movie. (The model of gameplay immersion discussed here is largely based on research published in Ermi *et al.*, 2004, and Ermi and Mäyrä, 2005).

The immediately noticeable aspect of immersion as offered by *Doom* is the powerful overall quality of the interactive moving images and sounds, which is likely to provide strong *sensory immersion* for the player. In present studies this phenomenon has been related with the degree to which the medium controls the user's access to stimuli (Tamborini and Skalski, 2006: 229). In this respect it is understandable that many *Doom* players have reported switching off lights while playing the game or using headphones to isolate their sensations from any external stimulus. As the senses are blocked from perceiving ordinary reality, the focus of player's attention will be solely on the simulated game environment.

Secondly, the freedom of movement, the speed and immediacy with which the game environment reacts to one's actions and the hectic tempo of the game are likely to induce another kind of immersion, as the player becomes immersed in actions of play. This has been commonly perceived as one of the core elements in gameplay experience; even such seemingly simple digital games as *Pong* or *Space Invaders* can hold players' attention for extended periods of time, as they remain focused on their efforts to improve their achievements in controlling the ball or in shooting down the aliens. The enjoyment of losing oneself in the flow of skilful action can be powerful, and the phenomena have been made widely known through the work of psychologist Mihaly Csikszentmihalyi (1991; see also Chapter 3). However, the flow phenomena relates to the optimum balance between player skills and game challenge, and can actually rarely be sustained while playing digital games for extended periods. Rather, games are regularly designed to present new kind of challenges that frustrate players who approach them with a skill set and strategy that was successful earlier in the same game (Gee, 2003: 67–71, 111–27). Therefore, rather than talking about flow as an essential part of gameplay experience, it is more appropriate to speak about *challenge-based* form of immersion into games. This involves being immersed in solving problems that are blocking a player's advancement, as well as the rewarding element associated with successful and skilful passing of these challenges. The challenges of *Doom* are largely requiring skilful manipulation of controls, capacity to navigate in high speed and accurate hand–eye coordination while shooting. But there are also more strategic challenges that test a player's intellect as the correct course of action needs to be decided. Some of the puzzles require a combination of dedicated thought, sustained effort and dexterity as well as intellect to solve.

Thirdly, there is yet another kind of immersion involved, as the player becomes emotionally as well as intellectually absorbed in the game world. *Doom* can certainly be emotionally gripping. The player experience involves narrow corridors, threatening snarls coming from somewhere close by, and sometimes also sudden loss of light and an attack from the dark. Elements like these have many of the visceral qualities of a roller-coaster, but the power of experience is also related to the fictional threats represented, as in a 'haunted house' ride. When it was launched, *Doom* was capable of provoking reactions that ranged from exhilaration and an adrenaline rush to genuine terror. Some critics claimed that for the first time, a digital game was capable of inducing shocks as powerful as a horror novel or movie. Approaching immersion to games and virtual realities from the perspective of literary studies, Marie-Laure Ryan (2001) has pointed out that readers of literary texts have long evidenced effects of powerful immersion, even without the help of any advanced audiovisual technologies. Crucial for this kind of strong involvement in a story is the use of imagination: the reader constructs a fantasy of 'text as world' while becoming immersed in text, often also becoming emotionally involved in the life of characters and course of events depicted in this illusory reality. While this kind of involvement takes place in digital games, we can call it *imaginative immersion*. The life of game-fictional characters and environments in the imagination is not necessarily connected with any particular representational or interactive technology, as the text-based adventure games from 1980s prove. Imagination is finally a player activity rather than a property of any technology or media. The three types of immersion are parts of the more general gameplay experience model (see Figure 6.6).

The multiple types or aspects of immersion in games underline the multidimensional character of digital games and related gameplay experience. Research shows that different players have different experiences while playing games they consider as their favourites; the challenge-based immersion reported by a player of *Nethack* or *Civilization III* (Firaxis, 2001) appears higher than that described by a typical *The Sims 2* (Maxis, 2004) player, for example. On the other hand, the sensory immersion into a text-based roguelike game (*Nethack*) is rather low, as compared with the experiences of players of a FPS-style adventure game with modern technology like *Half-Life 2* (Valve, 2004). And the players of a modern RPG adventure (*Knights of the Old Republic 2*; Obsidian Entertainment, 2005) appear to experience rather strong imaginative immersion. (Ermi and Mäyrä, 2005.) Being able to make such distinctions

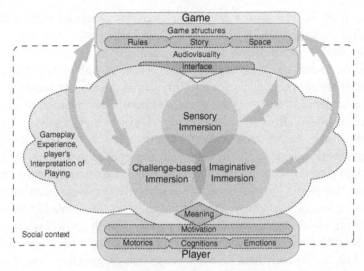

Figure 6.6 Gameplay experience model with three types of immersion. (Ermi and Mayra, 2005.)

within and among gameplay experiences is important – as, like Johan Huizinga (1938/1971: 2) writes in *Homo Ludens*, 'in this intensity, this absorption, this power of maddening, lies the very essence, the primordial quality of play'. Studying the multiple dimensions of gameplay experiences finally teach us to appreciate and understand the complexity and multidimensionality of human nature.

Doom was a powerful experience as solo play, but there was also a strong social element in its popularity. During the development of *Doom* John Romero coined the term 'Deathmatch' for the new style of high-speed, aggressively competitive collaborative play mode, implemented by linking several PCs with one another. Playing in deathmatch mode meant engaging in a multiplayer shooter tournament of player-vs.-player action. There existed a long earlier history of multiplayer, player-vs.-player gaming, starting with the first tennis games and two player space battles of the early *SpaceWar!* The deathmatch mode that was introduced in *Doom* was a distinctly new kind of an experience, however. The size of weapons and the graphic quality of the violence in *Doom* had a manifestly over-the-top, humorously exaggerated tone – at least for those who understood this kind of black humour. In a deathmatch, it was possible to turn those simulated bazookas and plasma guns on the virtual versions of one's real friends or foes. In offices, schools and garages – wherever it was possible to set up a LAN (Local Area Network) game – thousands of people were suddenly fragging each other to smithereens. ('Frag', a term of FPS gamer slang, was originally a term used in the Vietnam War, referring to the act of killing one's team member, usually with a fragmentation grenade.) At the core gameplay level, deathmatch also had many familiar features, reminiscent of such childhood games as tag, or Cops and Robbers.

Later, deathmatch-style tournament play increased in popularity with the release of subsequent FPS games like *Quake* (id Software, 1996) and *Unreal Tournament* (Epic, 1999). The multiplayer phenomenon continued to expand during the late 1990s, and also public games tournaments were arranged and advertised, sometimes with sizeable money prizes. From now on, there existed the possibility of making a career as a professional game player, similar to those of others professional athletes, albeit an option open only for the selected few most skilful players in powerful gamer cultures as in those of North America, Europe or South Korea. The multiplayer modes also continued to develop. In addition to deathmatch, *Doom* also had a 'co-operative' multiplayer mode where two to four players collaborate in fighting the computer-controlled monsters. However, human opponents remained to offer the most interesting challenge for most players, and it was only when later FPS games implemented team-based play modes where teams of players compete against each other, did all-against-all mayhem of deathmatch start to lose popularity. This was particularly related to the release of player-created game modifications, which introduced team roles, strategic planning and coordination as explicit parts of their FPS gameplay.

The popularity of 'mods' or player-created game modifications remains as one of the central contributions of *Doom* to the digital game cultures. Mods and machinima are also examples of emergent gameplay, meaning non-intentional uses created by the players for various game mechanisms. Much of the versatility and diversity of the FPS genre can be related to widespread modding activities, and this was due to the availability of tools and game software with program structure that supported modifications. In *Doom* the program code (game engine) existed in separate executable (EXE) files from those of game levels and objects, which were located inside files known as WADs ('Where's All the Data'), and thereby available to be edited and distributed separately from the actual commercial program code. The necessity and value attached to easy modifiability was well and early understood by John Carmack and the rest of id Software, who had in fact created their first own game demonstration, 'Dangerous Dave in Copyright Infringement' by duplicating and modifying the entire first level of Nintendo's popular *Super Mario Bros. 3*, this time by using PC technology rather than that of a Nintendo console. The original technical programming decision gradually evolved into entire hacker-friendly ethics and active support of mod communities, called 'communities of networked gamers' by Henry Lowood (2006). It nevertheless remains that id Software initially required all who would develop and distribute editing tools for *Doom* to sign a 'Data Utility Licence' (id Software, 1993) and the *Doom* modifying community seems to have developed in the beginning without any official encouragement from the part of game industry (Killough, n.d.).

Around the time of the release of *Doom II* (1994), id Software started providing editing tools and some source code for free distribution, thereby actively encouraging modification of *Doom*, and later *Quake* (1996), their next major FPS release. id Software also collaborated with other companies that licensed their game engines and expanded the field of FPS modifications with several successful games, like *Heretic* (Raven, 1994), *Hexen* (Raven, 1995), and *Half-Life* (Valve, 1998). Some of the most influential player-created mods include 'Capture the Flag' (CTF), a digital remediation of popular outdoors game with the gameplay focus on teams competing to capture each other's flag and bring it back to the team base. Another key mod was 'Team Fortress' (TF) which featured a further modified CTF game mode with an added class system. Particularly, CTF has become popularized as a mode of play that is readily available as a built-in team-play option in contemporary FPS games. Even more ambitious modification known as *Counter-Strike* (Minh Le and Jess Cliffe, 1999) has unquestionably become the most popular mod of all time. *Counter-Strike* is a modification of *Half-Life* in which the gameplay is team based and the players join a team of either terrorists or counter-terrorists. In 2002, *Counter-Strike* was the most popular of all games played online with its over 30 000 *Counter-Strike* servers on the Internet and large number of players.

There had been game modifications before *Doom*, and as Tero Laukkanen (2005) has noted, it is difficult to pin down the actual emergence of modding culture. At the early history of computer game programming, all games were constantly modified, and in any case hacking or modifying existing code was the dominant attitude among programming enthusiasts. Nevertheless, the arrival of home computers radically expanded the popularity of game modding. One important step towards authorized game modification was the platform game *Lode Runner* (Brøderbund, 1983) which was shipped with level editors which facilitated the emergence of player-created content for this game. On the less authorized front of gaming culture, there developed already in the late 1970s and early 1980s the practice of cracking copy protection from commercial games and then distributing them with a personalized 'intro screen' advertising the skills of groups or individuals responsible. One of the earliest actual game mods as they are understood today was 'Castle Smurfenstein', a mod of the original *Castle Wolfenstein* (Silas Warner/Muse, 1981) that was made by Andrew Johnson and Preston Nevins (with some help from Rob Romanchuk), all teenage fans of the game (see Figure 6.7). This was a transformation of the original game in which the Nazi guards were replaced by blue Smurf cartoon characters. The parody proved popular and is an important case study for anyone interested in the origins of the game modding scene in general. Even if many academics would prefer otherwise, it remains questionable to present mod communities as some kind of cultural counterforce to the games industry. As Olli Sotamaa's (2005) research points out, many modders engage in their activities just to get recognition for their skills, and perhaps even to get a job in the game industry. Modders are also providing 'free labour' to the

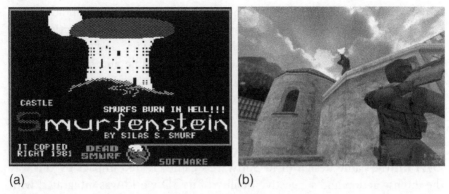

(a)   (b)

Figure 6.7   (a) Screenshot from 'Castle Smurfenstein' mod (1981) and (b) screenshot from *Counter-Strike* (1991). [Image credits: (a) Andy Johnson, (b) *www.counter-strike.net*, Valve Corporation.]

games industry, which exploits their efforts to provide added value for their games and thereby aims to extend the life-time of their product (Jeppesen, 2004). Modifications remain a conflicting site for creative pursuits, need for attention or prestige, production and marketing strategies, as well as for artistic or ideological resistance (see, e.g. Kerr, 2006: 121–4). Adding nudity into character graphics and modifying the weapon properties are typical examples of the mainstream, simple modding activities.

For the history of game cultures, the significance of *Doom* is manifold. It was important as a step in the application of new game technologies, and while doing so it introduced the FPS gameplay style to large audiences. Later in the 1990s, 3D computer graphics started to dominate game development, also for platform games, as in the case of *Super Mario 64* (Nintendo, 1996). In other family oriented games like those in the *Harry Potter* franchise (published by Electronic Arts) the influence of '*Doom*-era' is even more clear, as this type of game has their fair share of 3D shooter-style action, combined with the third-person adventure game format in this case. Along with the other key conventions, including the 2D top-down map interface (e.g. in *Pac-Man*, *Civilization*), 2D sideways perspective into game space (as in *Donkey Kong* and other 2D platform games) and isometric 3D perspective with no perspective shortening (as e.g. in *SimCity*), the first person, 'insider view' into a realistically rendered 3D environment became one of the key interface languages that most gamers today recognize and understand. The fairly simple control scheme that *Doom* also popularized is particularly suitable and often used in games that have plenty of immersive action in them. It is tailor-made for speed, rather than for complex manipulations of large numbers of game elements, such as is necessary in strategy games, for example.

It should be noted that there has been a further increase in multimodal or cross-genre gameplay in many games in recent years. For example, in the popular (and controversial) *Grand Theft Auto III* (GTA III; Rockstar, 2001) and in its sequels, the player can experience both free exploration as in adventure games, driving as in rally games, and more task-oriented and linear action game modes, alternating fluently between the third-person view and the first-person 'firing mode'. Such combinations have become possible and popular due to the historical developments in game design and an increasing familiarity with various elements of digital game lexicon or 'game interface literacy' within the digital game cultures.

Controversy has also been part of *Doom*'s legacy for action games. In its difference from the representations of realistic urban violence in games like *GTA III*, the game design of id Software's game created impact by the way the intense action and suggestive quality of its 3D world was integrated with particular themes inspired by horror and science fiction. Occult imagery was one of the elements that contributed to the controversy surrounding the game: with its penchant for violence, pentagrams and demons, *Doom* was easily identified as a work of evil by conservative or religious groups. Similar accusations of Satanism in rock music or other works of popular culture generally fail to ask why demonic imagery is common in this kind of culture in the first place.

One way of interpreting the demonic imagery is to see it as a signal for repressed and conflicting impulses and discourses, typical for situations of cultural discord and polyphony – co-existence of multiple, conflicting voices. A demon is historically a figure of alienation and ambiguity in the construction of identity: a demon is often active as an expression of tension at the borders of 'self' and 'otherness' (Mäyrä, 1999). Thus, the cultural interpretation of *Doom* should pay attention to the significance contributed by its imagery as well as gameplay. The 'digital demons' inhabiting the game world include such evocative figures as the Cyberdemon and Spider Mastermind, which mix technology with corporeal in their surreal, hybrid bodies. The players navigating the 'other world' of *Doom* will be involved in a ritualistic confrontation with images of technology-mixed subjectivity, thereby effectively exploring their own condition as digital game players. A cultural analysis will thereby reveal playing of *Doom* as an act that dramatises and examines players' own condition as subjects and objects that are ambiguously both empowered by and made dependent by information technology.

As discussed earlier in Chapter 3, the cultural roots of games and play can be derived from its ritualistic nature, with such rhetorics as 'play as power', 'play as identity' and 'play as frivolity' close to each other in the carnivalesque of game playing. The occult and grotesque imagery in *Doom* and the ritualistic killing of cybernetic demons during its gameplay can be related to this same ambivalent dynamics. For a student approaching the game from a cultural perspective, playing *Doom* must surely be recognized in its role as digital entertainment, but she also needs to pay close attention to how the powerful gameplay experience resonates with multiple symbolic and ritualistic dimensions that we are normally only partially aware of. A game like *Doom* is capable of removing its players temporarily from the logic of mundane world of work and study, and transporting them into a carnival world, full of riotous laughter, violence and the breaking of the rules of normative social reality. Rather than providing a peaceful fantasy of unconstrained wish fulfilment, it is worthwhile to notice the dangers, difficulties and symbols of threat facing the players taking their 'escape' in this dark digital fantasy.

Summary and conclusions

- This chapter has further introduced the role of technology for digital games with focus on such elements as the system CPU and bus bit width, which provide ways to differentiate between the increasingly powerful 8-bit, 16-bit, 32-bit, 64-bit and 128-bit generations of gaming hardware. Also, such key elements in computer graphics as memory size, polygons, rendering and textures were introduced, relating to the largely technology-driven pursuit for increasingly realistic appearance of digital games, sometimes criticized as part of the 'movie envy' within games industry. The introduction of new computing technology had nevertheless crucial effects on the look, feel and popularity of digital games within the parallel evolutions of consoles and home computers. One of the major trends concerning the foundations of games production has been the consolidation of ownership among media industry, relating to the concept of media convergence; also, games are increasingly produced as one part of franchises released in multiple media formats at the same time.
- The increasing power and memory size of digital games technology has provided opportunities for expanding the spatial aspects of game environments. Two different examples were provided of the direction spatial representation took in the popular 1990s' games. The first was Sid Meier's *Civilization* which featured two-dimensional representation of space, but rather extended gameplay on the global battle of different civilizations over the course of recorded human history and into the future. *Civilization* provides an example why it is analytically necessary to separate 'game session' from 'play session', the former potentially consisting of several of the latter type.
- *Civilization* also illustrates how the significant elements of the game can be interpreted in different ways, and thereby the entire meaning and character of the game can become an object of debate. Those scholars who emphasize the core gameplay as the sole source of significance, differ in their views from those who also take into account the shell or representational aspect of *Civilization* as a game played with and among various signs and symbols resonating with the Western-dominated history of colonization.
- The second example, the shooter game *Doom* by id Software, is open for similar conflicts in interpretation, but it is primarily introduced here as an important precursor for the 'era of 3D'. The representation of space as three-dimensional would be a dominant feature of most successful games produced after *Doom*. Immersion as an important element for gameplay experience was discussed through the distinction between three kinds of immersion: (1) sensory immersion, (2) challenge-based immersion and (3) imaginative immersion, relating to digital games' multiple dimensions as technology, interaction and fiction or fantasy.

- The role of particular game interface element, point of view into game space, was discussed by contrasting *Doom* with the games in the *Tomb Raider* series. When a player is controlling avatar (player character) in a game from the third-person perspective view as in *Tomb Raider* games, it is bringing the character design more to players' focus of attention, as the popularity of Lara Croft proves. Nevertheless, major differences remain in the degree to which players actually identify with a game character.
- The emotional involvement with a game is better illustrated by the powerful reactions *Doom* is able to elicit with its use of careful level and monster design. The fundamental character of *Doom* has powerful ritualistic and symbolic undertones, available for analysis at the level of its core gameplay, where the focus is on conquering increasingly powerful demons while navigating cavernous spaces. At the representational level *Doom* utilizes occult and science fictional imagery which contributes to the powerful gameplay experience it has been reported providing. The grotesque violence and demonic imagery in *Doom* have also created controversy, while these features can also be interpreted as continuation of the tradition of the carnivalesque in digital games. Finally, it is important to recognize the role of the fans of *Doom* in the early phases of modding and machinima cultures.

Suggested further reading

 David Kushner, 'Dangerous Dave in Copyright Infringement.' In: David Kushner (ed), *Masters of Doom*. New York: Random House, 2003, pp. 29–52.

Assignments on 3D and turn-taking

Benefits or Disadvantages of 3D?

What are the upsides and downsides of the recent years' emphasis on 3D in games? Find an example of a game or a game series that has appeared in both 2D and 3D versions (preferably from the 1990s). Make some quick comparisons, giving grounds for your views on which areas 3D is beneficial in and in which maybe not.

Real-Time and Turn-Based

A change in the way turn-taking is handled has many repercussions for the gameplay experience. The assignment involves describing and analysing these differences. Pick a game with either real-time or turn-based action. (It does not need to be a strategy game.) Describe its core game mechanics and explain how the player experiences the consequences of them being implemented either as real-time or as turn-based.

Concept Design for a Real-Time Board Game

This assignment involves writing a game concept document for a novel game. A concept document is typically just one or two pages long, and it tries to communicate the key features of game idea as clearly as possible. The starting requirement for your game design is that this game needs to be a board game, but rather than turn-based as most board games, this one should involve real-time interaction. In your description of the game include a short narrative that explains how this game is played, what are its key features, particularly focusing on verbs – what are the key gameplay actions that the player is involved in the game? Optionally, you might even build a prototype of your game using materials like paper and cardboard pieces and test out how your game would work out in reality. Conclude your game concept document by some self-critique or reflection: why this kind of board game might be interesting and what are its probable weak points?

(Associated research methods: structural gameplay analysis, comparative game analysis, analytical game playing as a research method, experimental game concept design.)

7

THE REAL AND THE GAME: GAME CULTURE ENTERING THE NEW MILLENNIUM

Games as worlds, the world as a game

A look at the contemporary game cultures reveals both its continuity and some signs of change. There were several important developments in the technologies underlying digital games during the late 1990s and early 2000s, which proved important particularly for the social quality of play experience. The cultural role of games remained still rather marginal when compared with the status of fine arts, literature or even cinema and television, and one of the remaining concerns was the 'juvenile' quality of games' thematic or representational content. On the other hand, the increasing critical discussion was also related to the rising self-awareness of games cultures and was followed by discussions on the nature and history of games and play appearing in both print and electronic media. A new phase of academic game studies commenced and was accompanied by some major newspapers also opening special sections dedicated to digital games and television shows, which were focused solely on digital games. The real boom was, however, happening in the Internet, where innumerable webpages and discussion forums were dedicated to the different aspects of game cultures.

In commercial terms, digital games have no longer repeated the 'from boom to collapse' pattern familiar from the previous decades. Even in the midst of the decline of the IT sector in general, digital games continued to attract millions of people, but there has been some signs of declining sales in recent years. The audiences for even the most best-selling digital games continue to be rather narrow, and even if the statistics of media usage and consumer spending on digital games show a steady rise, the estimated time spent with video games for an average US citizen was yet just 69 hours per year in 2003, as compared with the average 1745 hours of television viewing during the same year (US Census Bureau, 2006: 736). The available statistics for other Western countries appear roughly similar. Although electronic audiovisual media such as television and games continued to gain in popularity, there was a slow but perceptible decline in time spent with print media, such as newspapers, books and magazines, giving some concern about the changing role of literacy in the society.

While the early and mid-1990s had witnessed some overtly enthusiastic claims related to new media and 'cyberspace', and the turn of the millennium marked an economical crash to some of those dreams, some important developments in digital culture have indeed taken place during these years. One of them has been the slow but remarkable transition in many everyday behaviours, as people have acquired mobile phones and computers with Internet access to their homes and started using them for various tasks, ranging from social exchanges and online shopping to searching for information. Multiplayer game playing occupies a prominent place among these online activities (ibid.: 752). This chapter will focus on related developments within game cultures and introduce some key concepts for their analysis; the dialogue and changing relationships between 'world' and 'game' is at the main focus.

The growth of online games

There exist many different forms of multiplayer gaming, some of the most traditional forms being two people sharing the same game machine and play environment, each equipped with their own set of game controls, as in *SpaceWar!* and in *Pong*. Later varieties generally involve either split-screen technique, where two players can explore the game environment at their own speed, or the linking of several computers or consoles together so that they can communicate with each other, each player having their individual screen. One should neither underestimate the significance of perhaps the most traditional form of 'multiplayer' activity of all, where a single-player game experience is being observed and shared by one or several more or less helpful onlookers. The simple 'Hot Seat' multiplayer mode takes this social game situation a bit further by providing turn-based gaming on a shared set of input devices, for example by requiring use of the same keyboard and mouse for each player to make their game move before the next person comes to the same seat and takes the controls.

Any gameplay session carries social significance, regardless of how many players are involved in a particular in-game action at the same time. For example, the time invested in playing games can have various kinds of consequences on our social lives. Also the location of game playing should be considered. As Dmitri Williams (2006) has written, at least in the United States there appears to be a historical evolution where the social life of digital game players has moved away from arcades and where people of different ages, ethnicities and classes used to mix in relative freedom, into individual homes. In family homes, research has found game playing to be intertwined with existing social networks, bringing family members more into contact with each other (Mitchell, 1985). At the same time, it is a notable feature that game developers are predominantly male (IGDA, 2004), a fact further consolidating the culture of games as a male-gendered domain. Henry Jenkins

(1998) has noted how the nineteenth-century 'boy culture' often included such socially 'undesirable' elements as physical violence or scatological humour, as well as friendship and evolution of self-reliance, but largely cultivated in the backyards, outside of adult supervision. The twentieth (and twenty-first)-century childhood is increasingly affected by diminishing access to space and children's remaining in constant 'protective custody'. Digital games in their single player, and online multiplayer varieties provide intensity of experience and escape from adult regulation that can fulfil some of the same roles the physical space used to have for previous generations. One should nevertheless note that the trust and access issues related to unsupervised space are not necessarily the same in other parts of the world as in the modern United States.

Even if the societal role of digital games remains ambiguous as replacements of real physical space or movement, research suggests that the traditional stereotype of digital game play as socially isolating or crippling is not accurate, but rather that there exists a long history of empowering social play (Mitchell, 1985; Funk, 1992; Holmes and Pellegrini, 2005). The rise of online multiplayer gaming represents a return to intensively social forms of play, but rather than playing with people that we know or have physically met, the contemporary games open access to new social contacts via networked console systems and PCs. This will have an effect on the way our social networks are constructed (Williams, 2006).

Online gaming can be divided into various subcategories and historical phases. The expression 'Internet games' has currently started to refer particularly to those games that a casual gamer can access with their web browser, perhaps equipped with an add-on Flash plug-in, proving that Internet has commonly become synonymous with its graphical World Wide Web extension. The wide installation base of Internet browsers in network-connected computers of homes, schools and homes alike is often overlooked in the histories of game cultures, but this platform is actually numerically much more significant than even the most best-selling console platform for the mainstream of digital game play – in 2006, some estimates claim that over a billion people were being Internet users (Computer Industry Almanac, 2006). Web browsers can particularly be accredited with making it possible for us to play traditional card or board games online with other people, as well as for the popularity of various digital puzzle games. There has been a significant rise in popularity among such 'casual games', and there is also an interesting difference to the young 'hard core' console gamer audience, as typical casual game players are 35 to 65 years old, with slightly more women players than males. Casual gamers are also increasingly willing to spend money on their games, making casual game production and distribution into one of the strong growth areas within the games industry (IGDA, 2006). Some of the best-known casual games for Internet have been produced by PopCap Games, including *Bejeveled* (2001) and *Zuma* (2003). However, even more popular are the digital versions of the classic card game *Solitaire* developed and distributed with the Windows operating systems by Microsoft (1990–) as well as the *Snake* series of games bundled with Nokia mobile phones (1997–). (Kallio *et al.*, 2007.)

Much of the casual game playing is a solitary phenomenon, but social online play is also a popular feature of such games. Multiplayer online bridge, poker and *Scrabble* are popular examples of this game type. While for some it is no doubt more interesting than playing against the computer AI, an online social game often lacks in the area of informal social interaction between players, which is precisely the reason why many people play social games in the first place. A fast-paced action game does not rely that much on social interaction, which is one of the reasons why dial-up multiplayer services dedicated to action games (like DWANGO) were so popular in the 1990s. By dialling up the service provider line, these services linked together players from various parts of the country or even the world. These served particularly those participants in the early action game cultures who were not able to find fellow gamers from their neighbourhoods or who were not willing or able to carry their machines over for a LAN party. Specialized dial-up multiplayer companies eventually died out as Internet Service Providers (ISPs) took on the role of providing online access. Yet, there exist services both in PC and console environments (e.g. *gamespyarcade.com*, Xbox Live) which have persisted as there still exists a market for specialised services that keep player profiles, provide easy access to multiplayer games, do 'buddy positioning' (locating friends), provide chat functions, news and other such enhanced online game services. The fundamental features of online game worlds had nevertheless moved into the Internet by the end of the 1990s.

The history of Internet games is complex in its own right, including several types of games played on the multi-user systems of early Unix machines, as well as any kind of games that can be played by mail – email was already available within the early ARPAnet in 1971. One important platform was the PLATO system, introduced and patented by the University of Illinois in 1961; by 1974 it had grown into a substantial multi-user network of mainframe workstations, including many multiplayer games, such as the Star Trek inspired *Empire* (1972), and *Avatar* (developed in 1977–1979), which is considered as the first 'Multi-User Dungeon' type adventure game. PLATO was designed for computer-based education and in addition to multiplayer games it included many advanced features for communication and learning, but was displaced by low-cost PC-based solutions in the late 1980s (Woolley, 1994).

Avatar remained in a closed computer system, available only for PLATO users, but it marked an important new kind of game experience, capable of motivating and maintaining strong social networks or online communities among players. Known as MUDs, these Multi-User Dungeons, Dimensions, or Domains (depending on who was calling), were born in the late 1970s, inspired by early text adventure games, roguelike games and *Dungeons & Dragons* style RPGs. *Avatar* already had such genre features as navigating a graphically represented dungeon while fighting monsters and collecting treasure, and *Avatar*'s screen also displayed statistics of the character, items worn and creatures encountered. An important part of the gameplay was communication with other players and the capability to join character parties by tracking another player character; these small groups were more successful facing challenges than any single player would have been alone. The groups of player characters were an important emergent gameplay feature, showing future directions for much of the later online game developments.

The first MUD to carry that name (later known as 'MUD1') was designed and programmed by Roy Trubshaw and Richard Bartle at the University of Essex during 1979–1980. A challenge both in adventure game design and in multi-user database programming, this text-based game pioneered the use of rooms, objects and commands typical to many subsequent MUDs. An important element for the future of player-created content was the powerful 'Wizard mode' that Bartle introduced. In many MUDs, the more advanced players were awarded with the status of a wizard, being able to gain some 'godly powers'. Wizard status was a way to distribute some of the administrative work to experienced players, while the actual game administrators remained as the all-powerful 'gods', capable of overriding wizard (and arch-wizard) actions also. The hierarchical distribution of power became a standard feature of massively multiplayer games, as these were gathering hundreds or thousands (later millions) of players.

While many typical MUDs were focused on the competitive collection of experience points by fighting and gathering treasure ('level-hunting'), there were varieties early on, in which social interaction and role-playing were more central – notable example being TinyMUD (James Aspnes, 1989). The derivatives from this line of development are often referred to by terms such as MUSH, MUCK or MOO. MOOs (short for 'MUD, Object-Oriented') facilitate collaborative world creation and are sometimes used in distance education or other virtual world experiments. The social MUDs and MOOs are often important places for their user communities to meet and chat, the main differences from IRC (Internet Relay Chat) and other chat systems being those of the world metaphor and the added levels of world, action and character description. Several influential discursive conventions were developed in MUD discussions, and particularly notable was the innovative utilization of emotes, including not only 'smiley faces' familiar from email and IRC writing, but also more advanced 'poses' as descriptive texts of actions (Reid, 1994; Cherny, 1999).

As social worlds, MUDs and MOOs are not free of the social problems that eventually occur in most social contexts. The sociology and psychology of 'cyberspace' relate to both issues of common everyday social interactions and some specific features which are due to the mediated character of communication. Some such phenomena were recorded by Chip Morningstar and F. Randall Farmer, the designers of Habitat, an early virtual world with simple graphical interface, for LucasFilm (later LucasArts) in 1985.

The complexity of large-scale human action, and its consequences for any detailed central planning of events in this type of a game world was one of their key lessons, which is central for understanding the nature of massively multiplayer games, and worthy of quoting here at length:

> Our original, contractual specification for Habitat called for us to create a world capable of supporting a population of 20,000 Avatars, with expansion plans for up to 50,000. By any reckoning this was a large undertaking and complexity problems would certainly be expected. However, in practice we exceeded the complexity threshold very early in development. By the time the population of our on-line community had reached around 50 we were in over our heads (and these 50 were 'insiders' who were prepared to be tolerant of holes and rough edges).
>
> Moreover, a virtual world such as Habitat needs to scale with its population. For 20,000 Avatars we needed 20,000 'houses', organized into towns and cities with associated traffic arteries and shopping and recreational areas. We needed wilderness areas between the towns so that everyone would not be jammed together into the same place. Most of all, we needed things for 20,000 people to do. They needed interesting places to visit – and since they can't all be in the same place at the same time, they needed a *lot* of interesting places to visit – and things to do in those places. Each of those houses, towns, roads, shops, forests, theaters, arenas, and other places is a distinct entity that someone needs to design and create. Attempting to play the role of omniscient central planners, we were swamped. (Morningstar and Farmer, 1991: 286–7.)

The design and gameplay experience issues related to a single-player RPG or adventure game are distinctly different from those of games with several thousands of players. A particular adventure or story-setting can be tailor-made around a single player, or even a small group of them, but providing appropriate challenges and items to be constantly available for thousands of simultaneous players is a massive challenge for the art and engineering of the game. For a contemporary massively multiplayer game, the development budget for game's content can be between $5 million and $10 million, plus between $2 million and $5 million for creating and distributing the multiplayer infrastructure necessary for game's launch. Jessica Mulligan and Bridgette Patrovsky (2003: 55, 215) claim that actually 90 per cent of the production work takes place after this initial investment, when the game has launched and is operated live. The development team will change into a 'live team', which will try to manage the communications, resolve player requests and add to the game content, features and fix its problems. The size of investment required by state-of-the-art games is also on the rise; when the most popular massively multiplayer game so far *World of Warcraft* (WoW; Blizzard, 2004) launched in November 2004, it had over a four-year period of development behind it, with a reported associated cost of over €50 million ($63 million). Maintaining an active *World of Warcraft* operation in America, Europe and Asia, by June 2006, Blizzard had set up 9000 servers and had hired over 1300 game masters running the game service, which had then over 6.5 million subscribers (Vivendi, 2006).

Among populations of this size, there are inevitably differences in the needs, play styles and expectations with which different groups of players approach the same game, and this regularly leads to conflicts. One early example, the 'great debate' in *Habitat* was centred on guns, and the related activity of 'player-killing' (PKing). There was much debate among the players as to the form that the Habitat society should take. At the core of much of the debate was an unresolved question about the status of game's 'reality', and should an avatar or game character be considered as an extension of a real human being, thus entitled to be treated as you would treat a real person? Or, should player representations in a game be approached as Pac-Man-like critters, destined to be constantly killed and resurrected, or something else entirely? Thus, the discussion revolved into the fundamental philosophical and legal issues – is a 'Habitat murder' a crime? (Morningstar and Farmer, 1991.)

Later, in 1992, in a text-based environment called *LambdaMOO* (created by Pavel Curtis) social issues of virtual worlds were also much discussed. Curtis and the users agreed that a central control would not work and the users were left to manage their culture and community by themselves. In the spring of 1993 an event in *LambdaMOO* was reported by *The Village Voice* in the famous article 'The Rape in Cyberspace' by journalist Julian Dibbell. As reported, in this case a player with a character called 'Mr. Bungle' had got access with an object (actually a subprogram) 'voodoo doll' which attributed actions to other characters, unauthorized by their players. As the shared social reality in MUDs and MOOs is based on players submitting textual descriptions of their characters and their actions, this was a very powerful tool. Mr. Bungle used his powers to play out some sadistic fantasies on other players' characters, including textual descriptions where they were violated and sexually attacked.

The reaction, as voiced later by an attacked player (one behind the character 'exu'), in a discussion list message was powerful and emotional, reportedly written in tears:

'Mostly voodoo dolls are amusing,' wrote exu on the evening after Bungle's rampage, posting a public statement to the widely read in-MOO mailing list called *social-issues*, a forum for debate on matters of import to the entire populace. 'And mostly I tend to think that restrictive measures around here cause more trouble than they prevent. But I also think that Mr. Bungle was being a vicious, vile fuckhead, and I...want his sorry ass scattered from #17 [the 'living room'] to the Cinder Pile. I'm not calling for policies, trials, or better jails. I'm not sure what I'm calling for. Virtual castration, if I could manage it. Mostly, [this type of thing] doesn't happen here. Mostly, perhaps I thought it wouldn't happen to me. Mostly, I trust people to conduct themselves with some veneer of civility. Mostly, I want his ass.' (Dibbell, 1993/1998.)

The player community debated the issue for several days but was unable to reach complete consensus. Partly this was due to differing opinions on the degree of remorse felt by 'Mr. Bungle', and his intentions, partly to differing views on whether player punishment and control should be elements in these kinds of games, partly to deeper differences on how real the life and events in the game world were felt to be related in the first place. Finally, a wizard decided to take action and 'toaded' Mr. Bungle, which meant erasing the related player account, effectively a virtual death. Compared with how player-killing and similar forms of ludic aggression are approached among the players of *Doom*, and other FPS games, the difference in LamdaMOO's case is clear and related to both the game types and the game cultures surrounding them. When interpreted in terms of gameplay immersion discussed above, it, firstly, appears that there is a clear divide between those who immerse mostly with challenges and often adopt a 'gamist' distance from the fiction of game world, as compared with the states of powerful character involvement, which is typical to players drawn more into experiencing imaginative immersion. Secondly, the player of Mr. Bungle violated the ethos and culture of LamdaMOO, which was very social and community oriented. LamdaMOO's main focus was on the area of virtual community, and interpersonal actions were therefore carrying more weight than in some, more typically gamist MUDs or MOOs. It is important to note that even if MOOs are often socially oriented environments, there exists several different cultural and behavioural norms and expectations within them, and the interactions encouraged and tolerated vary (Hess, 2003: 36).

Rather than a distinct division, actually there exists much variety and overlap between those people who feel online game worlds to be very real and take them seriously and people who have little emotional attachment and regard for other game characters. Research into the complex issues in psychology and sociology of computer-mediated communication (CMC) has long debated the effects of online interactions. On the other hand, the anonymity and distance of CMC has a disinhibiting effect: when people believe their words and actions cannot be attributed directly to them personally, they are likely to become less inhibited by social conventions and express their aggressions more freely (Wallace, 2001: 124–5). Other researchers, like Nancy K. Baym (1995) critique the view that reduction of face-to-face signals would automatically lead into deterioration of communication; she refers to the dynamic and rich social networks in the Internet and identifies several areas where various contextual as well as game system, group and participant characteristics have an effect on the quality of social communication. 'Social presence', or the degree to which a person is perceived as a 'real person', is thus not a direct consequence of the media, but a complex part of the socially constructed reality that needs to be examined very carefully and closely at the microlevel of personal relationships to be understood correctly (Gunawardena, 1995).

In addition to social presence, there are many other elements to player psychology of online games that deserve attention. Many of these are such that

THE REAL AND THE GAME

they require lengthy participant observation within online game communities, and much of the early work has been based on observations made by online gamers or game designers rather than those of professional social scientists or trained psychologists. In 1996 Richard Bartle published his four-type classification of MUD players. Named 'Hearts, Clubs, Diamonds and Spades,' the different groups of players in Bartle's categories have their principal focuses on (1) achievement within the game context, (2) exploration of the game, (3) socializing with others, and (4) on the imposition upon others, respectively (Bartle, 1996). Also known as Achievers, Explorers, Socializers and Killers, these basic types have remained as the most widely known and popular classification of game players to date. Later, there has also appeared some critiques and competing ways to conceptualize various differences in player attitudes.

Another pioneering researcher working on the social psychology of MUD players has been Sherry Turkle. Her book *Life on the Screen* (1993) mostly focuses on the more general relationship that people have with computers and the Internet, but her most illustrious examples come from people who have become 'addicted' to MUDs. For these people, the fascination of online game worlds seems to stem mostly from the particular attractions of mediated human relationships. Turkle's work is somewhat characterized by the revolutionary 'cybercultural' spirit of the early 1990s, and she is often focusing on groups of individuals who are rather extreme in their dedication to technology, and not representative of population more generally. Spending extensive periods of time in front of the computer, some of the people Turkle has interviewed have developed a way of thinking in which life consists of different 'windows' and 'RL' (Real Life) is just one of them – and 'not necessarily their best window'. (Turkle, 1993: 13). Writing about one of her informants, a young man, Turkle says, 'It seems misleading to call what he does playing. He spends his time constructing a life that is more expansive than the one he lives in physical reality' (ibid.: 193).

The sharp opposition set up by such early studies between lives in the virtual game worlds and physical reality is, however, not the dominant position in current research. In one newer study (Jones and the research group, 2003) over 1000 college students were surveyed on their game-playing behaviours, and game playing was generally found to be an integrated part of their social lives. Two-thirds of the respondents (65 per cent) said gaming had little or no influence in taking away time they might spend with family and friends. One out of every five (20 per cent) of gaming students felt moderately or strongly that gaming helped them make new friends as well as improve the existing relationships. No opposition between life in online game realities and other social life emerge from this study. Some tensions in emphasis nevertheless remain; close to half of the gaming students (48 per cent) agreed that gaming keeps them from studying 'some' or 'a lot'. There appears little evidence of any serious 'gaming addiction', and digital game playing emerges in this study as integrated among other leisure time activities, forming part of a larger social multitasking setting alongside listening to music and interacting with other students face to face. Seventy per cent of all those surveyed reported playing digital games at least once in a while, and all of them had at least some experience with games.

We will next take a closer look at some features of popular online worlds and discuss their related social and even economic game dynamics, and also provide examples on the intermixing of digital and physical realities in contemporary games. Whereas the following discussion is centred on role-playing–style virtual worlds, it is worth remembering that these games represent only one particular type of online social play. There are many popular services that are focused on social interaction, casual gameplay and chat, including *Habbo Hotel* by the Finnish company Sulake. This one service alone claims over 83 million registered characters and reports 6 million unique visitors each month into its 31 national 'hotels' (Sulake, 2007). These figures appear not to be an exception, as many casual online games continue to attract sizeable audiences. Just to give another example, *Neopets* (1999), an online virtual pets game site, has reported over 136 million accounts and over 200 million pets being created by 2006 (Neopets, n.d.). Also such sports statistics-based games as fantasy football or fantasy baseball are reported to attract millions of users (see, e.g. *http://fantasy.premierleague.com*). Online role-playing games nevertheless remain as one of the most complex and visible forms of online game culture, while the above-mentioned other forms of play point towards interesting cultural growth and diversity that merits also scholarly analysis on its own terms.

EverQuest (1999), *World of Warcraft* (2004) and other virtual worlds

At the end of the 1990s and during the early 2000s, new types of digital games were drawing increasing public attention. These games had at their core gameplay many features that were familiar from text-based MUDs, but they looked different. These new games were easier to perceive as 'virtual worlds' as they were graphical, and many of the newer games displayed their characters and landscapes in increasingly detailed 3D. The emphasis in this subchapter is on introducing some of the key features and concepts that are crucial for understanding the distinctive characteristics of modern virtual world–style games, here discussed mostly with the help of *EverQuest* (Verant Interactive/Sony Online Entertainment, 1999), but also several other online games are mentioned. *EverQuest* is one of the more popular games of this kind, and it is taken here into main focus because it has already a long enough history to benefit from a body of dedicated research.

There were several notable games released during the latter part of the 1990s that pawed the way for the success of later graphical virtual worlds. Known as 'Massively Multiplayer Online Role-Playing Games' or MMORPG for short, these games continued the legacy of table-top, paper-and-pencil style role-playing games and computer role-playing games much in the same way as MUDs did, but they appeared visually more like descendants of the 1990s' graphical action games. MMORPG is no *Doom*, however. The core gameplay of a MMORPG is typically distinctly different from those of 3D action shooters. When one is playing *Doom* or *Quake* online, one is concerned with getting a low 'ping' (fast network response) since these are games of skill and accuracy at their core. Ping measures the lag or delay in the network connection to the server and it has a powerful effect on whether one hits or misses in the game. Combat in a typical MMORPG is handled differently and is based on the war game roots of *D&D*-style RPGs: when a player clicks the opponent with a readied weapon, the system calculates the odds and 'throws dice' (uses random numbers) to come up with the outcome of the encounter. Thus, gameplay in MMORPGs is not sensitive to a slow network connection. Some people, however, feel that battles which are not based on skills can quickly become uninteresting. *EverQuest* introduced an 'auto-attack' combat system, which some players do not like as for them it appears to transform them into an audience as their combat is being automatically played out. The main gameplay focus of *EverQuest*-style games is not on skills of hand–eye coordination but on other aspects of strategic play and life in these extensive virtual worlds.

Meridian 59 (3DO, 1996) was arguably the first commercial graphic MMORPG in the open Internet, although there had been numerous online games with some kind of a 'graphic' interface before. The sense of graphics had changed, however, from the grid-style graphic dungeons designed for the PLATO system games like *Avatar* or *Pedit5/Orthanc* (Rusty Rutherford, 1974), for example, to more or less realistically detailed 3D graphic worlds of the late 1990s. It is an interesting question, whether this leap in the visuals of a game is a mere incremental change or whether it represents a qualitative shift, transforming the whole gaming experience. Looking back at the discussion of types of gameplay immersion (Chapter 6), it seems clear that the introduction of interactive 3D representation added to the audiovisual quality and sensory immersiveness of a game. The quality of imaginative immersion is probably affected as well, as these aspects of the experience are not separate from each other. But as discussed, the imaginative immersion is not similarly dependent on the representation at the game interface. Imaginative players are able to build their fiction and fantasies on top of games with text-based, 2D as well as 3D graphical interfaces.

Probably of equal importance than the graphic design of *Meridian 59* were its flat monthly rates, before the introduction of which players were paying by the minute or the hour. There had been several MMORPG-style online games offered in proprietary networks, including *Islands of Kesmai* (1984, in CompuServe), *Habitat* (1988, in Q-Link) and *Neverwinter Nights* (1991, in AOL), but online play time within these worlds cost from $6 to $12 per hour. As MMORPG-style games have persistent game worlds, there is always something happening in the game and the game state changes continuously. Therefore, it is typical to invest rather substantially into play time when engaged with this kind of games – the term 'virtual worlds' rather than 'online games' appears appropriate precisely since these are environments for cultivating an online life and persona, and thus not primarily designed for unconnected moments of gameplay. The revenue models of game industry have an impact on how these games are experienced by their players, and a flat-rate subscription model was an important precondition for the modern virtual worlds to be able to gain their current sizeable populations. As Jessica Mulligan (2002) has noted, hourly rates have the effect of focusing the game mostly on the hardcore gamers who are willing to pay more when they play more. The flat rate changes the nature of the game and makes it appear inviting also for some of the more casual players.

The revenue models of online games are important elements to consider, since at their commercial essence, these games are more like services than products. The player may still need to buy the game client in a retail box and get with it some free subscription time to test the game, but those gamers who stay, pay regular fees to the game service provider. Rather than a one-time interaction between game developer and game player at the moment of buying decision, the economical relationship changes into a more enduring one, where the players may experience game developers as people who are doing a good or bad job in maintaining and developing their world. There may also emerge eventual conflicts between 'commercial ownership' of the producer company and the 'social ownership' of the player community. During extended gameplay a rather powerful sense of community can develop among the regulars of a virtual world, and such community spirit is likely to encourage players to experience and value other players and interactions with them as the real focus of gameplay and thus the core content in game.

Along with the increasing role of networked social play and online distribution of digital content, the legal questions related to the ownership of games, media and cultural content in general are turning into a quite complex and debated field. Games and players have emerged as one prominent area of participatory media culture, where the interests of fans and media industry do not necessarily coincide; online game companies sometimes react to player actions by cancelling their game accounts or even by threatening them with legal actions. The actions of the game industry have in such cases been driven by their claimed interests both in protecting legitimate players' gameplay experience from hacker activities and in protecting the public image of their intellectual property or brand from any 'undesirable' representations (Jenkins, 1992; Taylor, 2006: 125–50). Some researchers of law and legal studies claim that virtual worlds are becoming as significant as real places for human work and economical as well as other interactions, and that justifications for property should apply to virtual-world objects in similar way as to real-world property (Lastowka and Hunter, 2003).

At the time when the role of graphics was minimal, the subscriber base was still in a few thousands of simultaneous players, and the social or cultural consequences of virtual worlds did not receive similar public attention. At the early stage of massively multiplayer game development, many games could be more appropriately referred to as 'graphical MUDs' rather than virtual worlds in the modern sense. A good example is *The Realm* (later *The Realm Online*; Sierra On-Line, 1996), which featured a simple point-and-click graphical interface, but as in *Meridian 59*, a text-entry window, or console, held a prominent place in the game interface. Based on the successful Ultima computer role-playing game series, *Ultima Online* (UO; 1997) by Origin became the first real hit in the emerging market. Ultimately reaching 250 000 simultaneous subscribers in 2003, *Ultima Online* was based on the isometric, third-person graphics engine of *Ultima VI* that was already old fashioned in appearance at the time of the game's release (King and Borland, 2003: 155). Technical challenges for developing a stable massively multiplayer platform have appeared considerable. The launch of *UO* was a slow, multistep process where even the Beta (pre-release) version of the game was released with an associated price of $2 for players to participate. *UO* also familiarized players to the constantly evolving nature of online worlds through the process of patching – the process of downloading and installing patch files for fixes and updates of the game. For comparing the graphical evolution of MMORPGs, see Figure 7.1.

Having an effect on the way persistence and continuity of the game world is experienced, *UO* pioneered the use of 'shards' (called 'instances' in *EverQuest*). As a single server was not technically capable of supporting hundreds of thousands of simultaneous players, the solution that Origin introduced was to have identical copies of the game world running on multiple servers. All of them were presented as miniature copies or 'shards' of the Britannia, which was explained to have been 'magically' splintered in the game fiction. *UO* also incorporated support for player-run organizations, and thereby also made them into tools for social engineering of the large player populations. Called as guilds in *UO*, this kind of social networks of game players had been created around many games to facilitate social play and strategic teamwork. In *UO* there exists several special functions that are available by formally establishing a player guild: the guild interface allows access to the guild roster (listing and searching of guild members), and diplomacy functions where declarations or war or alliance with other guilds are among the most central functions. *UO*'s guild system also strengthens and systematizes the hierarchical character of social player networks, as there is support for a five-tier rank system implemented, including Guild Leader, Warlord, Emissary, Member and Ronin (the mercenary) (Origin, n.d.). Adding a further layer, guilds can in turn join the larger faction system, which consists of four factions all aggressive towards each other.

Virtual worlds differ greatly in how player-versus-player (PvP) conflicts and battles are integrated into the game. In *EverQuest*, fighting other player characters is allowed only in special PvP servers, apart from consensual duels, but the main focus is on group play where players team together to combat monsters ('mob') and gain experience and better equipment in PvE (players

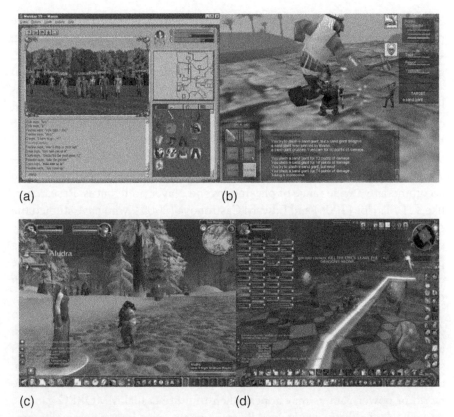

(a) (b)

(c) (d)

Figure 7.1   (a) Screenshot from *Meridian 59* (3DO, 1996). (b) Screenshot from
EverQuest (Verant Interactive, 1999). (c & d) Screenshots from *World of Warcraft* (Blizzard
Entertainment Inc, 2004). [Image credits: (a) *www.drewslinks.com*, NearDeathStudios.
(b) Arstechnica.com. PlayStation and PSP are trademarks of Sony Computer
Entertainment Inc. Images appear by kind permission of Sony Computer Entertainment
Europe. (c) Frans Mäyrä. (d) Markus Montola.]

versus environment) play. Groups are smaller teams of players who support
each other through their characters' complementary strengths and weaknesses.
The most challenging monsters or battle operations, however, can require the
coordinated effort of over fifty experienced players. *EverQuest* was originally
designed by Brad McQuaid, Steve Clover and Bill Trost, who derived much
inspiration from an earlier text-based online game world called *DikuMUD*. The
world of *EverQuest* has all the usual thematic elements familiar from Tolkien-
inspired sword and sorcery fantasy fiction. As more treasure and experience
points are collected, the more experienced game characters become more
powerful, but a single-minded focus on this dimension of the game can make
EverQuest gameplay reminiscent of *Progress Quest* (Eric Fredricksen, 2002) –
an *EverQuest* parody where a player has nothing to do except to follow the
statistics about the automated life of a game character. MMORPGs with
experience of point and level system are susceptible to 'powerlevelling' and

131

'grinding', which are terms relating to the highly goal-oriented, repetitive play style aimed to make the character more powerful as quickly as possible. Grinding, known also as 'treadmilling', means engaging in some experience-generating action like fighting a monster or using healer skills repeatedly in order to gain the related small experience boost. Despite widely criticized as being uninteresting, grinding is a widespread practice and related to the pursuit of status as much as the expected more interesting gameplay waiting at the higher experience levels of the game.

There exists multiple goals and gameplay focuses in a typical virtual world–style online game – these games are multi-modal in the sense that they try to accommodate a wide range of play modes and player preferences. Researchers like T. L. Taylor (2006) and Edward Castronova (2005), who have studied the culture and social life of virtual worlds in detail, emphasize the fundamentally social character of these worlds, but also recognize the differences among players. One of the most typical distinctions made in these worlds is among the cultures of role players and power gamers. Typically, role players are known to value characters with deep back-stories, who are engaged in elaborate, often dramatic plots and alliances with each other, all elements that aim to cultivate the game as shared imaginative fiction (cf. Fine, 1983). Power gamers, as interviewed by T. L. Taylor (2006: 67–92), on the other hand, have a strong focus on instrumental orientation to the goals in the game and share a commitment to understand and master the underlying game mechanics. The world of power gamers may appear alien to more casual MMORPG gamers, since they are effectively playing 'different games' even if they nominally carry the same name.

Psychologist Nicholas Yee (2002b) has studied the players of *EverQuest* and other MMORPGs and after conducting a statistical factor analysis to a survey answers from a sample of 6700 gamer respondents, he compacts most of the holding power of these games into five core factors:

- the desire to form and sustain supportive and meaningful relationships;
- the desire to accumulate power in different forms;
- the desire to be immersed in a fantasy world;
- the desire to taunt, annoy or irritate other people;
- and the appeal of group strategy and coordination.

Yee's starting point was Richard Bartle's (1996) model of player types we discussed above, but this research was focused on finding motivations which can also be overlapping, rather than identifying clear-cut categories for players to fit in. It nevertheless appears that Relationships, Immersion, Grief, Achievement and Leadership as powerful online game player motivations correlate with several of Bartle's categories, too. However, Yee says he did not find support for Explorer type as a motivational factor of its own, and his study also appears to point out that role-play does not correlate strongly with socializing but should rather be considered within the context of its own motivational factor, Immersion (Yee, 2002b).

Any study of virtual worlds as games has the challenge of properly acknowledging the multiple layers where gameplay takes place. Our dual model of distinguishing and analysing the core and shell elements of a game helps here only to a limited degree, since different players appear to have a whole range of different aspects of the game as their main gameplay focuses. Much of the core gameplay elements shared by players of this kind of game relates to their RPG roots: there is a distinct focus on the properties of game characters and the player aiming to advance the character by gaining experience with multiple means. Much of the common representational layer relates to medieval, sword-and-sorcery style fantasy, but there exists many players who mostly ignore it and play these games as an endless monster and treasure hunt or as a competitive player-versus-player combat game. Part of the analysis of virtual worlds therefore needs to address players and the behaviours in the scale of populations where the general outlines of these games become apparent.

EverQuest was for a long time the most popular MMORPG, and it can be considered as an important step in the evolution of genre; during the *EverQuest* era, the online game cultures and play conventions developed into their current complex forms from their initial roots in adventure games, MUDs and online chat rooms. When considered from a wider perspective, *EverQuest* remained relatively difficult to approach and demanding for non-hardcore players to engage with. At its peak time in 2003–2004 *EverQuest* had 400,000 to 500,000 subscribers, but these numbers have subsequently declined sharply. Another important development in the global history of online game cultures was the rise of popularity of Korean MMORPG games. The South Korean game *Lineage* (NCsoft, 1998) and its sequel *Lineage II* (NCsoft, 2003) reached soon after their release subscription numbers that far surpassed anything achieved by Western games. For the first time, several millions of players were subscribed to an online game world – an unprecedented popularity that has been related to many reasons, some of them being historical and cultural factors in the rapidly industrializing South Korean society, and some relating to the adopted subscription models. The PC cafés or 'PC baangs' in which most Korean gamers play pay for their customers' subscriptions. Despite the fact that new MMORPGs are constantly being developed, no Western game had reached similar figures until *World of Warcraft* was published in November 2004 and the market was quickly transformed. A notable exception among the high production value, 3D worlds, *RuneScape* (Jagex, 2001) has quickly risen in popularity and thereby proved a successful model where the online game world is provided with a freely playable, web browser–based game client (see Table 7.1).

The number of players yields very superficial information about the nature of play or game cultures involved. Yet a microlevel study of such large populations is challenging, and there is always the danger of presenting the play styles

Table 7.1   Available subscription data for twenty popular online game worlds.

MMOG	Current active subscriptions
1. World of Warcraft	6 600 000
2. Lineage	1 497 287
3. Lineage II	1 302 340
4. RuneScape	781 776
5. Final Fantasy XI	500 000
6. EverQuest	200 000
7. EverQuest II	175 000
8. Star Wars Galaxies	170 000
9. City of Heroes / Villains	160 000
10. Ultima Online	135 000
11. Eve Online	125 625
12. Dark Age of Camelot	125 000
13. Toontown Online	110 000
14. Dungeons & Dragons Online	90 000
15. Dofus	80 000
16. Tibia	67 397
17. Second Life	65 000
18. The Sims Online	35 500
19. Puzzle Pirates	34 000
20. EverQuest Online Adventures	30 000

Source: http://www.mmogchart.com, July 2006.

and values typical to researcher or his closest friends as truths about all game players. Yet there exists some more qualitative information from game players of *EverQuest* and *World of Warcraft*, which also points out how much and in which ways players are engaged with these game worlds.

According to published research, *EverQuest* players have appeared to be very dedicated to their game, proving to be comparatively hardcore as regards the time they spend with it. The average respondent in Yee's earlier study was 25.6 years of age and reported playing *EverQuest* 22.4 hours per week (Yee, 2001). In a later study Yee did found two main massively multiplayer game player groups to be the younger males (of ages between 12 and 28 years) and older females (of between 23 and 40 years). The basic demographics of online world play do not appear to have changed dramatically with the introduction of *World of Warcraft*, since according to Yee's survey, the average age of the *WoW* player is 28.3 years, and also in this game female players appear significantly older than male players (with median ages of 32 and 28 years respectively). *WoW* players also spend about the same average number of hours (22.7) playing their game per week than the *EverQuest* players did (Yee, 2003–2006). As *WoW* player numbers have gone up while *EverQuest* numbers decreased, it is likely that many of these people are actually the same players, following their friends in transferring from an older game to a more modern one. It should also be noted when interpreting the weekly online play time numbers that even if these appear to be relatively high for digital gameplay, they nevertheless remain around or below the numbers of hours that an average US citizen consumes while watching television. (Castronova, 2005: 61–2; Yee, 2003–2006.)

The amount of time spent with this type of game has been much discussed as it is often claimed to be excessive and having negative effects on active players' lives. For *EverQuest*, the nickname 'EverCrack' was applied, and also a support group 'EverQuest Widows' was established for partners, family and friends of people who play *EverQuest* compulsively. The group mailing list had over 6800 members in July 2006 (EverQuest-Widows, 2006), and there are many other online forums dedicated to discussing the issues related to having a relationship with an active gamer. There also exists some research linking the typical overlapping reward structures of MMORPGs to randomized reinforcement mechanism that is known to be linked with behavioural conditioning and addiction (Yee, 2002a; Castronova, 2005: 63–5).

One of the addictive aspects of the game – or, in positive terms, an explanation for its high holding power – is that games like *EverQuest* have a persistent game world. The player can see the results of their adventures accumulate in time, and the world itself can reflect the changes brought in by some major events. Technically, the *EverQuest* universe is divided into hundreds of play zones, and the game system loads the graphics, NPCs, monsters and other elements in that zone when one crosses a zone line. The extent of game world and its challenges also continues to expand, while the social universe created on top of it is constantly alive. There are several expansions that have been marketed as additions to the original game, adding new continents, races or character classes. This is also an important business strategy, and one way to extend the life cycle of game service by updating the used technology. In 2006, the list of *EverQuest* expansions included twelve additions to the original game in retail box and downloadable formats, as well as the release of the sequel or game world's parallel future in *EverQuest II* (Sony Online Entertainment, 2004) which has then released its own expansions and 'adventure packs'.

One of the key features of the fictional world of Norrath and the rest of the *EverQuest* universe is the range of alternatives this kind of fantasy realm offers for the creation of player characters. As familiar from fantasy literature in the tradition of J.R.R. Tolkien, these kinds of worlds are populated by multiple intelligent races like humans, halflings, elves, dwarfs and trolls, each having their distinctively different character and appearance, offering multiple opportunities for role-play. Other elements adding variety to the character creation are the character classes, familiar from *D&D* tradition of games. Classes add particular strengths and weaknesses to the templates of player characters, ranging from melee-oriented Rogues or Warriors to Wizards and Clerics who are weaker in melee battles but can use various kinds of magic. The physical looks of characters have also an effect on the player experience, and fine tuning the clothing and gear of one's player character is a popular activity among virtual world players. One way to interpret *EverQuest* or *WoW* is to see them as tools or toys to explore the multiplicity of our personae. Having both an ugly troll and an ethereal elf to choose when picking one's avatar character increases the expressive range available for exploring the various internal states that players might want to project into these fantasy worlds. The parallel lives conducted in game worlds may also be opportunities to act out unresolved conflicts or study aspects of the self that are kept hidden in real life (Turkle, 2005). At the same time, elements such as player characters need to be recognized at the level of their value for game mechanics; in this perspective the power balance between character classes is important for fair gameplay. Understanding this duality – the dynamics between character-based fantasy and core gameplay mechanics – is one of the keys for appreciating virtual worlds as digital games.

It is also important to notice that the 'magic circle' as originally conceived by Johan Huizinga is not complete even when powerfully immersed into playing in virtual worlds. As one example, there is evidence that men and women prefer noticeably different character classes; according to Yee (2003–2006), female *WoW* players are more likely to prefer a priest, hunter or druid character, whereas male players will more likely create a rogue, warrior or shaman character. In the early phases of online game player research (as in Turkle, 1993) the freedom of exploring alternative identities in cyberspace was emphasized and presented as almost complete. However, as T. L. Taylor (2006: 18) writes, more recent research tends to be more critical in this and points out how the lives of virtual characters and their real-life counterparts are intertwined in multiple and complex ways. Deep ties such as value systems, forms of identity, pre-existing social contexts and networks as well as culturally determined uses for technologies are cutting across the lines of magic circles. Nevertheless, there exist such practices as 'gender-blending' (adopting an online persona that is of opposite sex), giving evidence for some degree of escape from real-world identities. But this kind of practice is not without its social determinants, either. According to Yee's (2003–2006) figures, male players of *WoW* are about seven to eight times more likely to gender-blend their characters than females – according to his survey about one out of every two female *WoW* characters is actually played by a man, while only one out of one hundred male characters is played by a female.

The modes of separation and differences produced by entering the virtual worlds should thus be paid same degree of attention as to the similarities between the human life and society in virtual and physical realities. Edward Castronova (2005: 147) likens the boundary line between realities to an organic membrane; a virtual world is like an organism surrounded by a semi-permeable barrier. The magic circle needs to exist in order for there to be a game state, as that is maintained by our adherence to game rules. Yet this boundary line cannot be sealed completely, as people are crossing it all the time in both directions while carrying their behavioural models and assumptions with them.

Given the significance of social contacts in MMORPGs, the tools for communication hold a special place in this game type and are also an important entryway into studying the dynamics within and around these worlds. The original *EverQuest* was not particularly advanced in this area, but the player community itself has developed or appropriated various tools for their communication needs and purposes. The basic communication commands available from the text console are representative of the main communication modes in a game of this genre:

[enter] ('say', for sending a message heard by anyone in the local vicinity),

/tell [name] (for sending a message only to a certain person),

/shout (for sending in-character speech, heard by anyone in the same zone),

/ooc (for typing out-of-character speech, heard by anyone in the same zone),

/g (for speaking to group members, not zone specific),

/rs ('raid say' command, for speaking to everyone participating in the same raid event),

/guild (for messages to all online members from the same guild),

/auction (for buying or selling goods and services, heard by anyone in the same zone).

Separation of 'in-character' and 'out-of-character' speech is a loaded one, as mixing the channels and registers will be disapproved by many players. It is also possible in *EverQuest* to set up additional chat channels to have more targeted discussions for various purposes, as well as to use command '/ignore' to block all messages from some player. Later this kind of games have extended the communicational range by introducing character animations as well as recorded voices that can be used as 'emotes'. *WoW* supports a rather extensive set of commands that can be used to wave, cough, agree, deny, plead, call for help, dance or point, for example, each in the style of the race of the character in question.

With several discussions constantly going on multiple levels, the player of a MMORPG can be at a veritable nerve centre of messages flowing from various parties, having an effect on the total gameplay experience. At the same time, the social nature of this type of game can also be overestimated. In their study Nicolas Ducheneaut *et al.* (2006) discuss *WoW* and emphasize its accessibility, which has made it a 'more casual multiplayer game'. They also note specific balancing game mechanics such as how *WoW* rewards casual players with 'rest state' bonuses, which make it easier to keep up with more hardcore players in collecting experience. The researchers developed a custom application that allowed them to collect 'census' data from entire game servers, useful for analysing the development of player characters along time.

One of the main findings from this study was that *WoW* players appeared to play the game mostly solo, rather than with a player group. Only the characters at the higher experience levels, near the then-current top 60 level of progression, spent more time joined into groups. At this point of their careers, these game characters are also likely to be members of a player guild, as this is necessary for facing the challenges of the high-level quests and dungeons. The prevalent feature of *WoW*, however, appears to be playing alone but surrounded by others, rather than playing together. Authors suggest that other players provide an audience, social presence and social spectacle that make social online play appear inviting, even if the incentives in *WoW* for more tight team-play and social organization do not appear strong enough in themselves. The experience-level system can still rather easily produce such significant power differences between more and less active players' characters that it makes little sense for them to continue playing together after a while. According to authors, more powerful social navigation tools would be required to make group formation and guild maintenance genuinely central for *WoW* gameplay. The research points at the easy accessibility and carefully designed reward structure as the main success factors for *WoW* among the competing virtual worlds.

The longevity of virtual worlds have traditionally been associated with the strength of their social networks. The substantial amount of time spent playing a game and the intensity of the communication have been interpreted to lead into formation of virtual communities. Even if in *WoW* there does not appear to be much direct and durable involvement between majority of players, the constant sharing of play and communication spaces with other players creates a sense of social presence. In several other online games with smaller player populations, the intense, community-like interaction patterns have appeared to be more prevalent. According to Susana Tosca, typical *EverQuest* player networks have all the general characteristics of communities: (1) membership, (2) relationships, (3) commitment and generalized reciprocity, (4) shared values and practices, (5) collective goods and (6) duration (Tosca, 2002; the categories are based on Thomas Erickson's work on virtual communities). The players of *EverQuest* can be considered to constitute 'speech communities' that share certain linguistic features, some of which are typical of chat discussions on the Internet in general, some unique and born through spending much time within this game.

According to Jesper Juul (2002), a game like *EverQuest* has a double structure at its core. By this he means that *EverQuest* is a game of emergence, which has embedded progression structures. (This is attested to by the popularity of 'level-hunting', for instance.) Emergence here means that this large world, governed by a *D&D*-style rule system (character statistics, a class system, skills, hit points, experience points and levels), does not dictate the way one should play within it, but certain strategies and styles of gameplay emerge from this substratum. For example, sooner or later it becomes obvious to *EverQuest* players that some higher level monsters can only be defeated by team-based attacks in which different characters perform various roles suitable for their different abilities. As the formation of group strategies and the orchestration of joint attacks take time, it is an emergent feature of *EverQuest* that it becomes a group-oriented game with long gameplay sessions. On the other hand, the example of *WoW* proves that group or community orientation does not necessarily emerge within games of this type and that community is not always needed for these games to become popular among players. Ducheneaut *et al.* (2006) emphasize that the case of *WoW* points out how 'MMORPGs are BOTH games and communities'; a beautiful fantasy world enhanced with a rich structure of solo quests can alone sustain substantial major population of online players, even if the associated social networks remain sparse.

Some of the recent media attention and controversy surrounding games like *EverQuest* or *WoW* has focused on the value of virtual property. Edward Castronova, a professor of economics, raised the issue to greater academic attention. Since the beginnings of the game, there have been some real-life commercial exchanges related to the in-game valuables. Considered generally as a form of cheating, and forbidden by the game producers, the sale of in-game objects and whole characters for real currency has nevertheless continued to grow. In 2001, Castronova calculated that, considering the rates in the (illegal) trading at *eBay.com* and other Internet sites, the value of Norrath's currency exceeds that of the Japanese yen and the Italian lira. Furthermore, Castronova writes:

> The creation of dollar-valued items in Norrath occurs at a rate such that Norrath's GNP [Gross National Product] per capita easily exceeds that of dozens of countries, including India and China. Some 20 percent of Norrath's citizens consider it their place of residence; they just commute to Earth and back. To a large and growing number of people, virtual worlds are an important source of material and emotional well-being. (Castronova, 2001.)

As discussed earlier in Chapter 3, one of the fundamental characteristics associated with games is that they involve a degree of separation from the common reality: their meaning is endogenous, or produced and contained within its own structure. The real money trade of virtual game property is blurring or transgressing the boundaries of such classical conception of games. While virtual economies have continued to grow, critics have been quick to point out various problems it presents to digital game play. Richard Bartle (2004), for example, argues that acceptance of virtual property trading will effectively ruin the game as a game and that enforcing property rights of players would create impossible responsibilities for online game producers to indefinitely maintain these characters and objects in their servers. Vili Lehdonvirta (2005) has identified ten different attitudes towards virtual property (based on Yee's updated model of MMORPG player motivations),

Table 7.2 Ten different player perceptions of RMT [real money trade].

Achievement	Social	Immersion
Advancement	Socializing	Discovery
If RMT enables rewards to be bought, it violates the achievement hierarchy	RMT allows players to express themselves through their buying behaviour	RMT breaks the magic circle, but gives more choice over which content to experience
Mechanics	Relationship	Role-Playing
RMT makes it easier to obtain different asset configurations to examine	RMT allows those with less time to catch up and play together with their friends	RMT allows players to obtain the props that are needed for their chosen fantasy
Competition	Teamwork	Customization
RMT is cheating if it can be used to obtain competitive advantages	RMT provides objectives for teamwork and motivation for effective organization	RMT makes it easier to obtain a set of assets that correspond to player's taste
		Escapism
		RMT breaks the magic circle, introducing real-life worries into the virtual world

Lehdonvirta, 2005.

and even as a tentative framework that has not yet been empirically verified, it is helpful in pointing out the great range of issues involved for different players (see Table 7.2)

There already appears to exist a class of professional game players who derive their entire livelihood from virtual worlds (Dibbell, 2006). Stories circulate about Mexican, Chinese and Indonesian 'gold farming centres', where low-paid workers labour to produce in-game value that is then sold to wealthier, mostly Western players. But not all virtual worlds are trying to ban real money trading with virtual properties. *Second Life* (Linden Lab, 2003) is based on the concept of users designing content for the virtual world, which they can then sell or hire. *Second Life* operates with its own currency (Linden dollars), which can legitimately be sold and bought in LindeX, Linden Exchange. As the number and variety of virtual worlds continue to grow, so do the activities within. As increasingly popular places for work, leisure and socialization, their role for the future of society remains debated. Edward Castronova (2005: 260) claims that the distinction between online and offline lives will keep on fading away: 'it is all just a normal part of living – humans today, elves tonight, Martians tomorrow'. But Castronova also recognizes that a truly successful integration of the technology into everyday lives has not yet been achieved.

From a game studies perspective, virtual game worlds with their expansive social networks, fictional geographies and game mechanics remain as one of the central and most challenging subjects of study. Almost everything conceivable in real lives can probably have its virtual counterpart, but the additional layers provided by multiple levels of reality, game and associated rule-sets interacting together emerge as phenomena that can take place only in such ludic and computer-mediated setting. From a methodology point of view, analysing or researching subject like this requires careful thought and work in finding the appropriate approach to fit the research question. We will return to these challenges in our final chapter.

Multimodal and pervasive games

One of the long-standing critiques of digital games is that they are bad for your health; the physicality of digital games still also remains as one of their lesser known and researched aspects. In critiques, digital game play is connected with repetitive stress syndrome or possible epileptic seizures, caused by long hours of joystick wrenching in front of a flashing screen. In addition, obesity is a growing health problem in the Western world, and the increasing physical immobility while playing has been one of suspected reasons for this trend. There exists some research evidence linking digital game playing and overweight particularly among young children from immigrant background or from families with low-income status (Stettler *et al.*, 2004). There is also research (Vandewater *et al.*, 2004) pointing out a correlation between game playing and overweight for children under 8 years of age, who either play very much or play very little, as compared with children with no weight problem. Other studies (Giammattei *et al.*, 2003) rather point at too much television viewing than game playing as being linked to obesity: in this line of thinking, it is easy to consume soft drinks and snack food when watching television, while game playing requires more focused activity in controlling the game. Mark Griffiths (2005) has summarized the findings, noting that the causal connection between digital game playing and adverse health effects is not conclusive, and as there are also numerous positive uses or effects reported in research, gaming should be considered safe for most players, or even potentially useful in health care. There are also more physical uses of digital games, which will be discussed in this subchapter.

For those who have followed the current developments in game design and industry, the increasing popularity of physical games and more multimodal gaming has been plainly visible. In addition to the multiple modalities of gameplay discussed in Chapter 6, this kind of modern game will take advantage of multiple senses and modes of interaction, including the use of movement, voice or touch. An important contemporary subject of study in the laboratories of human–computer interaction, the history of multimodal control in games cultures reaches back to the 1970s. Television game systems like the Atari 2600 were provided with multiple controller devices – joysticks, paddles and light guns were among the typical devices of this era. The arcade gaming consoles were more robust in their construction and allowed more opportunities to react with the entire body while playing. But it was certain special controllers, often provided by external manufacturers, that provided home gamers with their first experiences of more physical style of play. Already in 1983 Amiga Joyboard was marketed to Atari 2600 players along with the *Mogul Maniac*, a slalom ski game. In 1987, Exus relased another Atari peripheral, Foot Craz, which was a small pad with coloured, touch-responsive spots the player needed to step on. The device was packaged with two games, *Video Jogger* and *Video Reflex*, requiring speed and agility in stepping motions for player to make advance. A year later Nintendo followed with a larger and more complex controller of same type, Power Pad, with games that featured gameplay simulating track and field sports, dance aerobics and various other tests in running or jumping skills (Bogost, 2005; Höysniemi, 2006b).

The early physical gaming devices met only with moderate success, and most successful games remained to be designed for mainstream controllers that were handled manually and required only minimal use of force, like joysticks, console control pads or the PC mouse and keyboard combination. The legacy of 1980s experiments grew into more substantial part of modern game cultures first in Japan, a country with a long history of experimental arcade game designs. One of the significant steps was the release of *Parappa the Rapper* (NaNaOn-Sha, 1996), an original rhythm game where a player is challenged to make rap music, and soon after that *Beatmania* by Konami (1997). *Beatmania* was followed by a subsequent line of Konami's 'Bemani' rhythm games, in which the audio has at least as important a role as the cues on the screen. The theme of *Beatmania* was inspired by music DJs: you have keyboard-like keys to press and a turntable to 'scratch'. The challenge is to keep in rhythm and hit the right keys (or spin the turntable) exactly at the right moment as horizontal notes cascade down on the arcade machine's screen. Jacob Smith (2004) has described how Japanese rap, music and dance games are linked to 'party rap' and such social performances as karaoke developing into integral parts of Japanese popular culture.

Konami has proved innovative in expanding the range of rhythm-based alternative game interfaces into other musical activities, as playing guitar and dancing. The most successful of Bemani games has been *Dance Dance Revolution* (DDR; Konami, 1998). It spearheaded the take-off of multimodal games all over the world. The core gameplay in *DDR* consists of dance moves: following a stream of arrow symbols on the screen, a *DDR* player tries to step on the corresponding arrow-marked square on the dance platform, or dance mat, in the case of a home system. Two simultaneous arrows demand a 'jump' step. The system keeps score and provides ratings based on how close to the beat the step was, ranging from 'perfect' to 'miss'. There exists several different versions of the game, with various musical mixes, and there are different songs for different difficulty ratings, ranging from light '1–3 feet songs' to very difficult '9 feet', or even '10 feet', songs.

A game like *DDR* requires players to have fast pattern-recognition capacity and quick reactions, as well as a good sense of rhythm. Extended gameplay sessions also entail having plenty of stamina, and some people have found dance games to be effective as physical exercise and use them for weight control. This use of physically exerting games for fitness purposes has its roots in the early aerobics-themed games and has also evolved into its own dedicated software like *Yourself! Fitness* (ResponDesign, 2004), which features a 'virtual personal trainer' designed to help in losing weight and keeping fit, even if this product can be seen as continuation of a training video as much as a game.

The mainstream of *DDR* culture is, however, rooted in game's basic character as game and dance performance. The arcade *DDR* device is constructed in the shape of a raised platform, enhanced with the use of colour lights, loud music, simulated commentary and virtual audience cheers or boos. When a gameplay session takes place in public spaces, often large crowds can gather around to follow *DDR* players' performances. Two distinctive subcultures have evolved as responses to this context; 'technical' or 'perfect attack' players focus on their gameplay to perfect timing and high score in difficult songs, whereas 'freestyle' players focus on the style of performance and may introduce complex dance routines into their gameplay. The main sites of activity for these subcultures are games arcades, *DDR* tournaments and online forums, each with their distinctive differences in forms of participation. The active *DDR* fandom has been an exception to the general trend of decline of Western games arcades; particularly in the United States, arcades with *DDR* machines have attracted a diverse blend of players from different backgrounds, including also a significant portion of female players. *DDR* tournaments in contrast are mostly male-dominated and more strongly competitive and performance-oriented events in nature. Online, fan websites like *DDRFreak.com* have made it possible to form discourse communities across regional boundaries and share gameplay videos or 'demos' of top players performing their routines in Asia, North America and Europe (Chan, 2004; Höysniemi, 2006a; Smith, 2004). For comparing the various multimodal interfaces, see Figure 7.2.

Another major line of physical and multimodal game development has been related to the introduction of computer vision and movement recognition techniques into digital games. Starting in 1969, American computer scientist and artist Myron Krueger had pioneered the development of 'responsive environments' and designed a system known as *Videoplace* in the early 1970s: a video projection that reacted to the movements of users. A combination of user's silhouette shape and computer-generated objects was allowed to interact in the projected video screens, producing an early 'artificial reality' or interactive simulation (Krueger *et al.*, 1985). There were many interesting innovations presented in scientific conferences and art galleries alike over the years, but it was a product called the Sony Eye Toy that became influential in introducing computer vision-based gaming to consumers. The Eye Toy is a digital camera, manufactured by Logitech for Sony's PlayStation 2 game

(a)　　　　　　　　　　　　　　　　　　(b)

(c)　　　　　　　(d)

Figure 7.2 (a) Foot Craz pad for Atari 2600 (Exus, 1987). (b) *EyeToy camera* (Sony, 2002). (c) DDR dance game players (Konami, 1998). (d) *Guitar* Hero package (Harmonix Music Systems, 2005). [Image credits: (a) www.atariage.com, AtariAge, (b) www.mag.awn, com. PlayStation and PSP are trademarks of Sony Computer Entertainment Inc. Images appear by kind permission of Sony Computer Entertainment Europe. (c) www.starbulletin. com, Honolulu Star-Bulletin. (d) www.codinghorror.com, RedOctane.]

console, and it provides vision-based gameplay when combined with the associated game software. The device was introduced in 2002, and the first game product for it, *Eye Toy: Play*, was launched in 2003. Eye Toy software was developed by Sony Entertainment Europe's London Studio, which has also designed *SingStar* (2004) line of karaoke games. As further music games with special control devices like *Guitar Hero* (Harmonix Music Systems, 2005) with its guitar-shaped control peripheral continue to gain popularity among Western players, the experimental varieties of multimodal gameplay do no longer remain as the speciality of Japanese game cultures.

The core gameplay of Eye Toy games is based on movement and pattern recognition technology: standing in front of the camera, the player is depicted on the game screen among the other game elements. Playing involves staying in a preset place on the screen and gesturing, while the software detects movement of hand, for example. Rather than offered as a general controller for navigating in traditional types of digital games, Eye Toy in its *Play* release includes 12 minigames specifically designed for movement recognition features and casual play. A typical minigame involves the players competing for a high score in such activities as window cleaning or boxing. In a later release, *Eye Toy: Antigrav* (Harmonix Music Systems, 2004) players are transported into a futuristic 3D world; the game involves competing while riding flying skateboards or hoverboards, as tilts in players' body movements are translated into those of an animated onscreen character.

Stopping for a while to gain a wider picture, and to contextualize this kind of ongoing developments, it soon becomes clear that there are no reliable ways to position elements like physically exertive gaming within the digital games cultures as a whole. The main reason is that contemporary game cultures still largely remain as little-researched areas. The few existing studies of broader demographics are usually the work of marketing research companies rather than the scientific community. Such published data as are available in a survey of game playing in the United Kingdom (BBC, 2005) currently mostly provides rough 'profiles' of typical players in different generations. Even this kind of survey is useful in pointing out how digital game playing has become such a common phenomenon that it is difficult to simplify in any single model. It appears that while the younger generation (less than 16 years) are happy playing the mainstream console action-adventure games, or best-selling PC games as those in *The Sims* (The Maxis, 2000) series, older players are more critical towards the direction game industry is taking. In the BBC-commissioned study the older informants, particularly from the age group of 36–50 years, offered most support for the statement: 'There are too many racing, shooting and fighting games'. Elder gamers (51–65 years old) also preferred puzzles, board games and quiz games to the high-production-value offerings of the game industry with their Lord of the Rings, Harry Potter, and 007 movie licences.

There are some signs, however, that the game industry is starting to react to the disparity between production and demand. Nintendo has been active in broadening the range of game design by introducing such products as *Dr. Kawashima's Brain Training: How Old Is Your Brain?* (Nintendo, 2005) the 'brain age' game based on popular book by Ryûta Kawashima, a Japanese neuroscientist, and the multimodal controller 'Wii Remote' ('Wiimote') for their Wii gaming console. Rather than reminding the usual console 'gamepads', this controller design is based on standard remote controls familiar from consumer electronics. The controller contains integrated accelerometer, allowing it to sense tilt and motion along three axis, an optical sensor, allowing detection of pointing direction, as well as basic audio and force feedback functionality. However, at the time of this writing, the effect of such new technologies in making digital games more diverse and appealing for a broader range of players remains to be seen.

Rather than relying only on new technology, or implementing the interface differently, there are also significant opportunities in alternative game design that can challenge the established paradigms or genres of digital games. The field of 'indie gaming' is one area where such alternatives are created independently from the game industry, usually for freeware, shareware or open source distribution over the Internet. Usually smaller in project size than those of mainstream industry products, indie games are often, but not necessary always, more accessible for casual play. Like the hobbyist-driven subculture of mod creation (see Chapter 6), some of the indie games feature original or even eccentric ideas that would probably not receive funding as commercial products.

Few digital games question the boundary between games and reality, and remain technically enclosed within the limits of a screen, even if the fiction of games may of course enter the life and imagination of player in multiple ways. A recent development called pervasive gaming attempts to probe and expand the domain of digital games in multiple ways.

Historically related to experimental branches of computer science called pervasive or ubiquitous computing, pervasive games involve game designs that break away from the bounds of traditional gaming devices and deliberately mix game reality with the real world. An Eye Toy game can be connected with this field, as many of those involve mixing the real-time video image of player with virtual, interactive objects or opponents. However, it is more typical to situate Eye Toy games in the family of augmented reality games, which is a close, but distinct, field of its own. Where the general aim of pervasive or ubiquitous computing is to 'bring the user back' from the virtual realities, and rather enhance real life with computing applications, augmented reality (AR) can be seen as a more direct extension of virtual reality technologies. A typical augmented reality system generates a composite view, where the user can see virtual objects overlaid or mixed with the real physical environment, often with the help of semi-transparent see-through displays or special eyeglasses. A demonstration of high-technology-augmented reality game is provided by the 'ARQuake', a modification of id Software's FPS game *Quake* as a mixed reality version, which was implemented in the University of South Australia. In this version, the demonic monsters and shooting action was overlaid to the reality of university campus area with the help technologies as Head-Mounted Displays (HMD) and Global Positioning System (GPS). (Weiser, 1993; Azuma, 1997; Thomas *et al.*, 2002.)

Augmented or mixed reality generally involves users maintaining a fixed position as in Eye Toy, in front of the camera, or wearing somewhat obtrusive special equipment, as in 'ARQuake'. In contrast to this, most existing commercial pervasive game productions have relied on existing hardware to reach larger audiences. A small Swedish game studio Its Alive! released the first game marketed as a pervasive game to be played with mobile phones. Mobile phones have grown in computing power and multimedia capabilities over the years and are currently one of the main gaming platforms, along with consoles, PCs and interactive television. However, rather than relying on the graphical or audio capabilities of mobile phones, the game *Botfighters* (2001) was based on movement. Players would adopt the roles of battle robots, using the SMS functionality to locate and attack other robots or players, while the cell identification in mobile phone network is used to determine whether players are close enough to hit. Thus, only ordinary GSM phones were needed to play the game, but a PC and web browser were required to build and upgrade the battle robots. (Sotamaa, 2002.)

In principle, using phones for location-based multiplayer experiences is a promising concept. Mobile games are, after all, almost always carried around by their users and since they are also connected to an operator network, it makes them effectively into an ubiquitous computing platform with user identification, readily available billing solutions and always on online access. In reality, implementing location aware games into mobile phones has proved challenging, due to the divergent features of different phone models, non-standardized support for various operator services and various telecom regulations for using positioning information. As an alternative example, geocaching is a simple treasure-hunt game self-organized by owners of GPS positioning devices. GPS provides more precise location information than mobile phone cell identification, but more importantly, players of geocaching are independent from commercial telecom operators. It is typical to use websites for sharing coordinates into a cache, which usually contains some small 'treasure', alongside pen and a log book. With historical roots reaching in the 'letterboxing' of the nineteenth century as well as treasure-hunting as a popular children's game, geocaching seems to have established itself as an outdoor activity with its own community and ethics.

There exists several research and development projects studying the future directions of game design and technology, within both the industry and the academia. Sometimes collaborations bring researchers from industry and universities together to work on issues relevant to game studies. In the case of pervasive games, one such example is IPerG, an EU-funded research project started in 2004. Looking at the variety of location-based, mobile and mixed reality games from perspectives of multiple disciplines, it has promoted a definition, according to which a pervasive game 'has one or more of salient features that expand the contractual magical circle of play socially, spatially or temporally' (IPerG, 2006). Discussing this definition, Markus Montola (2005) relates it to examples derived from games that blur the traditional conception of games in different ways, as by having a playing field size of cities or globe, by being ambiguous about when game starts and stops; or by complicating who is actually playing the game and who is not. Contemporary game design–oriented research projects like IPerG often attempt to combine social, humanist and technical research to produce a wide scale of different results. In this project, the practical opportunities as well as conceptual principles and player behaviours are investigated, while experimental game design prototypes are implemented and researched for massively multiplayer mobile games, pervasive larp (live action role-playing) and cross-media games, among others.

One of the important developments in recent years which has already proceeded quite far in realizing its own distinctive alternative game aesthetics is called alternate reality games (Gosney, 2005; Szulborski, 2005). Some of the earliest examples were created for advertisement campaigns and can therefore also be considered as examples of 'advergames' – games that also operate at some level as advertisement of company, product or political view. One of the earliest games of this type was *Majestic* (EA, 2001), which was a cross-media game that invited its players to solve a mystery with conspiracy elements. Released in five episodes, *Majestic* used the Internet, as well as IM chat messages, telephone and fax machine as well as numerous fake websites to mix game with the real lives of its players.

More successful in attracting community around it was the mysterious challenge designed to accompany the release of the Steven Spielberg movie *A.I.* (2001). Dubbed as the 'The Beast' because of initially having 666 elements, the game was created by a team at Microsoft, but the real identity of the organizers was kept secret even from other company employees. Sean Stewart (n.d.), the lead writer, has listed the design team's starting hypotheses as follows:

1 The narrative would be broken into fragments, which the players would be required to reassemble.
2 The game would – of necessity – be fundamentally cooperative and collective because of the nature of the Internet.
3 The game would be cooler if nobody knew who was doing it or why.
4 The game would be cooler if it came at you, through as many different conduits as possible.

Particularly the second item in the list has formed into a hallmark of the genre, as emergent player networks would be formed to address the game's challenges. The first clues of mystery were embedded into the end credits of *A.I.* the movie, which led to the establishment of Cloudmakers, one of the Beast player collectives. The producers have estimated that over one million people from different parts of the world were engaged with the game to some degree, but Cloudmakers remains as the most organized group, growing finally into a group of 7480 members, who had submitted a total of 42 209 messages when they closed on 24 July 2001. Jane McGonigal (2003) who has analysed the powerful hold this complex mystery had on the imaginations of participants has also discussed how even the 9/11 terrorist attacks were initially absorbed within the mentality of game play; some Cloudmaker members were suggesting to others that they should use their collective intelligence to solve the terrorist conspiracy. Being collective involved in a large-scale emergent network aimed at and unified by a joint purpose appears to have had a powerful cognitive and affective effect on the players.

Box 7.1 ON NEW GAMES MOVEMENT

It was somewhat ironic that Stewart [Brand]'s inspiration for developing the first new games was the Vietnam War. 'I felt that American combat was being pushed as far away as the planet would allow, becoming abstract and remote. It suggested to me that there was something wrong with our conflict forms here.' So in 1966, when the War Resisters League at San Francisco State College asked him to stage a public event for them, Stewart decided to create an activity which, instead of further entrenching people in their views and positions, would let them understand war by appreciating and experiencing the source of it within themselves. He called the event World War IV. It was to be convergence of people at play. [...]

George Leonard was intrigued with the notion of 'creative play' – the experience of a player placed in an open environment and encouraged to use his imagination to device new play forms. [...]

To Stewart's vision of softwar Pat [Farrington] added her own vision of 'soft touch' – games that develop trust and cooperation. [...] Softwar, creative play, and trust – the union of these three approaches to playing was the seed point for the new games that were developing. The one element that they all shared was participation – by everyone. (Fluegelman, 1976: 7–10.)

McGonigal has continued to research this phenomena, calling it 'supergaming'. A 'tactical combination of network-based play and spectacle', supergaming as described by McGonigal (2005) is massively scaled play behaviour and culture that is superimposed in public environments and has personally, socially and culturally transformative power. The characteristics of this collective experience McGonigal relates both back to the communal roots of 1970s New Game Movement (Fluegelman, 1976; DeKoven, 2002) and to contemporary theories of emergent systems and social computing networks. Practical examples include alternate reality games such as 'The Beast', 'I Love Bees' (42 Entertainment, 2004) and 'flash mobs', which are self-organized groups of people who suddenly appear into public space, engage in some startling behaviour and then disperse. Flash mobs are arranged both for fun and as social experiments, and for political commentary, sometimes also as an advertisement.

The contemporary field of digital game cultures has expanded and diversified to the point where it can contain several, even contradictory, trends of development. At the same time when production lines and sales charts are dominated by sequels and action adventure games from popular licences, there are also signs of alternative or counter-cultural elements rising within cultures of digital game play and design. The alternatives are significant within every cultural context, whether it here involves making a distinction between two games from different genres, or more or less original games within the same genre, or between a commercial game product and an indie game. For some, a meaningful alternative may be provided by the different ways of engagement offered by an online multiplayer game or by the physical interface and social spectacle of a dance game, while some are drawn into the problem-solving collectives of alternate reality games. It should be considered a positive sign for the future and viability of game cultures that such alternatives exist.

Summary and conclusions

- This chapter has focused on social online game worlds as an important form for contemporary games cultures, while also discussing some alternative developments. Evolved from text-based MUD environments, modern graphical massively multiplayer games typically appear as extensive virtual worlds that are characterized by persistence and continuity. Focused on long-term development of player characters through battles and search of treasure, they invite social collaboration and often engage their players with the life of player-created organizations or guilds.

- As the player populations in these games can reach millions, social and psychological issues have risen into important role in their research. This chapter introduced Richard Bartle's four-category classification of MUD players, as well as the more recent work by Nicholas Yee in surveying the behaviour and attitudes of players in virtual worlds. Some researchers emphasize the continuum between real-world social life and that in virtual worlds, whereas others have emphasized that the distance and difference of these worlds is important for them to function in their role as sites for experiments of identity and exploring an alternative social reality.

- Due to the social nature of these games, the analysis of social networks and communication has taken a prominent place in research of virtual worlds. These games have also attracted the interest of economists because of the vibrant market of virtual property that has grown within and around these games. The multiple, often conflicting, attitudes towards virtual property are one way of highlighting the different ways in which the fundamental character of these virtual worlds is experienced by their players. It is equally important to notice the various ways in which the in-game value related to the rules and game mechanics is intertwined with and underlying the other forms of value, created by the players through their imaginative immersion and various social interactions.

- This chapter also discussed multimodal game controls and related type of games where physical exertion plays an important role. Notable as a counterexample to the claimed physically crippling effects of digital games, this type of gameplay is also important in providing a link between traditionally physical forms of play and sports, and contemporary forms of digital games. Dance and rhythm games and computer vision-based games are offered as examples of this development.

- There are several alternative directions where game culture can proceed in the future. This chapter concluded by discussing experimental game design research in the area of pervasive games. Such experiments study the multiple ways in which the traditional boundaries of digital games can be extended or called into question. Games utilizing mobile phones and positioning technology is one example, but the 'magic circle' of games can be blurred by means of many media, such as fictional websites, phone calls or mysterious email and instant messages. These are some ways that an experimental game type known as alternate reality games is often using to engage its players with its web of fiction. As large numbers of players join forces in solving the complex puzzles, these games can become powerfully immersive experiences for their players. The emergent properties of self-organizing networks are also evidenced by such phenomena as 'flash mobs' that gather together for some brief playful spectacle and then quickly disperse again.

- The discussed examples point towards the necessity to analyse the relationship between 'reality' and 'game' with increasing degrees of sophistication, as different 'virtual' or 'augmented' realities with their social or game contracts intermingle with the commonsense reality, itself a product of certain shared social agreements.

Suggested further reading

Jane McGonigal, ' "This is not a Game": Immersive Aesthetics and Collective Play.' In: *Proceedings of DAC 2003*. Melbourne: RMIT University, 2003. Online: *http://www.seanstewart.org/beast/mcgonigal/notagame/paper.pdf*.

Assignments on mixed reality and multiplayer games

Reality as a Game Board?

As digital technologies and networks are becoming more ubiquitous, it is becoming possible to probe many aspects of physical reality with sensors and thus potentially also use such information to create gameplay. Consider some aspect of reality (from natural phenomena to human behaviours) that is common enough, but not yet used as a mechanism in any game that you know about. Write a short game concept paper, describing your idea based on such novel game mechanic, and give grounds why this would be an interesting and worthwhile experiment in game design. A game concept document is discussed earlier (see assignment 'Concept Design for a Real-Time Board Game', Chapter 6).

Multiplayer Means More Fun?

Are there immediate gains to be derived by designing and playing digital games in multiplayer format, rather than alone? Play some game that has both singleplayer and multiplayer mode in both versions. Experiment and take notes of your gameplay experiences. Pay attention to the kind of multiplayer experience you are talking about (split screen on a console, LAN party, Internet online play). What are the strong and weak points of the single-player mode and what are those of the multiplayer one? Also discuss can these two be meaningfully compared at all?

(Associated research methods: game concept design, comparative gameplay analysis.)

8

PREPARING FOR A GAME STUDIES PROJECT

Learning to ask

At this point it should be clear that the range of both valid subjects of study and concepts and methods to address them is very broad within the multidisciplinary field of game studies. Each professor, department or faculty will make use of their individual expertise and academic history while approaching games and therefore they will each offer a slightly differently focused version of game studies. Typically, there will also be specific practical guidelines available for students to conduct their game studies work on certain line of issues and in a certain manner. Most students will soon also face the exciting freedom as well as the many challenges that are ahead of those choosing to specialize within this emerging field. This final chapter will briefly discuss some of the most central issues involved in preparing for an independent study project or other larger assignment in game studies.

A crucial step into successful research is finding and formulating a good research question. Discovering the right question and topic of inquiry might require some dedicated effort, though. The subject matter defines the phenomenon you are interested in, while the research question will determine the particular point of view and line of approach required to answer that question. Both the subject matter and the research question should be something that you are genuinely interested in and something that you would like to learn more about. Is there a game that you are curious about or some aspect of player behaviour you have observed and which has caught your attention? While considering your options, it is important to note that some questions are more appropriate for a Ph.D. dissertation subject than the first game studies project – some major questions are enough to trouble entire groups of researchers over several years. Estimating the time and effort required by researching the topic is an important consideration that will be discussed further below, in methodological issues.

One aspect to consider is also the availability of previous research on the subject. The paper should obviously not duplicate the efforts of some earlier study, but generally when still early in one's studies, it is easier to get started when there already exists some previous, roughly comparable analysis or research to discuss, criticize or use as a model for one's own inquiry. There are many fascinating topics to research in games, and many of them are such that virtually no previous academic work exists to open the road. This is by no means a reason to abandon the subject, as your paper might be the first step on the road into an important academic study which will fill in this particular gap. But the lack of academic sources will raise the bar; there will be added conceptual and theoretical challenges ahead of the first researcher mapping an uncharted area. What is the nature of the phenomenon? How to situate it within the broader field of human behaviour or forms of culture? Which are the correct concepts to use while discussing it? This last issue is by no means trivial, since science and scholarship are socio-cultural activities in themselves, and a research paper should communicate its message to the scientific community. If works within game studies fail to take into account the long history of scholarship within multiple relevant disciplines, they will easily be perceived as ignorant and isolated attempts. Academic life is based on love of learning, and there is no better advice than to read widely and well, and to write often. For my experience, it is more common for a student in game studies to have many original ideas, but lack awareness of how existing academic work can contribute to her study, than to be over-reliant or dependent on scholarly sources.

Finding a good and productive research question for one's study is part of the hermeneutic circle of research process. As originally discussed by the German philosopher and theologian Friedrich Schleiermacher (1768–1834), the hermeneutic circle appears superficially as a paradox: in order to understand the subject of study correctly, one first has to pay attention to its various details and particulars. But it is impossible to appreciate the significance of these details and particulars correctly without first having a correct idea about the whole (Jasper, 2004: 21). During the process of study, hermeneutic inquiry actually operates more like a spiral: as more is learned about the details, a better conception of the whole is acquired, which in turn helps researcher to understand the role of each particular detail better (see Figure 8.1).

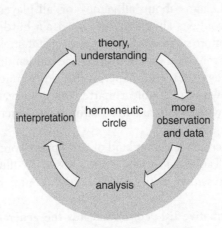

Figure 8.1   Hermeneutic circle as a spiralling process of inquiry.

The hermeneutic circle helps to comprehend why a change in the topic of paper is often a good sign. As a student learns more about the nature of phenomenon, or comes across a method or concept that opens up a fresh perspective into it, the precise focus and formulation of a research question is likely to change. Too early fixation on a particular approach means easily missing the point, as the research question has not yet been informed by the research process at this point; but the decision of subject should not be postponed too late, either. To give a very rough guideline, one could imagine dividing the available time for a game study project into three parts, and then dedicating the first third to 'pre-study' (playing games, searching of literature, reading, making notes and outlining the work), the second third to gathering and analysing data and the last third to writing and proof-reading the actual research paper. It is easy to underestimate time and effort required by each of these phases. The final selection of subject matter, research question and approach is fixed during the first of these three phases, and one should always consult one's academic supervisor while considering these fundamentals – having consultations as early and as much as is needed at this stage is crucial.

One practical way of scaling down the workload associated with certain research questions is to focus the paper on a certain subset within one's field of interest. The ultimate goal might be to understand the nature of interaction in a multiplayer FPS game, for example, or the character of related gameplay experience; but the start might involve describing some of the core gameplay features in one particular map of one particular game. Even this kind of narrowed-down approach can require substantial amounts of work, as there are surely many differences between the same map as played alone, against bots of certain difficulty level, or when experienced in a deathmatch tournament against experienced players.

Some of the central principles of scientific thought are important to consider while selecting one's research subject. Particularly, be cautious while aiming to make substantial claims about 'all games' or 'all players'. Claims of facts made in academic contexts always involve a certain burden of proof, which becomes higher the more substantial the findings or statements claim to be. The motivation of study might be on discovering the hidden universals behind all games and play, but as an academic paper, your study is much more convincing if it is narrowed down into a subject matter that you really can confidently claim to know very well and discuss in an informed manner from an academic perspective as well.

To give you a concrete idea what kind of titles papers presented in scientific conferences carry, Table 8.1 offers a list chosen to illustrate the variety of research work presented in the DiGRA 2005 conference in Vancouver, Canada.

A good and informative title communicates the general idea of what the paper is about to discuss. The title is, nevertheless, not the same as the research

Table 8.1 Selected titles of papers presented in *Chancing Views – Worlds in Play*.

Build It to Understand It: Ludology Meets Narratology in Game Design Space

Frame and Metaphor in Political Games

Shadowplay: Simulated Illumination in Game Worlds

Towards an Ontological Language for Game Analysis

Fundamental Components of the Gameplay Experience: Analysing Immersion

Push. Play: An Examination of the Gameplay Button

The Things We Learned on Liberty Island: Designing Games to Help People Become Competent Game Players

Presence Experience in Mobile Gaming

Designing Goals for Online Role-Players

Girls Creating Games: Challenging Existing Assumptions about Game Content

Understanding Korean Experiences of Online Game Hype, Identity, and the Menace of the 'Wang-tta'

Early Games Production in New Zealand

Evolution of Space Configuration in Videogames

Interactive Story Writing in the Classroom: Using Computer Games

Playing Through: the Future of Alternative and Critical Game Projects

Playing with Non-Humans: Digital Games as Technocultural Form

Learning Games as a Platform for Simulated Science Practice

The Design of Narrative as an Immersive Simulation

Opening the Production Pipeline: Unruly Creators

Who Owns My Avatar? – Rights in Virtual Property

Source: Digital Games Research Association's Second International Conference. Vancouver, Canada, 16–19 June 2005. Via *www.digra.org/dl*.

question which should be formulated early in the paper and which relates intimately to the methodological considerations discussed next.

Selecting and building the toolbox of methods

Individual methods can be described as means to do research and pursue knowledge, and together a set of methods and rationale for employing them form a methodology. As the interdisciplinary range of game studies includes studies with distinctly humanities and social sciences -related approaches as well as research work with mostly technical or artistic emphasis, there is no single methodology organizing work done within game studies; rather, every researcher needs to construct their own toolbox of methods to suit their particular approach. This can occasionally be a communication problem within the game studies community, since the choice of methodology is tightly related to the overall goals of research and its underlying philosophy. Within a more mono-cultural field, the underlying assumptions of methods can easily be passed over, but in an interdisciplinary field like game studies it is important to state explicitly what kind of knowledge one is aiming at and why. Such fundamentals form the ontological and epistemological basis of research. Ontology is concerned with the existence of what games or play are fundamentally. Epistemology deals with the nature of knowing and knowledge. How can we study and learn to know games and play as they are ontologically defined? According to Thomas Kuhn (1996), a sociologist of science, these basic assumptions form scientific paradigms, consisting of accepted views on the subjects of study as well as of proper ways to structure research questions, methodologies and interpretations of results. Even if it is still too early to talk about established paradigms within or among varieties of thought in game studies, it is nevertheless useful to be aware of how even the terms used in academic contexts carry with them entire systems of thought. Thus, both the adopted methods and the language used to discuss them are interconnected as forms of social practice or as academic discourses of power.

In discussing methodology issues on the basis of their central subjects of study, there appears to be currently at least three main areas within game studies. The first area is research that principally aims to study games and their structures; the second kind of research is mostly focused on understanding game players and their play behaviour; a third distinctive area involves researching game design and development – even if in reality there is much overlap and interaction between and within the research done in all these three main areas. The disciplinary history of game studies was discussed in the first chapter of this book, and it is relevant also in this context, as scholars working in each of these three areas bring with them the methodologies typical for their original disciplines. Studies that involve analyses of individual games or cultural interpretations of their significance are often rooted in a methodology typical for the humanities, whereas play and player studies are generally informed by social sciences methodologies. Studies in game design research have a variety of methodological traditions to draw upon, including those of technical and computer sciences, and approaches in art and design studies. Some of the most interesting current work in game studies consists of attempts to fit together and synthesize these diverse traditions into unique new approaches and methodologies. This book is also promoting such efforts, perceiving important strengths and opportunities being available for game studies as a field of learning dedicated to understanding both game, game design and players, and their dynamic relationships in the practices and processes of games cultures.

There is no room in this book to discuss thoroughly the multiplicity of relevant methods, nor their theoretical backgrounds, and the reader is advised to consult specialized volumes while starting their own study projects. The following will briefly present some important approaches and related considerations to offer an introductory overview. Particular attention here is paid to the methods related to the social sciences traditions because of their overlap, utility and application for cultural studies and design research methodologies alike.

Humanities methods

The methodological range of humanities is great, and numerous approaches have been applied to the study of games. The influence of such fields as literary and textual studies or music and performance studies has already been mentioned in earlier chapters of this book. Much of contemporary research into games will involve some of the conceptual tools or underlying philosophy derived from semiotic and structuralist thought. These traditions involve studying systems like human language, psyche, society or, as in our case, a digital game, through an analytical process which involves identifying the constituent elements and their underlying structures, as well as describing the rules for their combination within the subject of study. The process of semiotic analysis focuses on the signifying potentials in such systems through identification of its most important signs (or 'signifiers' in semiotic parlance), describing how these combine into larger structures and finally interpreting how meaning is produced within the context of this sign system.

Generally known as 'textual analysis', this kind of methodology often also involves discussing games as texts, or in textual terms as complex and multimodal signs that are constituted by other signs. When called 'discourse analysis', the emphasis is on uncovering how conventions in language (or in games, when they are considered as media) make certain ways of representing or thinking to appear as self-evident and natural, even if they carry certain power relations within them. Within such approaches, intertextual or intermedial comparisons are used to highlight hidden similarities and differences between games, or areas of media and culture, thereby extending the range of interpretation. Textual analyses are influenced to a varying degree by post-structuralist thought which rejects the structuralist search for universal cultural logic, or any single authorial meaning, and rather aims to reveal how the signification processes are always inherently multiple and conflicting. Literary and media studies have contributed to this assemblage of humanistic game studies methodologies its own conceptual tools, ranging from discussions of character, narration, dramatic arc or theme, to point of view, cut scenes and camerawork familiar from film studies. Cultural studies style of analysis often also subjects the text to ideological critique that is informed by Marxist, feminist or psychoanalytic thought. The works of British game researchers published in *ScreenPlay* (King and Krzywinska, 2002) and *Game Cultures* (Dovey and Kennedy, 2006) are good examples of such approaches.

Such humanities disciplines as history and visual art studies also have much to contribute to the methodological range of game studies. There are many special challenges related to the archival and identification of software and hardware histories, and the systematic approaches developed within library and information studies are useful for such studies. The study of language, literature and beliefs created and circulated among game cultures can also draw upon the methodological traditions of various humanities disciplines. This book has, to a large degree, been influenced and informed by games research work done using humanistic methodologies, while the impact of the next two groups of methodologies has also been great.

Going back to the sample assignments featured earlier in this book, particularly 'Remediation of a non-digital game' (Chapter 3) is based on a humanities approach: it involves adopting an analytical stance towards games, making analytical distinctions between such key elements as game controls, game mechanics and visual representation of the game interface. It also involves comparative structural analysis, since it requires comparing non-digital game with its digitalized version. Also the assignment 'Alternative Games History' (Chapter 4) with its historiographic approach is rooted in the humanities.

Social sciences methods

The methodological toolbox available from within traditions of social sciences into game research is equally extensive. The main difference to humanities is the influence of natural sciences and how scientific method is often perceived within this tradition. Where research in humanities is generally strong in providing original and insightful interpretations about the meaning of the studied phenomenon, social sciences can provide some verifiable facts about the use or influence of this phenomenon. Verification is at the heart of classic scientific method, which is rooted in a view of science as study of empirical, objectively observable reality. However, not all social scientists adhere to this view, also known as positivism. Deriving from such nineteenth-century early social scientists as Auguste Comte (1798–1857), positivism holds to the view of science as logical and coherent structure of statements that can be confirmed or falsified by empirical tests or observations and that results attained through such methods are independent of culture or the person doing the observation.

Studies into the effects of game playing generally rely on scientific method and involve setting a hypothesis to explain and predict how a relation between certain measurable variables function and then creating an experiment to support or falsify the hypothesis. While many social science studies involve observations in natural settings, preparing a controlled experiment requires two groups of test subjects, where the other group acts as a control sample compared with the results derived from testing the experimental sample. Both groups are tested before and after the treatment, and experiment is normally conducted in a laboratory to eliminate any extraneous effects. A typical laboratory research may involve, for example, comparing how much aggressive behaviour can be observed in a group of children who spent some time playing a violently themed digital game to the behaviour of a control group who was watching television or playing a non-violent game. While laboratory studies usually have good internal validity (the design of experiment itself is scientifically solid), they may have problematic external validity, which means that results derived in a laboratory are not necessarily generalizable to the real world. The researcher also has to be careful while conducting the statistical analysis of her data; for example, the proof of strong correlation between two variables does not necessarily imply their causality, as the explaining causal link may be in a third variable hidden from the researcher. Also, proving the reliability of measurements does not automatically mean their validity, since a test may be reliably measuring something that is actually not a valid measure for the phenomena research was supposed to be focusing on.

One particular method often used in social sciences to derive information on the attitudes and behaviours of larger populations is survey. Many surveys involve providing large groups of people with a set of questions, usually in the form of a questionnaire. A caveat, though, people are not very reliable in answering questions that ask them to quantify precisely their behaviour, like reporting the exact time they spend daily playing games, nor do they always answer truthfully to what they feel as sensitive personal questions. A survey can be administered by the researcher over the phone, or face to face in the street, as is common for various marketing surveys. A survey study can also take the form of a self-administered survey questionnaire through mail or by the Internet. While creating a survey to provide data for a game studies project, standard questionnaire design guidelines apply; you must first clarify the objectives of study to yourself, think carefully how the answers will be analysed, write as clear and unambiguous questions as possible, while avoiding biased language or leading questions. Open questions provide the informants with more freedom, but require much more work to analyse than closed questions where the informant is required to choose from alternatives given.

It is also a good idea to test the questionnaire by doing a small-scale pilot study and try analysing its data, as this will help detecting any flaws in the survey design. Note also that the longer and more detailed the survey is, the lower the response rate is likely to be. In game studies, as in general, it is also worth considering carefully how to distribute and focus the survey. It is relatively easy to get many responses to an online questionnaire by advertising it in game-related websites or discussion forums, but this kind of random collection of answers is likely to be biased to those who are active participants in those sites and interested in your subject of study. A representative sample requires first identifying the population which is the subject of survey; for example, all 15- to 20-year-old females in Finland. As it is usually impossible to survey a whole population, a sampling frame needs to be set that is representative of this population. In our example, the Population Register Centre of Finland may be used to acquire a random sample of names and addresses for posting the survey, but this kind of service has an associated cost. There exists statistical guidelines for determining the appropriate representative sample size, but it is important to also take into account that low response rates may necessitate respectively growing the size of the target sample.

Statistical analyses are an important part of quantitative methodology within the social sciences, but there exists also many important traditions of qualitative studies. This broad 'alternative' field of social sciences is an area where social sciences cross paths with the traditions of humanities and cultural studies. Qualitative research is concerned with the experiences and meanings people attach to phenomena, and therefore it takes cultures and real-world contexts into account. Rather than aiming to operationalize the research questions into mathematically quantifiable variables, knowledge provided by qualitative research is often narrative and illustrates how different groups and individuals experience life by observation and dialogue. Qualitative research uses various 'rich' data: people's speech, texts, photos, other media or participation in their activities. All this contributes to providing the researcher with a holistic understanding about the whole surrounding the particular phenomenon she is interested in analysing. Pertti Alasuutari (1995: 7) has compared qualitative analysis with riddle-solving; the analyst will look at the rich data and carefully check for clues, sometimes coming up with a surprisingly new way to combine them and explain the evidence.

Interviews are one of the central methods for qualitative social sciences. Also quantitative research may use interviews, as the face-to-face administration of survey can also be interpreted to be a structured interview. Semi-structured interviews are more common in qualitative research. This type also relies on a pre-designed framework, but rather than repeating the same detailed questions to every informant, a semi-structured interview is based on a list of topics which set the themes for interview. A completely unstructured interview takes the form of free-flowing discussion between the informant and the researcher. Semi-structured and unstructured interviews have the benefit of informality as they encourage two-way communication. Both individual and group interviews are used; group interviews of people selected within a certain demography are in marketing research called 'focus groups'. On the other hand, the analysis of interview materials requires more work than is typically the case for survey-style questionnaires. The interviewer takes notes while making sure the interview covers all topics listed in the interview framework, but recording the interview is also common. A recorded interview can then be transcribed into text, and subjected to detailed content analysis, which can use techniques of textual analysis mentioned above, or adopt a more quantifiable approach with a detailed coding scheme and possibly the use of dedicated analysis software (like NUD*IST or ATLAS.ti). Transcription and analysis of interviews is work intensive and usually qualitative studies using this approach do not aim to produce statistical proof, and sample sizes are rather small. Increasingly, game researchers are also combining qualitative and quantitative approaches, thereby profiting from their different strengths. An interview is an efficient way to find out how certain people are thinking about the research themes and provide the basic understanding necessary for constructing a larger-scale survey instrument. The downside is the possible over-reliance on anecdotal evidence that the interviewed people provide, or inexperienced interviewers imposing their own preconceptions on to the informants. Having a team of interviewers working together and discussing their findings and interpretations generally improves results, as does doing practice interviews before starting the actual study.

Other qualitative social science methods that are useful for studying players and game cultures involve inviting informants to keep a diary of their game playing practices. Particularly for getting a better idea of how play interfaces and mixes with other everyday activities, a time-diary method provides useful data. Traditionally in a time-diary approach, informants are recruited for keeping a detailed, hour-by-hour record of their activities during a certain day or during an entire week. This requires a significant contribution of effort on part of the participants and the final cooperation rate can easily be rather low. A more free-form diary-keeping method may be used to stimulate informants to write about the reasons and feelings behind their activities with games, which also provides useful starting points for a later, in-depth interview. Another interesting group of methods relying on informant creativity are the various biographical methods, which provide more longitudinal, qualitative information about the role of games and play in the course of human lives. With some specific, motivational and instructive guidelines, the researchers invite informants to contribute life stories focused on their experiences with games and play. Autobiographical accounts are rich and deep sources of information, and can contain the sum of individual experience and reflection on the topic over several years or decades. As such they call for a certain respect and strictly ethical approach from the researchers' part – the ethical guidelines of research of course apply always, regardless of methodology. The means of textual or discourse analysis can be used while analysing life stories, and many social scientists also rely on narrative methods developed within literary studies. While analysing and interpreting biographical accounts, the researcher needs to be aware that human memory is not perfect and that fantasy commonly mixes with real past experiences. Nevertheless, biographical accounts are a popular and important source of information about how individuals view their actions, norms, values and life events.

Lastly, ethnography is an important social sciences methodology, derived from cultural and social anthropology. A central part of doing ethnography is the field work, which means the researcher observing, participating and experiencing first-hand the life of people she is interested in analysing. A game studies ethnography may involve participating in the life of an online guild or observing the behaviours, norms and customs typical for a group of people who are frequent patrons in a location like a local games arcade. Keeping an open mind is important for an ethnographer, but it is also important to develop a rigorous routine for documenting events, social relationships and discussions in field notes or journals in order to provide evidence for any conclusions. When reporting, an ethnographer is both scientist and storyteller, being ideally able to act as a conduit for the 'insider' view of a particular culture to interface with the systematic and objective requirements of scientific knowledge.

Many chapters discussing recent studies of game players in social science or psychology are included in *Playing Video Games: Motives, Responses and Consequences* (Vorderer and Bryant, 2006), while interesting ethnographies of certain gamers and game cultures are provided by *Shared Fantasy: Role-Playing Games as Social Worlds* (Fine, 1983), *Play between Worlds: Exploring Online Game Culture* (Taylor, 2006) and *Synthetic Worlds: The Business and Culture of Online Games* (Castronova, 2005). An example of using surveys to probe the behaviours and attitudes of online game players is the 'Daedalus Project' (Yee, 2003–2006).

Among the sample assignments featured in this book, particularly 'Game Culture Survey' (Chapter 2) is based on a social sciences approach. It involves doing small-scale ethnographic field studies, making notes and organizing the findings concerning the role of games in lives of different groups of people into a structured report.

Design research methods

The third methodology group introduced here is related to games being software products as well as creative industry. Game research can make a contribution in the development of games by opening up alternative directions for game design or by providing important feedback from users to the developers during the game production. Design research also involves the processes of 'meta-design', or researching the game design methods and their underlying logic. Also the studies into the cultures of game design and detailed analyses or critiques of the operations within the game industry are related to this area of game studies. It should nevertheless be noted that while humanities or social sciences are established academic fields, evaluated through their contributions to scholarship and peer review publications, the main emphasis in game design is on producing games rather than research papers. Still, there is much room for fruitful overlap between research and design.

The analysis of economics, internal company cultures, production practices and marketing strategies of the games industry mostly falls beyond the scope of this book, but should nevertheless be mentioned here. An approach into these directions can profit a great deal from classic studies of the entertainment and electronic industries, such as *Doing Cultural Studies: The Story of the Sony Walkman* (du Gay *et al.*, 1997). Looking at the construction of consumer products as complex combinations of particular conditions of ownership, investment, design choices, technological innovation or appropriation, as well as of strategies of hype, advertisement, distribution and market launch, this kind of study can help to demystify the games industry. The commercial realities that underlie digital games as electronics and software products are also explored by Stephen Kline *et al.* (2003: 297) in their work *Digital Play*, while they also point out the potential for conflict as a multitude of voices, ranging from 'brand-loyal gamers to dissident hackers, to concerned parents, to other media industries and beyond' compete. Aphra Kerr's (2006) analysis of digital games as texts as well as a cultural industry complex tangled into global networks and multiple cultures of production is also useful in uncovering the larger image that is necessary for understanding the contexts where game design practices take place. Much of the originality and diversity of digital game design is nevertheless rooted in innumerable innovations created daily in processes of game design, and studying them is an important part of game studies. It is important to realize that research that has an effect on how games are designed is going to impact the overall direction of digital culture.

Game design research can make use of many of the methods discussed above, either directly or as applied into the purposes of deriving information about the way certain designs or changes in them are experienced by different players. There are established practices of play-testing and quality assurance within the game industry, which seek information about the learning curve, game-balancing issues and software bugs that plague products under development. Researchers working for Microsoft Game Studios (Davis *et al.*, 2005) have described the process they use to play-test different game titles as a set of procedures which goes beyond finding and reporting bugs or usability problems. This method involves standardized means for inviting a group of about thirty participants from the game's target audience to play it for an hour, after which participants fill in an electronic survey questionnaire. The questions used are focused on asking about 'fun' of particular gameplay elements or mechanics, like 'How fun was combat?' or 'How fun was Quest 1?' The survey also includes other gameplay-related questions that address players' experiences with the music, graphics and sound effects in the game. The authors emphasize that their approach is motivated by the industry needs for quick and efficient testing methods; they use standardized testing conditions, questions and a relatively large sample size while iteratively testing multiple games, allowing the researchers to do statistical analyses and comparisons between games rapidly and with a low cost.

The player experience with game can also be studied with the help of focus group interviews, observations, ethnography and usability research methods. Some computer game designs will allow the collection and analysis of log files, which can point out certain patterns, like players repeatedly failing at a certain point of the game. The methodology of usability engineering includes a range of approaches, where laboratory testing includes an important group of methods which can also be applied in game studies. A video recording of events captured from inside the game can be combined and synchronized with another video feed which records the expressions, gestures and verbal comments made by players during the play, opening many opportunities for later analysis. However, while traditional usability testing involves measuring the efficiency and ease of use for utility software, game studies needs to take into account the special character of games as enjoyable challenges, as well as the wide range of different player preferences and types of immersion discussed in this book. A combination of multiple methodologies is again recommended: for example, having both questionnaires, interviews and recordings of gameplay will provide the researcher with a rich array of data – with the downside of substantial challenge in analysis and interpretation.

Approaches that involve designing games are closely related to the field and processes of software engineering. A rapid prototyping technique might involve 'extreme programming', for example, where program code is developed through improvization, starting from the 'simplest thing that works', adding complexity when it is required. But not all approaches to game design require programming at all. Both the initial game concept document and the first experiments in core game mechanics can be designed with pen and paper. The conceptualization phase can be supported by multiple different brainstorming techniques, which may involve team work, followed by editing and refining phases. The game design can also draw inspiration from different sources, including 'game design games' (Järvinen, 2005) or collections of 'game design patterns' (Björk and Holopainen, 2005). Many of the core game rules and interactions can be first implemented into a board or card game, or social game with an innovative use of physical objects and environments. This phase can already tell much about the dynamics of the game concept and may inspire redesign. Some aspects of the game concept can be illustrated or narrated in short scenarios which can then be researched with the help of focus group interviews. Such early steps can provide designers with a better idea about the reactions and attitudes of players early on the design process, but they are not actual play-tests. When a playable version of software prototype is available, the design process involves further iterative rounds of play-testing and redesigning, checking the design for functionality, internal completeness and balance, as well as for making sure that the controls, interfaces and the core activities which players are engaged with are enjoyable enough.

There exists a broad range of technical literature on digital game development, but theories and methods of game design are not addressed by all of them. Various game design approaches are discussed in the wider context of digital design and the study of design in *Design Research: Methods and Perspectives* (Laurel, 2003). *Rules of Play: Game Design Fundamentals* (Salen and Zimmerman, 2004) includes a thorough discussion of its core concepts, including rules, play and culture, while *Game Design Workshop: Designing, Prototyping and Playtesting Games* (Fullerton *et al.*, 2004) is useful in introducing several practical approaches into game conceptualization and design.

In this book, both assignments 'Concept Design for a Real-Time Board Game' (Chapter 6) and 'Reality as a Game Board?' (Chapter 7) involve creating an experimental game design idea and writing a game concept document. Optionally, they can also be taken into prototype design phase by using paper prototyping or some other suitably lightweight and quick approach.

Game playing as a method

The last but most crucial element in any methodology of game studies involves playing games. Any student who is serious about gaining deeper expertise and understanding in the field of game studies needs to play a wide range of games. This may appear as a welcome suggestion and a pleasurable way to spend the entire term. However, analytical appreciation involves being able to communicate and critically examine one's experiences with the subject of study. Thus, analytical play as part of one's studies is different from leisurely play. Such more 'utilitarian' playing involves making notes and relating games to wider contexts of historical, conceptual and social range of thought that constitutes game studies and game cultures in their reflexive form. It may still be fun, but becoming a professional in game studies also means that game playing becomes a part of one's work. Playing as a part of research should not be limited to researcher's own favourites, but it may involve getting acquainted with an entirely new genre that is at the focus of study and learning the language and ways of thinking of those people who form its active player community. Playing is thus part of a larger range of activities which all contribute to the overall qualitative understanding of studied phenomena, necessary for formulating well-informed research questions.

The analytical play needs to be responsive and observant of the game in several levels. It involves all the key concepts discussed within this book and probably will also involve developing more detailed distinctions for needs of that particular object of study. To start with, it is useful to differentiate between the *structural gameplay analysis*, which responds to the core gameplay, and *thematic analysis* of games. While the first is derived from analytical play by paying special attention to how game rules and interactions with game objects and other players are structured, the latter involves studying those parts of the game we have called in this book its shell. Structural understanding of a game is important for any analysis, since it involves those parts and processes which have strongest influence on people engaged with its actual gameplay. The representational aspects, game world, characters and fiction of games are also very important, and these have an emphatic significance to the interpretations concerning game's cultural character. A thematic analysis highlights the experience of players sensitive to the symbols and messages conveyed by game's operation as a cultural medium. Such thematic understanding deals with the central idea or message as revealed by the total game experience and its interpretation by an analytical player. There are also added dimensions of play that become appropriate, depending on the genre, research focus and methodology in question; for example, *social analysis* of game-related communication networks and communities is a relevant part of analytical play within many online multiplayer games.

It is likely that every critic of games will develop their own style of playing and appreciating games, and it should be pointed out that a game professional's approach is not necessarily a typical way of playing. Indeed, it is worth considering if there exists a 'typical' player or play style; every player has their individual history and preferences, having roots in their personality and experiences. Learning to understand and appreciate the diversity of players, play styles and associated experiences is crucial for developing a more encompassing and inclusive comprehension of games and their multiple roles within different game cultures.

Espen Aarseth (2003) has distinguished between seven different 'strata' or layers in engagement that are open for the analytical player:

> First, we have superficial play, where the analyst plays around with the game for a few minutes, merely to make a quick classification and get a 'feel' for the game, but without learning interface commands or structural features. Then there is light play, where the player/analyst learns enough to make meaningful progress in the game, but stops when progress is made. Then there is partial completion, when a sub goal or a series of sub goals has been reached. Total completion is of course only possible in games with defined endings, and not in games such as *Tetris* or *Space Invaders*. Repeated play and expert play are strata that usually come after total completion, unless the game genre is so familiar to the analyst that no substantial learning is necessary. The expert player is also, typically, a winner of multi-player games. The seventh stratum, innovative play, is seen when players invent totally new strategies and play the game not to win, but to achieve a goal by means that are not previously recognized as such by other players.

It is important to be aware of the great range of player engagement as well as differences in skill level, while it is equally important not to make such differences in play style or mastery into a scale between more and less significant play experiences. There are many players who remain at the level of superficial or light play in most of their game playing but, nevertheless, have their personal relationship with the experience of gameplay, albeit more casual. Aarseth (ibid.)

also calls for a balance between free play, analytical play and research in 'non-play' mode. Playing games is an essential part of being a scholar in game studies, but it should be combined with a selective and thoughtful use of other sources for information, such as observing others play or interviewing players.

All game playing requires time and practice for a player to develop their skills, no matter what kind of game is in question. But some research projects are more intensive undertakings than others; particularly adopting an ethnographic approach into some of the virtual game worlds will involve playing the game for extended periods not only to become familiar with its core gameplay mechanisms and different areas of the game world, but to gain a deeper insight in the social life taking place in various game servers and online forums. But while possibly arduous, they also feature their fair share of adventure and challenge – humorously illustrated by a quote from Edvard Castronova's field diary on his humble beginnings in the world of *EverQuest*:

> Journal entry, 20 April. I have made my first kills, mostly rats. They did me a great deal of damage and I have been killed several times. I do return to life but it is a pain to go through. Nonetheless, I have to attack the rats. I need money to buy edible food and water, and rat fur, and other similar junk, is about the only thing I can get my hands on that the vendors will pay money for. I was hoping to do more exploring and less work, but a woman named 'Soulseekyre' told me that beyond Freeport lie biots so powerful they could kill me instantly. My problem is that I am under-equipped. Soulseekyre was wearing an elaborate suit of armor and she had impressive weapons. I have been basically naked, carrying only a simple club, a caveman in a world of cavaliers. My poverty is oppressive – no amount of rat fur is sufficient to buy even a simple tunic at the ludicrously high prices of the merchant biots. Fortunately I just killed enough rats to gain a 'level' of experience, and I seem to have become a much more effective rat killer. (Castronova, 2001.)

In this book, assignments 'Gameplay Experience of a "Classic Game"' (Chapter 4), 'Real-Time and Turn-Based' (Chapter 6) expressly involve engaging in analytical game playing, but it is difficult or impossible to do most of the other assignments without some kind of analytical play or replay to refresh one's memories.

Writing for an audience

The subject matter, research question and methodology issues discussed above each contribute to the way the final research paper needs to be structured. The presentation of study is not an external part of the research process, but at its very core, science and scholarship are communication of knowledge, and work that does not convey its message to anyone does not exist as far as academic community is concerned. Similarly, solid argumentation, logical structure and clear language will reveal the merits of research work to the reader. It should also be possible to recognize the limits and possible weaknesses in the work. It is not a fault of scholarship not to cover every issue in a research field; on the contrary, these kinds of gaps need to be recognized as opportunities for further research. Preparing for comments and critique is therefore an integral part of study. It is easy to perceive the finished paper to be the final and complete word on the matter, but there are always alternative viewpoints or approaches that can contribute or even question the claims of the research. A central part of any progressive view of science is the concept of dialogue, where it is in the joint interests of academics to make research stronger by questioning, testing and building upon each others' work. This fundamental principle should also guide the work and debate in classroom and in seminars. Presenting a game studies paper should not be a deathmatch.

While thinking about the overall organization of any course assignment, the first thing is to check again all the provided instructions and what the course supervisor is saying. There are established conventions in presentation and use of references that vary between universities and departments. A key part in organizing your presentation is identifying the main argument. After doing your pre-study, reading all relevant literature and doing your own research, what is it that you want to say? Why is it interesting?

Game studies is a broad and diverse field, and an author cannot rely on the homogeneous background in one's audience as in some other fields. Thus, it is a good idea to take less as granted, and spend some time in describing the background and character of both the subject of study and the adopted methodological approach. In more advanced courses a certain level of proficiency is expected, in terms of both scholarly and game-related expertise, which should be reflected in the style of writing in those cases. Being brief and informative is a skill in itself. Often it is useful to provide references to sources that allow readers to gain more background knowledge than is appropriate to fit into the paper. The motivation for study and clarification why a certain approach was adopted to study this phenomenon is nevertheless something that should be presented to the reader early in the paper.

Some dedicated thought is required to construct a logical outline for the paper. There are numerous different modes of arrangement that might suit the purpose, ranging from arrangement that focuses on description of phenomenon, or some process and its course of events, to narrative or story-like arrangements, which also are an option. The logic of the paper can also rely on division and grouping of your findings into distinctive categories, as well as on utilizing comparisons and contrasts to highlight the key differences and similarities among research findings. The logic of cause and effect is one of the classic modes for arrangement, which progresses by giving an explanation to phenomenon through a process of discovery of its underlying reasons or mechanisms. A riddle and solution structure is also a way to capture the attention of readers; a curious phenomenon or challenging problem is presented in the beginning, and the paper explores one or more hypotheses as solutions, giving evidence and comparing their respective merits and weaknesses. Factual clarity is nevertheless the dominant tone of academic papers, rather than the thrills or poetic allusions familiar from drama or detective stories.

While there is no single structure or stylistic convention that would cover game studies, it is useful to be aware of the standard scientific article structure that dominates publishing in many disciplines. This involves presenting the argument within an 'IMRaD' template, which has four main parts: introduction, methods, results, and discussion. This kind of paper format typically also includes title, author information, abstract and keyword list in the beginning, and a list of references at the end. While using such structures, it is important to put enough weight to the analysis and results as the key part of paper; all the other sections are traditionally brief when compared with the part where the real 'beef' is presented. Beware particularly the part containing the introduction and background from taking up too much room in the paper, as the attention of reader needs to be focused on the key results and claims made in this particular research. Within the macrostructure of main parts, there is a microstructure, with each part consisting of series of paragraphs, each carrying one thought, logically linked with each other. Thus, the main argument of the entire paper is sustained by a logical line of thought carried coherently through it.

There are many good guides for scientific writing, but few issues are particularly pertinent in this context. One of the most important is the use of references. All scholars need to ground their claims either to data that they have themselves gathered and documented or through references into other scientific work. Making claims that carry no reference pointers makes a vague impression and can even be a sign of plagiarism, when text and information is provided without clearly marking it as a paraphrase or quotation that is followed by reference. Since much current discussion and thinking around games takes place among both academics and non-academics in various forums of the Internet, special attention needs to be given to the use of electronic sources. The quality of sources and how they are used is one of the key elements in determining the quality and substance of scholarly work. The core argumentation in academic papers should not rely on Internet sources that are not qualified through academic editing and peer reviewing processes. At the same time, there is much value and substantial expertise invested in various individual and communal online projects, and modern scholarship should not close its eye on this work. However, critical evaluation of sources is something that is needed also for printed publications as much as while using online sources. As a general recommendation, when multiple sources are carefully compared, it becomes easier to point out inconsistencies and conflicts within information obtained from different resources.

Finally, game studies is discussion of games and players, informed by research and scholarship. Recognizing the cultural value and significance of games should be visible in the way games are discussed and treated by students and scholars alike. The existing guidelines for academic writing and referencing rarely take into account all the needs of games-focused research. In addition to a list of bibliographic references, many researchers are including a ludography, or detailed list of games into their reference section. An entry in such list needs to include at least the name of the game, year of publication and usually the studio responsible for its design. However, research projects discuss games production-related issues with a varying level of detail, and in some cases even minor differences between the various released versions of a game are significant. Thus, a more thorough ludography might include also publisher, names of such key individuals as the main designer, programmer, writer or artist, as well as version information including the platform such as PlayStation 2 or Xbox. In the end, in this as generally in formal details, it is most important to be consistent, whatever the adopted reference practice is.

* * *

This book has aimed to provide an introductory perspective into the main dimensions of digital games and play, providing a multidimensional view of games' meanings and roles in culture. There are many issues that concern studying games and writing research that cannot be discussed within the scope of this work, but hopefully in these chapters, as well as the recommendations in further online resources, game studies bibliography and other materials at the companion website (*www.gamestudiesbook.net*) are helpful for getting into the road of learning and appreciation of games and the associated rich game cultures. Good luck – play well!

REFERENCES

All online sources accessed in July 2006.

Aarseth, Espen (1997) *Cybertext: Perspectives on Ergodic Literature*. Baltimore and London: Johns Hopkins.

Aarseth, Espen (2003) 'Playing Research: Methodological Approaches to Game Analysis'. *Proceedings of DAC 2003*. Melbourne: RMIT University. Online: *http://hypertext.rmit.edu.au/dac/papers/Aarseth.pdf*

Aarseth, Espen (2004) 'Genre Trouble: Narrativism and the Art of Simulation'. In: Noah Wardrip-Fruin and Pat Harrigan (eds), *First Person: New Media as Story, Performance, and Game*. Cambridge (MA): The MIT Press, pp. 45–55.

Alasuutari, Pertti (1995) *Researching Culture: Qualitative Method and Cultural Studies*. London: Sage Publications.

Aliaga-Buchenau, Ana-Isabel (2003) *The 'Dangerous' Potential of Reading: Readers and the Negotiation of Power in Nineteenth-Century Narratives*. New York: Routledge.

Altman, Rick (1999) *Film/Genre*. London: British Film Institute.

Arnold, Matthew (1869/1909) *Culture and Anarchy: An Essay in Political and Social Criticism*. London: Nelson.

Avedon, Elliott M. and Brian Sutton-Smith (1971) *The Study of Games*. New York and London: John Wiley and Sons.

Azuma, Ronald (1997) 'A Survey of Augmented Reality'. *Presence: Teleoperators and Virtual Environments*, 6(4): 355–85.

Baer, Ralph (1996) 'PONG: Who Did It First?' In: David Winter (ed), 'Pong Story' 1996–2006. Online: *www.pong-story.com/inventor.htm*

Baer, Ralph H. (2005) *Videogames: In the Beginning*. Springfield (NJ): Rolenta Press.

Bakhtin, Mikhail (1965/1984) *Rabelais and His World*. Trans. Helene Iswolsky. Bloomington: Indiana University Press.

Barker, Martin and Julian Petley (eds) (2001) *Ill Effects: The Media Violence Debate* (2nd edn). London and New York: Routledge.

Barthes, Roland (1972) *Mythologies*. New York: Paladin.

Bartle, Richard (1996) 'Hearts, Clubs, Diamonds, Spades: Players Who Suit MUDs'. *The Journal of Virtual Environments*, 1(1). Online: *http://www.brandeis.edu/pubs/jove/HTML/v1/bartle.html*

Bartle, Richard (2004) 'Pitfalls of Virtual Property'. *The Themis Group*. Online: *http://www.themis-group.com/uploads/Pitfalls%20of%20Virtual%20Property.pdf*

Bates, Daniel G. and Elliot M. Fratkin (2002) *Cultural Anthropology* (3rd edn). Boston (MA): Allyn and Bacon.

Baudrillard, Jean (1988/1994) *Simulacra and Simulation*. Ann Arbor: University of Michigan Press.

Baym, Nancy K. (1995) 'The Emergence of Community in Computer-Mediated Communication'. In: Steven G. Jones (ed), *Cybersociety*. Newbury (CA): Sage Publications, pp. 138–63.

BBC (2005) 'Gamers in the UK: Digital Play, Digital Lifestyles'. Commissioned by BBC Creative Research and Development, authored by Rhianna Pratchett. Online: *http://crystaltips.typepad.com/wonderland/files/bbc_uk_games_research_2005.pdf*

Bennett, Andy and Keith Kahn-Harris (eds) (2004) *After Subculture: Critical Studies in Contemporary Youth Culture*. Houndmills: Palgrave Macmillan.

Bittanti, Matteo (ed) (2005) *Civilization: Storie Virtuali, Fantasie Reali*. Videoludica, Game Culture series. Trans. Valentina Paggiarin. Milan: Costa and Nolan.

Björk, Staffan and Jussi Holopainen (2003) 'Describing Games: An Interaction-Centric Structural Framework'. In: Marinka Copier and Joost Raessens (eds), *Level Up: Digital Games Research Conference Proceedings*. Utrecht: DiGRA and University of Utrecht. Online: *http://www.digra.org/dl/db/05150.10348*

Björk, Staffan and Jussi Holopainen (2005) *Patterns in Game Design*. Hingham (MA): Charles River Media.

Bogost, Ian (2005) 'The Rhetoric of Exergaming'. *Proceedings of DAC 2005*. Copenhagen: IT University.

Bolter, Jay David and Richard Grusin (1999) *Remediation: Understanding New Media*. Cambridge (MA): The MIT Press.

Brand, Stewart (1972) 'SPACEWAR: Fanatic Life and Symbolic Death among the Computer Bums'. *Rolling Stone*, 7 December 1972. Online: *http://www.wheels.org/spacewar/stone/rolling_stone.html*

Bryce, Jo and Jason Rutter (2003) 'Gender Dynamics and the Social and Spatial Organization of Computer Gaming'. *Leisure Studies*, 22(1): 1–15.

Burghardt, Gordon M. (1984) 'On the Origins of Play'. In: Peter K. Smith (ed), *Play in Animals and Humans*. Oxford and New York: Basil Blackwell, pp. 5–41.

Burnham, Van (2001) *Supercade: A Visual History of the Videogame Age 1971–1984*. Cambridge (MA): The MIT Press.

Byers, John A. (1984) 'Play in Ungulates'. In: Peter K. Smith (ed), *Play in Animals and Humans*. Oxford and New York: Basil Blackwell, pp. 43–65.

Caillois, Roger (1958/2001) *Man, Play and Games*. Champaign: University of Illinois Press.

Campbell-Kelly, Martin (2003) *From Airline Reservations to Sonic the Hedgehog: A History of the Software Industry*. Cambridge (MA): The MIT Press.

Carr, Diane (2002) 'Playing with Lara'. In: Geoff King and Tanya Krzywinska (eds), *ScreenPlay: Cinema/Videogames/Interfaces*. London: Wallflower Press, pp. 178–80.

Carr, Diane (2007) 'The Trouble with Civilization'. In: Barry Atkins and Tanya Krzywinska (eds), *Videogame, Player, Text*. Manchester: Manchester University Press, pp. 222–36.

Carter, Cynthia and C. Kay Weaver (2003) *Violence and the Media*. Buckingham: Open University Press.

Castro, Radford (2004) *Let Me Play: Stories of Gaming and Emulation*. Tucson (AZ): Hats Off Books.

Castronova, Edward (2001) 'Virtual Worlds: A First-Hand Account of Market and Society on the Cyberian Frontier'. CESifo Working Paper No. 618, December 2001. Online: *http://papers.ssrn.com/sol3/papers.cfm?abstract_id=294828*

Castronova, Edward (2005) *Synthetic Worlds: The Business and Culture of Online Games*. Chicago: University of Chicago Press.

Chan, Alexander (2004) 'CPR for the Arcade Culture: A Case History on the Development of *Dance Dance Revolution* Community'. Unpublished coursework, History of Computer Game Design, Stanford University. *Online: http://pdf.textfiles.com/academics/ddr-case-history-chan.pdf*

Cherny, Lynn (1999) *Conversation and Community: Chat in A Virtual World*. Stanford (CA): CSLI Publications.

Clarke, John, Stuart Hall, Tony Jefferson and Brian Roberts (1975) 'Subcultures, Cultures and Class: A Theoretical Overview'. In: Stuart Hall and Tony Jefferson (eds), *Resistance Through Rituals*. London: Routledge, 9–74.

Cohen, Stanley (1972/2002) *Folk Devils and Moral Panics: Creation of Mods and Rockers* (3rd edn). London and New York: Routledge.

Computer Industry Almanac (2006) 'Worldwide Internet Users Top 1 Billion in 2005'. Computer Industry Almanac, Inc. Press Release, January 4, 2006. Online: *http://www.c-i-a.com/pr0106.htm*

Costikyan, Greg (2002) 'I Have No Words & I Must Design: Toward a Critical Vocabulary for Games'. In: Frans Mäyrä (ed), *CGDC Conference Proceedings*. Studies in Information Sciences. Tampere: Tampere University Press, pp. 9–33.

Crawford, Chris (1982/1997) *The Art of Computer Game Design*. The electronic edition. Online: *http://www.vancouver.wsu.edu/fac/peabody/game-book/ACGD.pdf*

Csikszentmihalyi, Mihaly (1991) *Flow: The Psychology of Optimal Experience*. New York: Harper Perennial.

Culin, Stewart (1907/1992a) *Games of the North American Indians. Vol. 1: Games of Chance*. Lincoln and London: Bison Books/University of Nebraska Press.

Culin, Stewart (1907/1992b) *Games of the North American Indians. Vol. 2: Games of Skill*. Lincoln and London: Bison Books/University of Nebraska Press.

Davis, John P., Keith Steury and Randy Pagulayan (2005) 'A Survey Method for Assessing Perceptions of a Game: The Consumer Playtest in Game Design'. *Game Studies*, 5(1). Online: *http://www.gamestudies.org/0501/davis_steury_pagulayan/*

DeKoven, Bernie (2002) *The Well Played Game: A Playful Path to Wholeness* (3rd edn). San Jose (CA): Writers Club Press. Online: *http://www.deepfun.com/WPG.pdf*

Delaney, Kevin J. (2004) 'When Art Imitates Videogames, You Have "Red vs. Blue"'. *The Wall Street Journal*, 9 April 2004. Online: *http://interactive.wsj.com/dividends/retrieve.cgi?id=/text/wsjie/data/SB108145721789778243.djm&d2h converter=display-d2h&template=dividends*

DeMaria, Rusel and Johnny L. Wilson (2004) *High Score! The Illustrated History of Electronic Games* (2nd edn). New York: McGraw-Hill/Osborne.

Dibbell, Julian (1993/1998) 'A Rape in the Cyberspace (Or TINYSOCIETY, and How to Make One)'. In: Julian Dibbell, *My Tiny Life: Crime and Passion in a Virtual World*. New York: Henry Holt, pp. 11–30. Online: *http://www.juliandibbell.com/texts/bungle.html*

Dibbell, Julian (2006) *Play Money: Or, How I Quit My Day Job and Made Millions Trading Virtual Loot*. New York: Basic Books.

Douglas, Christopher (2002) '"You Have Unleashed a Horde of Barbarians!": Fighting Indians, Playing Games, Forming Disciplines'. *Postmodern Culture* 13: 1 (September 2002). Online: *http://www.iath.virginia.edu/pmc/text-only/issue.902/13.1douglas.txt*

Dovey, Jon and Helen W. Kennedy (2006) *Game Cultures: Computer Games as New Media*. Maidenhead: Open University Press.

du Gay, Paul, Stuart Hall, Linda Janes, Hugh Mackay and Keith Negus (1997) *Doing Cultural Studies: The Story of the Sony Walkman. Culture, Media & Identities*, Vol. 1. London: Sage Publications.

Ducheneaut, Nicolas, Nicholas Yee, Eric Nickell and Robert J. Moore (2006) '"Alone together?" Exploring the Social Dynamics of Massively Multiplayer Online Games'. In: *Proceedings of CHI 2006 Conference*. New York: ACM, pp. 407–16.

Duke, Richard (2003) 'Closing Remarks of Richard Duke, ISAGA 2003, Kisarazu, Chiba, Japan'. *ISAGA Newsletter* 1. Online: *http://www.isaga.info/newsletters/newsletter1.pdf*

Durkin, Kevin (1995) *Computer Games – Their Effects on Young People: A Review*. Sydney: Office of Film and Literature Classification.

Ermi, Laura, Satu Heliö and Frans Mäyrä (2004) 'Pelien voima ja pelaamisen hallinta: Lapset ja nuoret pelikulttuurien toimijoina'. (The Power of Games and Control of Playing: Children as the Actors of Game Cultures.) Hypermedialaboratorion verkkojulkaisuja – Hypermedia Laboratory Net Series; 6. Tampere: University of Tampere. Online: *http://tampub.uta.fi/haekokoversio.php?id=53*

Ermi, Laura and Frans Mäyrä (2005) 'Fundamental Components of the Gameplay Experience: Analysing Immersion'. In: Suzanne de Castell and Jennifer Jenson (eds), *Proceedings of Chancing Views – Worlds in Play. Digital Games Research Association's Second International Conference*. Vancouver: DiGRA and Simon Fraser University. Online: *http://www.digra.org/dl/db/06276.41516.pdf*

ESA (2006) 'Essential Facts about the Computer and Video Game Industry 2006: Sales, Demographic and Usage Data'. Entertainment Software Association. Online: *http://www.theesa.com/archives/files/Essential%20Facts%202006.pdf*

Eskelinen, Markku (2001) 'The Gaming Situation'. *Game Studies*, 1(1). Online: *http://www.gamestudies.org/0101/eskelinen/*

EverQuest-Widows (2006) EverQuest-Widows email discussion list. Online: *http://health.groups.yahoo.com/group/EverQuest-Widows/*

Fine, Gary Alan (1983) *Shared Fantasy: Role-Playing Games as Social Worlds*. Chicago and London: University of Chicago Press.

Fiske, John (1989) *Reading the Popular*. London and New York: Routledge.

Fluegelman, Andrew (ed) (1976) *New Games Book*. New Games Foundation. New York: Dolphin/Doubleday.

Frasca, Gonzalo (1999) 'Ludology Meets Narratology. Similitude and Differences between (Video)games and Narrative'. Originally published in Finnish in *Parnasso* 1999: 3, 365–71. Online: *http://www.ludology.org/articles/ludology.htm*

Frasca, Gonzalo (2001) 'Simulation 101. Simulation versus Representation'. Online: *http://www.ludology.org/articles/sim1/simulation101.html*

Frasca, Gonzalo (2003a) 'Ludologists Love Stories, Too: Notes from a Debate that Never Took Place'. In: Marinka Copier and Joost Raessens (eds), *Level Up: Digital Games Research Conference Proceedings*. Utrecht: DiGRA and University of Utrecht. Online: http://www.digra.org/dl/db/05163.01125.

Frasca, Gonzalo (2003b) 'Simulation versus Narrative: Introduction to Ludology'. In: Mark J. P. Wolf and Bernard Perron (eds), *Video Game Theory Reader*. London: Routledge, pp. 221–35.

Freedman, Jonathan L. (2002) *Media Violence and Its Effect on Aggression: Assessing the Scientific Evidence*. Toronto: University of Toronto Press.

Friedl, Markus (2003) *Online Game Interactivity Theory*. Hingham (MA): Charles River Media.

Fromme, Johannes (2003) 'Computer Games as a Part of Children's Culture'. *Game Studies*, 3(1). Online: *http://www.gamestudies.org/0301/fromme/*

Frow, John (2005) *Genre. The New Critical Idiom*. London: Routledge.

Fullerton, Tracy, Christopher Swain and Steven Hoffman (2004) *Game Design Workshop: Designing, Prototyping and Playtesting Games*. San Francisco (CA): CMP Books.

Funk, Jeanne B. (1992) 'Commentary: Video Games; Benign or Malignant?' *Developmental and Behavioral Pediatrics*, 13(1): 53–4.

GameSpot (1997) 'The Ultima Legacy'. Online: *http://www.gamespot.com/features/ultima/contents.html*

Gee, James Paul (2003) *What Video Games Have To Teach Us About Learning And Literacy*. New York: Palgrave Macmillan.

Gelber, Steven M. (1999) *Hobbies: Leisure and the Culture of Work in America.* New York: Columbia University Press.

Gelder, Ken and Sarah Thornton (eds) (1997) *The Subcultures Reader.* London and New York: Routledge.

Giammattei, Joyce, Glen Blix, Helen Hopp Marshak, Alison Okada Wollitzer and David J. Pettitt (2003) 'Television Watching and Soft Drink Consumption'. *Archives of Pediatrics and Adolescent Medicine,* 157(9): 882–6.

Giddens, Anthony (1991) *Modernity and Self-Identity: Self and Society in the Late Modern Age.* Cambridge: Polity Press.

Goffman, Erving (1959) *The Presentation of Self in Everyday Life* (Revised edn). (Orig. 1956.) New York: Anchor Books.

Goldsmith, Thomas T., Jr, Cedar Grove and Estle Bay Mann (1948) 'Cathode-Ray Tube Amusement Device'. United States Patent Office, Patent Number 2,455,992 (patent application filed in January 25, 1947). Online: *http://www.pong-story.com/2455992.pdf*

Goldstein, Jeffrey H. (ed) (1998) *Why We Watch: Attractions of Violent Entertainment.* New York: Oxford University Press.

Gosney, John W. (2005) *Beyond Reality: A Guide to Alternate Reality Gaming.* Boston (MA): Thomson Course Technology.

Griffiths, Mark (1999) 'Violent Video Games and Aggression: A Review of the Literature'. *Aggression and Violent Behavior,* 4: 2 (Summer 1999), pp. 203–12.

Griffiths, Mark (2005) 'Video Games and Health'. *British Medical Journal,* 331 (16 July 2005): 122–3.

Grossberg, Lawrence (1992) *We Gotta Get Out of This Place: Popular Conservatism and Postmodern Culture.* London: Routledge.

Grossberg, Lawrence (1997) *Dancing in Spite of Myself: Essays on Popular Culture.* Durham: Duke University Press.

Guillory John (1993) *Cultural Capital: The Problem of Literary Canon Formation.* London: University of Chicago Press.

Gunawardena, Charlotte N. (1995) 'Social Presence Theory and Implications for Interaction and Collaborative Learning in Computer Conferences'. *International Journal of Educational Telecommunications,* 1(2/3): 147–66. Online: *http://www.aace.org/dl/files/IJET/IJET12147.pdf*

Hall, Stuart (1980) 'Encoding/decoding'. (Orig. 1973.) In: Centre for Contemporary Cultural Studies (eds), *Culture, Media, Language: Working Papers in Cultural Studies, 1972–79.* London: Hutchinson, pp. 128–38.

Hall, Stuart and Tony Jefferson (eds) (1975/2002) *Resistance Through Rituals: Youth Subcultures in Post-War Britain.* First published as Working Papers in Cultural Studies, No. 7/8. London: Routledge.

Hebdige, Dick (1979) *Subculture: the Meaning of Style.* London: Methuen.

Herman, Leonard, Jer Horwitz, Steve Kent and Skyler Miller (2002) 'The History of Video Games'. *Gamespot* feature article. Online: *http://www.gamespot.com/gamespot/features/video/hov/*

Herz, J. C. (1997) *Joystick Nation: How Video Games Gobbled Our Money, Won Our Hearts, and Rewired Our Minds.* London: Abacus.

Hess, Elizabeth (2003) *Yib's Guide to MOOing: Getting the Most from Virtual Communities on the Internet.* Victoria: Trafford. Online: *http://www.yibco.com/*

Holmes, Robyn M. and Anthony D. Pellegrini (2005) 'Children's Social Behaviour During Video Game Play'. In: Joost Raessens and Jeffrey Goldstein (eds), *Handbook of Computer Game Studies.* Cambridge (MA): The MIT Press, 2005. pp. 133–44.

Höysniemi, Johanna (2006a) 'International Survey on the Dance Dance Revolution Game'. *ACM Computers in Entertainment*, 4(2), Article No. 8, April 2006.

Höysniemi, Johanna (2006b) *Design and Evaluation of Physically Interactive Games*. Dissertations in Interactive Technology, 5. Acta Electronica Universitatis Tamperensis, 544. Tampere: University of Tampere. Online: *http://acta.uta.fi/pdf/951-44-6694-2.pdf*

Huhtamo, Erkki (2005) 'Slots of Fun, Slots of Trouble: An Archaeology of Arcade Gaming'. In: Joost Raessens and Jeffrey Goldstein (eds), *Handbook of Computer Game Studies*. Cambridge (MA): The MIT Press, pp. 3–21.

Huizinga, Johan (1938/1971) *Homo Ludens. A Study of the Play-Element in Culture*. Boston: Beacon Press.

id Sofware (n.d.) 'id History'. Online: *http://www.idsoftware.com/business/history/*

id Software (1993) 'Data Utility License'. Online: *http://www.johnromero.com/lee_killough/history/dul.txt*

IGDA (2004) 'Quality of Life in the Game Industry: Challenges and Best Practices'. International Game Developers Association Whitepaper. Online: *http://www.igda.org/qol/*

IGDA (2006) '2006 Casual Games Whitepaper'. International Game Developers Association Whitepaper. Online: *http://www.igda.org/casual/*

Internet Systems Consortium (2006) 'ISC Domain Survey: Number of Internet Hosts'. Online: *http://www.isc.org/index.pl?/ops/ds/host-count-history.php*

IPerG (2006) 'Deliverable D5.3b: Domain of Pervasive Gaming'. Integrated Project on Pervasive Gaming. Authors: Markus Montola, Annika Waern, Eva Nieuwdorp. Online: *http://iperg.sics.se/Deliverables/D5.3b-Domain%20of%20Pervasive%20Gaming.pdf*

Järvinen, Aki (2002a) 'Gran Stylissimo: The Audiovisual Elements and Styles in Computer and Video Games'. In: Frans Mäyrä (ed), *Proceedings of the Computer Games and Digital Cultures Conference*. Tampere: Tampere University Press, pp. 113–28. Online: *http://www.digra.org/dl/db/05164.35393*

Järvinen, Aki (2002b) 'Kolmiulotteisuuden aika. Audiovisuaalinen kulttuurimuoto 1992–2002'. In: Erkki Huhtamo and Sonja Kangas (eds), *Mariosofia. Elektronisten pelien kulttuuri*. Helsinki: Gaudeamus, pp. 70–91.

Järvinen, Aki (2003) 'The Elements of Simulation in Digital Games System: Representation and Interface in Grand Theft Auto: Vice City'. *Dichtung-digital: Journal für digitale ästhetik*, 2004(4). Online: *http://www.dichtung-digital.org/2003/issue/4/jaervinen/index.htm*

Järvinen, Aki (2005) 'Theory as Game: Designing the Gamegame'. In: Suzanne de Castell and Jennifer Jenson, *Proceedings of Chancing Views – Worlds in Play. Digital Games Research Association's Second International Conference*. Vancouver: DiGRA and Simon Fraser University. Online: *http://www.digra.org/dl/db/06276.43287.pdf*

Järvinen, Aki, Satu Heliö and Frans Mäyrä (2002) 'Communication and Community in Digital Entertainment Services'. *Prestudy Research Report*. Hypermedia Laboratory Net Series, 2. Tampere: University of Tampere. Online: *http://tampub.uta.fi/tup/951-44-5432-4.pdf*

Jasper, David (2004) *A Short Introduction to Hermeneutics*. Louisville (KY): Westminster John Knox Press.

Jenkins, Henry (1992) *Textual Poachers: Television Fans and Participatory Culture*. New York and London: Routledge.

Jenkins, Henry (1998) '"Complete Freedom of Movement": Video Games as Gendered Play Spaces'. In: Henry Jenkins and Justine Cassell (eds), *From Barbie to Mortal Kombat: Gender and Computer Games*. Cambridge: MIT Press. Online: *http://web.mit.edu/cms/People/henry3/complete.html*

Jenkins, Henry (2000) 'Lessons From Littleton: What Congress Doesn't Want to Hear About Youth and Media'. *Independent School Magazine*, Winter 2000. Online: *http://www.nais.org/ismagazinearticlePrint.cfm?print=Y&ItemNumber=144264*

Jenkins, Henry (2006) *Convergence Culture: Where Old and New Media Collide.* New York: New York University Press.

Jenkins, Henry and Kurt Squire (2002) 'The Art of Contested Spaces'. In: Lucien King (ed) *Game On: The History and Culture of Videogames.* London: Laurence King, pp. 64–75. Online: *http://web.mit.edu/cms/People/henry3/contestedspaces.html*

Jeppesen, Lars Bo (2004) 'Profiting from Innovative User Communities: How Firms Organise the Production of User Modifications in the Computer Games Industry'. Department of Industrial Economics and Strategy, Copenhagen Business School Working Papers. Online: *http://ep.lib.cbs.dk/download/ISBN/8778690978.pdf*

Jones, Gerard (2002) *Killing Monsters. Why Children Need Fantasy, Super Heroes, and Make-Believe Violence.* New York: Basic Books.

Jones, Steve and the research group (2003) 'Let the Games Begin: Gaming Technology and Entertainment among College Students'. Washington (DC): Pew Internet and American Life Project. Online: *http://www.pewinternet.org/pdfs/PIP_College_Gaming_Reporta.pdf*

Juul, Jesper (1999/2001) 'A Clash Between Game and Narrative: A Thesis on Computer Games and Interactive Fiction'. (Orig. version in Danish; English translation, 2001.) Institute of Nordic Language and Literature, University of Copenhagen. Online: *http://www.jesperjuul.dk/thesis/AClashBetweenGameAndNarrative.pdf*

Juul, Jesper (2002) 'The Open and the Closed: Games of Emergence and Games of Progression'. In: Frans Mäyrä (ed), *CGDC Conference Proceedings. Studies in Information Sciences.* Tampere: Tampere University Press, pp. 323–9.

Juul, Jesper (2005) *Half-Real: Video Games between Real Rules and Fictional Worlds.* Cambridge (MA): The MIT Press.

Kallio, Kirsi Pauliina, Kirsikka Kaipainen and Frans Mäyrä (2007) 'Gaming Nation? Piloting the International Study of Games Cultures in Finland: Hypermedia Laboratory Net Series, 14 Tampere: University of Tampere. Online: *http://tampub.uta.fi/haekokoversio.php?id=202*

Kapell, Matthew (2002) 'Civilization and its Discontents: American Monomythic Structure as Historical Simulacrum'. *Popular Culture Review*, 13(2) (Summer 2002): 129–36.

Kelley, David (1988) *The Art of Reasoning.* New York: W. W. Norton & Company.

Kennedy, Helen W. (2002) 'Lara Croft: Feminist Icon or Cyberbimbo? On the Limits of Textual Analysis'. *Game Studies*, 2(2). Online: *http://www.gamestudies.org/0202/kennedy/*

Kent, Steven L. (2001) *The Ultimate History of Video Games: From Pong to Pokémon and Beyond – The Story Behind the Graze That Touched Our Lives and Changed the World.* New York: Three Rivers.

Kerr, Aphra (2006) *The Business and Culture of Digital Games: Gamework/Gameplay.* London: Sage Publications.

Killough, Lee (n.d.) 'Doom Editing History'. Online: *http://www.johnromero.com/lee_killough/history/edhist.shtml*

Kim, John H. (1998–2006) 'The Threefold Model'. Online: *http://www.darkshire.net/~jhkim/rpg/theory/threefold/*

King, Brad and John Borland (2003) *Dungeons and Dreamers: The Rise of Computer Game Culture from Geek to Chic.* New York: McGraw-Hill/Osborne.

Klein, Naomi (2000) *No Logo: No Space, No Choice, No Jobs.* London: Flamingo.

Kline, Stephen, Nick Dyer-Witheford and Greig De Peuter (2003) *Digital Play: The Interaction of Technology, Culture, and Marketing*. Montreal: McGill-Queen's University Press.

Knuth, Patricia (1994) 'Wargaming: A Selected Bibliography'. April 1994. U.S. Army War College Library. Online: *http://carlisle-www.army.mil/library/bibs/wargame.htm*

Kohler, Chris (2005) *Power-Up: How Japanese Video Games Gave the World an Extra Life*. Indianapolis (IN): BradyGAMES/Pearson Education.

Krueger, Myron W., Thomas Gionfriddo and Katrin Hinrichsen (1985) 'VIDEOPLACE: An Artificial Reality'. *Proceedings of CHI 1985*. New York: ACM, pp. 35–40.

Krzywinska, Tanya and Geoff King (2002) *Screenplay: Cinema/Videogames/Interfaces*. London: Wallflower Press.

Kuhn, Thomas S. (1996) *The Structure of Scientific Revolutions* (3rd edn). Chicago: University of Chicago Press.

Kuittinen, Jussi, Annakaisa Kultima, Johannes Niemelä and Janne Paavilainen (2007) 'Casual Games Discussion'. In: *Proceedings of the Future Play 2007 Conference*. Toronto: Algoma University.

Kushner, David (2003) *Masters of Doom. How Two Guys Created an Empire and Transformed Pop Culture*. New York: Random House.

Lammes, Sybille (2003) 'On the Border: Pleasures of Exploration and Colonial Mastery in *Civilization III Play the World*'. In: Marinka Copier and Joost Raessens (eds), *Level Up: Digital Games Research Conference Proceedings,* Utrecht: DiGRA and University of Utrecht, pp. 120–9. Online: *http://www.digra.org/dl/db/05163.06568*

Lastowka, F. Gregory and Dan Hunter (2003) 'The Laws of the Virtual Worlds'. Public Law and Legal Theory Research Paper Series, Research Paper No. 26. University of Pennsylvania Law School. Online: *http://papers.ssrn.com/sol3/papers.cfm?abstract_id=402860*

Laukkanen, Tero (2005) 'Modding Scenes: Introduction to User-Created Content in Computer Gaming'. Hypermedia Laboratory Net Series, 9. Tampere: University of Tampere. Online: *http://tampub.uta.fi/tup/951-44-6448-6.pdf*

Laurel, Brenda (ed) (2003) *Design Research: Methods and Perspectives*. Cambridge (MA): The MIT Press.

Lehdonvirta, Vili (2005) 'Real-Money Trade of Virtual Assets: Ten Different User Perceptions'. *Proceedings of DAC 2005.* II University of Copenhagen. Online: *http://www.hiit.fi/u/vlehdonv/publications/Lehdonvirta-2005-RMT-Perceptions.pdf*

Levy, Steven (1984/1994) *Hackers. Heroes of the Computer Revolution*. New York: Delta (1984).

Loftus, Geoffrey R. and Elizabeth F. Loftus (1983) *Mind at Play: the Psychology of Video Games*. New York: Basic Books.

Lowood, Henry (2006) 'A Brief Biography of Computer Games'. In: Peter Vorderer and Jennings Bryant (eds), *Playing Video Games: Motives, Responses, and Consequences*. Mahwah (NJ) and London: Lawrence Erlbaum Associates, pp. 25–41.

Mackay, Daniel (2001) *The Fantasy Role-Playing Game: A New Performing Art*. Jefferson (NC): McFarland.

Mäyrä, Frans Ilkka (1999) *Demonic Texts and Textual Demons: The Demonic Tradition, the Self, and Popular Fiction*. Doctoral Dissertation. Tampere: Tampere University Press. Online: *http://www.uta.fi/~frans.mayra/Demon_2005/*

McAllister, Ken S. (2004) *Game Work: Language, Power, and Computer Game Culture*. Tuscaloosa (AL): The University of Alabama Press.

McGonigal, Jane (2003) '"This is not a Game": Immersive Aesthetics and Collective Play'. *Proceedings of DAC 2003*. Melbourne: RMIT University. Online: *http://www.seanstewart.org/beast/mcgonigal/notagame/paper.pdf*

McGonigal, Jane (2005) 'SuperGaming: Ubiquitous Play and Performance for Massively Scaled Community'. Modern Drama, 48(3): 471–91. Online: *http://avantgame.com/McGonigal_SuperGaming_MODERNDRAMA.pdf*

McMahan, Alison (2003) 'Immersion, Engagement, and Presence: A Method for Analyzing 3-D Video Games'. In: Mark J. P. Wolf and Bernard Perron (eds), *The Video Game Theory Reader*. New York: Routledge, pp. 67–86.

Meyer, Leonard B. (1956) *Emotion and Meaning in Music*. Chicago: The University of Chicago Press.

Mitchell, Edna (1985) 'The Dynamics of Family Interaction Around Home Video Games'. *Marriage and Family Review*, 8(1): 121–35.

Montfort, Nick (2003) *Twisty Little Passages: An Approach to Interactive Fiction*. Cambridge (MA): The MIT Press.

Montola, Markus (2003) 'Exploring the Edge of the Magic Circle: Defining Pervasive Games'. *Proceedings of DAC 2005*. IT University of Copenhagen. Online: *http://iperg.sics.se/Publications/Exploring-the-Edge-of-the-Magic-Circle.pdf*

Morningstar, Chip and F. Randall Farmer (1991) 'The Lessons of Lucasfilm's Habitat'. In: Michael Benedikt (ed), *Cyberspace: First Steps*. Cambridge (MA): MIT Press, pp. 273–301. Online: *http://www.fudco.com/chip/lessons.html*

Morris, Jeff (n.d.) 'Civilization Multiplayer – A Fresh Approach'. Online: *http://www.civ3.com/devupdate_multi.cfm*

Morrison, Foster (1991) *The Art of Modeling Dynamic Systems: Forecasting for Chaos, Randomness, and Determinism*. New York: Wiley-Multiscience Press.

Muggleton, David and Rupert Weinzierl (eds) (2004) *The Post-Subcultures Reader*. Oxford: Berg Publishers.

Mulligan, Jessica (2002) 'Talkin' 'bout My... Generation'. Biting the Hand Column # 17. Online: *http://www.skotos.net/articles/BTH_17.shtml*

Mulligan, Jessica and Bridgette Patrovsky (2003) *Developing Online Games: An Insider's Guide*. Indianapolis (IN): New Riders.

Murray, Harold James Ruthven (1913/2002) *A History of Chess*. Oxford: Oxford University Press.

Murray, Janet (1997) *Hamlet on the Holodeck: The Future of Narrative in Cyberspace*. New York: Free Press.

Myers, David (1990) 'Chris Crawford and Computer Game Aesthetics'. *Journal of Popular Culture*, 24(2): 17–28. Online: *http://www.loyno.edu/%7Edmyers/F99%20classes/Myers_CrawfordGameAesthetics.pdf*

Myers, David (2003) *The Nature of Computer Games: Play as Semiosis*. New York: Peter Lang.

Myers, David (2004) 'The Anti-Poetic: Interactivity, Immersion, and Other Semiotic Functions of Digital Play'. In: A. Clarke (ed), *COSIGN 2004 Conference Proceedings*. Split, Croatia: Art Academy, University of Split. Online: *http://www.loyno.edu/%7Edmyers/F99%20classes/Myers_Antipoetic_ARCHIVE1.rtf*

Myers, David (2005) 'Bombs, Barbarians, and Backstories: Meaning-Making within *Sid Meier's Civilization*'. Appeared in Italian translation in: Matteo Bittanti (ed), *Civilization Storie Virtuali, Fantasie Reali*. Videoludica, Game Culture series. Trans. Valentina Paggiarin. Milan: Costa and Nolan, 2005. Original version online: *http://www.loyno.edu/%7Edmyers/F99%20classes/Myers_BombsBarbarians_DRAFT.rtf*

Myers, David (2006) 'Signs, Symbols, Games, and Play'. *Games and Culture*, 1(1): 47–51.

Nelson, Theodor (1965/2003) 'A File Structure for the Complex, the Changing, and the Indeterminate'. (Orig. In: Lewis Winner (ed), *Association for Computing*

Machinery: Proceedings of the 20th National Conference, 1965, pp. 84–100.) In: Noah Wardrip-Fruin and Nick Montfort (eds), *The New Media Reader*. Cambridge (MA): The MIT Press, pp. 134–45.

Nelson, Theodor (1980/1990) *Literary Machines, 90.1*. (Orig. 1980.) Sausalito (CA): Mindful Press.

Neopets, Inc. (n.d.) 'Pet Central'. Online: *http://www.neopets.com/petcentral.phtml*

Newman, James (2004) *Videogames*. London: Routledge.

Newman, John and Iain Simons (eds) (2004) *Difficult Questions About Videogames*. Nottingham: Suppose Partners.

Nielsen, Jakob (1993) *Usability Engineering*. Boston: Academic Press.

Origin (n.d.) 'Guilds'. Ultima Online Playguide. Online: *http://guide.uo.com/miscellaneous_2.html*

Paley, Vivian Gussin (2004) *A Child's Work: The Importance of Fantasy Play*. Chicago: University of Chicago Press.

Pearce, Celia (2005) 'Theory Wars: An Argument Against Arguments in the so-called Ludology/Narratology Debate'. In: Suzanne de Castell and Jennifer Jenson, *Proceedings of Chancing Views – Worlds in Play. Digital Games Research Association's Second International Conference*. Vancouver: DiGRA and Simon Fraser University. Online: *http://www.digra.org/dl/db/06278.03452.pdf*

Piaget, Jean (1966/2000) *The Psychology of the Child*. (Orig. La Psychologie de l'enfant. Trans., Helen Weaver.) New York: Basic Books.

Poblocki, Kacper (2002) 'Becoming-State: The Bio-Cultural Imperialism of Sid Meier's Civilization'. *Focaal – European Journal of Anthropology*, 39: 163–77. Online: *http://www.focaal.box.nl/previous/Forum%20focaal39.pdf*

Poole, Steven (2000) *Trigger Happy: The Inner Life of Video Games*. London: Fourth Estate.

Prensky, Marc (2001) *Digital Game-Based Learning*. New York: McGraw-Hill.

Radway, Janice (1984/1991) *Reading the Romance: Women, Patriarchy, and Popular Literature*. Chapel Hill and London: The University of North Carolina Press.

Rehak, Bob (2003) 'Mapping the Bit Girl: Lara Croft and New Media Fandom'. *Information, Communication and Society*, 6(4): 477–96.

Reid, Elizabeth M. (1994) 'Cultural Formations in Text-Based Virtual Realities'. Unpublished MA Thesis, Cultural Studies Program, Department of English, University of Melbourne. Online: *http://www.aluluei.com/cult-form.htm*

Rouse, Richard, III (2000) 'Gaming and Graphics: Computer Games, Not Computer Movies'. *ACM SIGGRAPH Computer Graphics*, 34(4) (November 2000): 5–7.

Ryan, Marie-Laure (2001) *Narrative as Virtual Reality: Immersion and Interactivity in Literature and Electronic Media*. Baltimore: The Johns Hopkins University Press.

Salen, Katie and Eric Zimmerman (2004) *Rules of Play: Game Design Fundamentals*. Cambridge (MA): The MIT Press.

Schechner, Richard (2002) *Performance Studies: An Introduction*. London: Routledge.

Schiller, Friedrich (1795/1983) In: *On the Aesthetic Education of Man: In a Series of Letters English and German Facing*. Elizabeth M. Wilkinson and L. A. Willoughby (eds), Oxford University Press.

Sellers, John (2001) *Arcade Fever: The Fan's Guide to the Golden Age of Video Games*. Philadelphia: Running Press.

Sheff, David (1999) *Game Over – Press Start to Continue: How Nintendo Conquered the World*. With new chapters by Andy Eddy. Wilton (CT): Game Press/CyberActive.

Simpson, Dan (2005) 'Ultima IV: Quest of the Avatar. FAQ/Walkthrough'. v. 1.61. Online: *http://db.gamefaqs.com/computer/doswin/file/ultima_iv.txt*

Smith, Jacob (2004) 'I Can See Tomorrow in Your Dance: A Study of *Dance Dance Revolution* and Music Video Games'. *Journal of Popular Music Studies*, 16(1): 58–84.

Smith, Peter K. (ed) (1984) *Play in Animals and Humans*. Oxford and New York: Basil Blackwell.

Sotamaa, Olli (2002) 'All The World's A Botfighter Stage: Notes on Location-based Multi-User Gaming'. In: Frans Mäyrä (ed), *CGDC Conference Proceedings*. Studies in Information Sciences. Tampere: Tampere University Press, pp. 35–44. Online: *http://www.digra.org/dl/db/05164.14477.pdf*

Sotamaa, Olli (2005) 'Creative User-Centred Design Practices: Lessons From Game Culture'. In: Leslie Haddon, Enid Mante, Bartolomeo Sapio, Kari-Hans Kommonen, Leopoldina Fortunati and Annevi Kant (eds), *Everyday Innovators: Researching the Role of Users in Shaping ICT's*. Berlin and New York: Springer Verlag, pp. 104–16. Online: *http://members.aol.com/leshaddon/Sotamaa.pdf*

Spencer, Herbert (1880) *The Principles of Psychology*. New York: D. Appleton and Company.

Spivak, Gayatri Chakravorty (1992) 'Acting Bits/Identity Talk'. *Critical Inquiry*, 18 (Summer 1992): 770–803.

Squire, Kurt D. (2004) 'Replaying History: Learning World History through Playing *Civilization III*'. Unpublished PhD Thesis. Indiana University. Online: *http://website.education.wisc.edu/kdsquire/dissertation.html*

Stahl, Ted (ed) (2005) 'Video Games: Golden Age'. In: *History of Computing* website. Online: *http://www.thocp.net/software/games/golden_age.htm*

Stettler, Nicolas, Theo M. Signer and Paolo M. Suter (2004) 'Electronic Games and Environment Factors Associated with Childhood Obesity in Switzerland'. *Obesity Research*, 12(6): 896–903.

Stewart, Sean (n.d.) 'The A.I. Web Game'. Online: *http://www.seanstewart.org/beast/intro/*

Strinati, Dominic (1995) *Introduction to Theories of Popular Culture*. London: Routledge.

Sudnow, David (1983) *Pilgrim in the Microworld: Eye, Mind and the Essence of Video Skill*. New York: Warner Books.

Suits, Bernard Herbert (1978) *The Grasshopper: Games, Life, and Utopia*. Toronto: University of Toronto Press.

Sulake (2007) 'Quick Habbo facts (November 2007)'. Online: *http://www.sulake.com/habbo/?navi=2*

Sutton-Smith, Brian (1997) *The Ambiguity of Play*. Cambridge (MA): Harvard University Press.

Szulborski, Dave (2005) *This Is Not a Game: A Guide to Alternate Reality Gaming*. Santa Barbara (CA): eXe Active Media Group.

Tamborini, Ron and Paul Skalski (2006) 'The Role of Presence in the Experience of Electronic Games'. In: Peter Vorderer and Jennings Bryant (eds), *Playing Video Games: Motives, Responses, and Consequences*. Mahwah (NJ) and London: Lawrence Erlbaum Associates, pp. 225–40.

TASP (n.d.) 'History of TASP'. The Association for the Study of Play. Online: *http://www.csuchico.edu/kine/tasp/history.htm*

Taylor, Alice (2002) 'My Story: Girls Playing Games'. In: Lucien King (ed), *Game On: The History and Culture of Videogames*. London: Laurence King, pp. 56–7.

Taylor, T. L. (2006) *Play Between Worlds: Exploring Online Game Culture*. Cambridge (MA): The MIT Press.

Thomas, Bruce, Ben Close, John Donoghue, John Squires, Phillip De Bondi and Wayne Piekarski (2002) 'First Person Indoor/Outdoor Augmented Reality Application: ARQuake'. *Personal and Ubiquitous Computing* 6(1): 75–86.

Todorov, Tzvetan (1990) *Genres in Discourse.* (Orig. Genres du discours, 1978; trans. Catherine Porter.) Cambridge: Cambridge University Press.

Tosca, Susana (2002) 'The EverQuest Speech Community'. In: Frans Mäyrä (ed), *CGDC Conference Proceedings.* Studies in Information Sciences. Tampere: Tampere University Press, pp. 341–53.

Toynbee, Arnold J. (1934–1961) *A Study of History.* Volumes 1–12. London and New York: Oxford University Press.

Trice, Harrison M. (1993) *Occupational Subcultures in the Workplace.* Ithaca (NY): Cornell University Press.

Turkle, Sherry (1993) *Life on the Screen: Identity in the Age of the Internet.* New York: Touchstone.

Turkle, Sherry (2005) 'Computer Games as Evocative Objects: From Projective Screens to Relational Artifacts'. In: Joost Raessens and Jeffrey Goldstein (eds), *Handbook of Computer Game Studies.* Cambridge (MA): The MIT Press, 2005, pp. 267–79.

Turner, Victor (1982) 'Liminal to Liminoid, in Play, Flow, and Ritual: An Essay in Comparative Symbology'. In: Victor Turner, *From Ritual to Theatre: The Human Seriousness of Play.* New York: PAJ Publications, pp. 20–60.

Tylor, E. B. (1879/1971) 'The History of Games'. In: Elliott M. Avedon and Brian Sutton-Smith, *The Study of Games.* New York and London: John Wiley and Sons, pp. 63–76.

US Census Bureau (2006) *Statistical Abstract of the United States: 2006.* U.S. Census Bureau. Washington (DC): Department of Commerce. Online: *http://www.census.gov/compendia/statab/2006edition.html*

US Department of Labor (1999) 'Computer Ownership Up Sharply in the 1990s'. *Issues in Labor Statistics*, Summary 99–4 (March 1999). U.S. Department of Labor, Bureau of Labor Statistics. Online: *http://www.bls.gov/opub/ils/pdf/opbils31.pdf*

van Gennep, Arnold (1908/2004) *The Rites of Passage.* London: Routledge.

Vandewater, Elizabeth A., Mi-suk Shim and Allison G. Caplovitz (2004) 'Linking Obesity and Activity Level with Children's Television and Video Game Use'. *Journal of Adolescence*, 27(1): 71–85.

Vivendi (2006) 'Introduction to Vivendi Games'. June 2006 investor presentation by Bruce Hack, Mike Morhaime, Jean François Guillemund and Nishul Bradford. Online: *http://www.vivendi.com/ir/download/pdf/VIVGames_EuropeRoadshow_June2006.pdf*

Vogel, Harold L. (2004) *Entertainment Industry Economics: A Guide to Financial Analysis.* Cambridge: Cambridge University Press.

Vorderer, Peter and Jennings Bryant (eds) (2006) *Playing Video Games: Motives, Responses, and Consequences.* Mahwah (NJ) and London: Lawrence Erlbaum Associates.

Vygotsky, Lev S. (1980) In: *Mind in Society: The Development of Higher Psychological Processes.* Michael Cole, Vera John-Steiner, Sylvia Scribner, and Ellen Souberman. (eds), Cambridge (MA): Harvard University Press.

Vygotsky, Lev S. (1934/1986) In: Alex Kozwin (ed), *Thought and Language* (Revised edn). (Ed. Alex Kozulin.) Cambridge (MA): The MIT Press.

Wallace, Patricia (2001) *The Psychology of the Internet.* Cambridge and New York: Cambridge University Press.

Weiser, Mark (1993) 'Some Computer Science Issues in Ubiquitous Computing'. *Communications of the ACM*, 36(7): 75–84.

Williams, Dmitri (2006) 'A (Brief) Social History of Video Games'. In: Peter Vorderer, Jennings Bryant (eds), *Playing Computer Games: Motives, Responses, and Consquences.* Mahwah (NJ) and London: Lawrence Erlbaum.

Williams, Patrick, J., Q. Hendricks Sean, and W. Keith Winkler (eds) (2006) *Gaming As Culture: Essays on Reality, Identity And Experience in Fantasy Games*. Jefferson (NC): McFarland and Company.

Wolf, Mark J. P. (ed) (2001) *The Medium of the Video Game*. Austin: University of Texas Press.

Woolley, David R. (1994) 'PLATO: The Emergence of On-Line Community'. *Computer-Mediated Communication Magazine* 1(3). Online: *http://www.december.com/cmc/mag/1994/jul/plato.html*

Yee, Nicholas (2001) 'The Norrathian Scrolls. A Study of EverQuest'. Version 2.5. Online: *http://www.nickyee.com/eqt/report.html*

Yee, Nicholas (2002a) 'Ariadne: Understanding MMORPG Addiction'. Online: *http://www.nickyee.com/hub/addiction/home.html*

Yee, Nicholas (2002b) 'Facets: 5 Motivation Factors for Why People Play MMORPG's'. Online: *http://www.nickyee.com/facets/home.html*

Yee, Nicholas (2003–2006) 'The Daedalus Project'. Online: *http://www.nickyee.com/daedalus*

INDEX

dialogue, 22, 81, 83, 99, 119, 160;
    in academic community, 5, 168
dial-up multiplayer service, 121
diary, 161, 162, 167
Dibbell, Julian, 124, 140
dice, 22, 34, 38, 41, 128
Digital Equipment Corporation (DEC), 41
digital game history; *see* history
Digital Game Research Association
    (DiGRA), 5, 10, 154–5
DikuMUD, 131
discipline, 4–8, 11, 13, 21, 23–4, 30, 33,
    147, 153, 156, 158, 168–9
discourse, 22, 44, 50, 88, 97, 114, 143,
    156–7, 161
discourse analysis, 157, 161
Disneyland, 101
divination, 38
divine, 45–6
doll's house, 22–3
domestication, 6, 26
Donkey Kong, 72–7, 86, 104, 113
Donkey Kong Junior, 74
Doom, 101–16, 125, 128
Doom II, 105, 112
Doom Bible, 105–6
dot-com crash, 57
dot-com frenzy, 90
Douglas, A. S., 40
Douglas, Christopher, 97, 98
Douglas, Mary, 48
Dovey, Jon, 27, 107, 158
*Dr. Kawashima's Brain Training: How
    Old Is Your Brain?*, 145
dramatist, 82, 87
du Gay, Paul, 163
dual model of core and shell, 17–18, 53, 63,
    65–6, 99, 115, 133, 165
Ducheneaut, Nicolas, 137, 139
dungeon, 79–80, 81, 121, 128, 138
Dungeon Master (DM), 78
Dungeons & Dragons, 3, 78, 102, 121, 134
Durkin, Kevin, 91
dynamics, 2, 20, 31, 49, 59, 64, 69, 105,
    114, 125, 127, 136–7, 157, 164

Eagle Games, 96
East Coast War Games Council, 7
Easter egg, 102
eBay, 139
economical dynamics; *see* dynamics
economics, 31–2, 95, 102, 120, 139–40,
    163, 167
Eddy, Andy, 56
Electronic Arts (EA), 90, 94, 113
electronic games, 40, 56, 58–62, 75, 118
Ellison, Harlan, 86

emote, 122, 137
emotion, 18, 24, 35, 48, 69, 82, 99, 102,
    109–10, 116, 124–5, 139
Empire, 95, 121
empowerment, 24, 65, 75, 104, 114, 120
entertainment, 46
Entertainment Software Association
    (ESA), 23
Epic Games, 111
epistemological basis of research, 156
Erfurt shootings, 90
Erickson, Thomas, 138
Ermi, Laura, 14, 24, 100, 108–10
Eskelinen, Markku, 53
ethics, 82, 85–6, 111, 147, 161
ethnography, 6, 13, 29, 162, 164, 167
ethos, 125
EverQuest, 127–8, 130–9, 167
EverQuest II, 134–5
EverQuest Widows, 135
Evil Dead, 103
exergames; *see* physically exertive games
Exidy, 65
experience, 6, 42, 45, 48, 49, 54, 58, 66, 75,
    94, 95, 160–1; of gameplay, 12, 14–17,
    21, 22, 25, 28, 35, 53, 59, 64–5, 67,
    72–4, 79–80, 82–7, 99–101, 104,
    107–10, 114–16, 118–21, 123, 128–30,
    135, 137, 142, 147–51, 154, 161,
    163–6; of interactivity, 6, 40, 52; of
    music, 18–19
experience levels, 81, 132, 137–8, 167
expert play, 11, 72, 99, 166
Explorers; *see* MUD player classification
Exus, 142, 144
Eye Toy, 143–6
Eye Toy: Antigrav, 145
Eye Toy: Play, 145

fairground attractions, 42, 63
fandom, 25–7, 143
fantasy, 3, 21, 26, 47–8, 78, 81–3, 88, 95,
    109, 115, 127, 131–6, 139–40, 161–2
fantasy baseball, 127
fantasy football, 127
FAQ; *see* walkthrough
Farmer, F. Randall, 122–4
Farrington, Pat, 149
Fate, 38, 44
feminist critique, 24, 158
Fey, Charles, 42
fiction, 26, 34–6, 42, 44, 63–5, 75, 81, 84,
    86–8, 95, 103, 107, 109, 115–16, 125,
    128, 130–2, 135, 140, 146, 150, 166;
    see also interactive fiction; *see also*
    science fiction
field notes, 162, 167; *see also* diary

Harmonix Music Systems, 144
Harris, Eric, 90, 104
Harry Potter, 77, 113, 145
Head-Mounted Display (HMD), 95, 146
health, 98, 104, 141
Hebdige, Dick, 25–6
hegemony, 27, 98
Heliö, Satu, 24, 64
Helwig, 7
Heretic, 112
hermeneutic circle, 153–4
Herz, J. C., 42, 56, 82, 100–1
Hexen, 112
Higginbotham, Willy, 40, 58
high score, 59, 63–4, 66, 72, 142–4
historiography; *see* history
history, 6–12, 13, 31–2, 49, 54–6, 65, 72,
    90, 95–9, 120–1, 152–3, 156–8, 166;
    of digital games, 30–2, 55–6, 66, 69,
    82, 103; historiography (meta-history),
    31–2, 56, 67, 158; microhistory, 32;
    prehistory of digital games, 30, 32,
    37–50, 56
Hitchhiker's Guide to the Galaxy,
    The, 79
hobbies, 22, 28, 44, 57
holding power of games, 38, 50, 64, 67,
    132, 135
Holmes, Robyn M., 120
Holy Scripture; *see Bible*
Homo Ludens; *see* Huizinga, Johan
Hopscotch, 22, 23
horror, 26, 84, 101, 103, 109, 114
Hot Seat play style, 119
Höysniemi, Johanna, 142, 143
Huhtamo, Erkki, 42
Huizinga, Johan, 1, 4, 11, 20, 34, 35, 43,
    47, 50, 110, 136
humanities methods, 156–8
Hunter, Dan, 129
hyperreality, 101
hypertext, 8–9

I Have No Mouth, and I Must Scream, 86
I Love Bees, 149
IBM PC, 61, 79, 93
id Software, 101–16, 146
identification, 69, 86, 107
identity, 17, 23, 25, 27, 29, 44, 56–7, 85,
    94, 114, 136, 148, 150
ideological critique, 73, 95–9, 113, 158
IEEE Computer Society, 31
ilinx, 21
imaginary, 44
immersion, 38, 82, 101, 107–8, 109, 115,
    125, 128, 133, 140, 150, 164;
    challenge-based, 108, 115; imaginative,

109, 115; SCI model of, 108, 110;
    sensory, 108, 115
immersive aesthetics, 151
IMRaD template, 169
in-character speech, 137
Indiana Jones and the Last Crusade, 106
indie games, 146, 149
Industrial Business Machines Corporation
    (IBM), 61, 79, 93
industry consolidation, 94–5, 115, 119;
    see also convergence
industry, 2, 4, 30–2, 41–2, 54, 57, 58, 60,
    62, 66, 68–9, 73, 77–8, 84, 90–1,
    94–5, 111–13, 120, 129, 135, 141,
    145–7, 162–3
Infocom, 78–9
innovative play; *see* player creativity
instance, 17, 130
instant messenger (IM), 148, 150
Integrated Project on Pervasive Gaming
    (IPerG), 147
Intel 386, 93
Intellivision, 61–2
interactive fiction, 8–9, 73, 80, 87
interactivity, 6, 9, 52, 65, 70–2
interdisciplinarity, 2–4, 6, 11, 24, 30,
    152–170
interface, 54, 66, 78–81, 84, 108, 110,
    113–16, 128, 130–1, 142–5, 149, 158,
    164, 166; multimodal interface, 141–5,
    150, 157; language of, 113–14
International Game Developers Association
    (IGDA), 119, 120
International Simulation and Gaming
    Association (ISAGA), 5, 7
Internet, 26–8, 58, 94, 103, 112, 118, 121,
    125, 128, 134, 138–9, 146, 148, 151,
    159, 169
Internet Relay Chat (IRC), 122
Internet Service Provider (ISP), 121
interpretation, 32, 45, 50, 53, 65, 73, 97,
    110, 114–15, 156–8, 161, 164, 166
interview, 14, 69, 82, 126, 132, 160–1,
    164, 167
intramusical meaning; *see* meaning
Islands of Kesmai, 128
isometric perspective, 113, 130
iterative design and testing, 64, 163–4
Its Alive!, 146
Iwatani, Toru, 69, 89

Jagex Ltd., 133
Japan, 10, 62, 69, 72–4, 76–7, 86, 93, 139,
    142, 144–5
Järvinen, Aki, 64, 91, 100, 104, 164
Jasper, David, 153

Nintendo Entertainment System (NES), 61, 92

Nishikado, Toshihiro, 63

non-linguistic meaning; *see* meaning

non-player character (NPC), 78, 135

norms, 19, 22, 48–9, 55, 115, 125, 161–2

North American Simulation and Gaming Association (NASAGA), 7

nudity, 113

observation, 7, 14, 18, 31, 38, 45, 47–8, 67, 82, 96, 100, 119, 126, 152–3, 158–60, 162, 164, 165, 167

Obsidian Entertainment, 109

online games; *see* Internet

online persona, 129, 135–6; *see also* avatar

ontological basis of research, 156

oppositional reading, 73

Origin Systems, Inc., 83, 101, 130

Orthanc, 128

Other, the, 26, 114

Otherness; *see* the Other

out-of-character speech, 137

overweight, 141

Pac-Man, 68–73, 86, 104, 113, 124

Pac-Man Vs., 72

paidia, 21, 34, 46; *see also* ludic attitude

painting, 22

Paley, Vivian Gussin, 47–8

paper prototype; *see* prototype

paradigm, scientific, 156

Parappa the Rapper, 142

parser, 78

patriarchy, 24

Patrovsky, Bridgette, 123

Pauline, 74

PC baang, 133

PC-Engine, 92

PDP-1, 41

Pearce, Celia, 10

Pedit5, 128

Pellegrini, Anthony D., 120

perfect attack, 143

performance, 14–17, 27, 44–6, 49–50, 142–3, 157

personal computer (PC), 25, 27, 53, 61, 79, 81, 91, 93–5, 103, 110–11, 120–1, 133, 142, 145–7

personality, 70, 73, 107, 166

pervasive gaming, 146–7

pet, 99, 127

Petley, Julian, 91

Pew Internet and American Life Project, 24, 126

physically exertive games, 141–5, 150

Piaget, Jean, 14

pilot study, 159

pinball machines, 42, 50, 59, 63, 69

Pirates!, 95

Planescape: Torment, 84

platform game, 73–4, 80, 83, 86–7, 105, 112–13

PLATO, 121, 128

Play and Culture journal, 8

Play and Culture Studies journal, 8

play style, 50, 82, 113, 124, 131, 133, 166

playability, 62, 64, 66

player character (PC), 70, 78, 85, 104–7, 116, 122, 135–7, 150

player creativity, 122, 164, 166; *see also* mod; *see also* machinima

player motivations, 24, 74–5, 87, 110, 132–3, 139–40

player psychology, 43, 48–9, 82, 91, 108, 122, 125–6, 132–3, 150, 157–8, 162

player-killing (PKing), 124

player-versus-environment (PvE), 131

player-versus-player (PvP), 130

playful behaviour; *see* ludic attitude

playing as research method, 67, 117, 165–7

PlayStation, 61, 93

PlayStation 2 (PS2), 61, 94, 143, 170

PlayStation 3 (PS3), 61, 94

play-testing, 78, 163–4

Pobłocki, Kacper, 97–8, 101

Pokémon, 55, 66, 77

Poker, 12, 17, 121

politics, 21, 31, 57–8, 97, 101, 148–9

polygon, 91, 93–4, 115

Pong, 41, 55, 58–60, 62, 66, 69, 72, 76, 83, 97, 108, 119

Pools of Radiance, 56, 99, 100

PopCap Games, 120

Populous, 99

pose; *see* emote

positivism, 100, 158

post-subculture; *see* culture

power gamers, 132

Power Pad, 142

powerlevelling; *see* grinding

powerup, 70, 104–5

practice theories of play, 43

prehistory; *see* history

Prensky, Marc, 100

primary schemas, 37

print media, 27, 55, 65, 69, 76–7, 84–5, 118

production; *see* game development

profane, 38, 50

professional gaming, 111, 140

programming; *see* code

Progress Quest, 131

prototype, 117, 147, 164–5
psychoanalytic critique, 158
psychology, 5, 11, 43, 82, 122, 125–6, 162;
    see also player psychology
psychology of the Internet, 125
punk, 25, 68
puzzle, 9, 22, 26–7, 50, 69–71, 73, 80,
    83, 85–6, 102, 105, 108–9, 120,
    134, 145, 150

Q-Link (Quantum Link), 128
Quake, 25, 111–12, 128, 146
qualitative research, 11–12, 20, 82, 128, 133,
    160–1, 165
quality assurance (QA), 163
quantitative research, 160–1; *see also*
    statistical analysis
questionnaire; *see* survey

racism, 86
Radway, Janice, 24
Railroad Tycoon, 95
rape in cyberspace, 124
rapid prototyping, 164
raster graphics, 53
reading; *see* literacy
Real Life (RL), 126, 136, 146
real money trade of virtual game property,
    139–40
real person, 124–5
realism, 54, 57, 61, 94–5, 100, 104,
    113–15, 128
Realm, The, 130
real-time strategy (RTS), 96, 101, 116–17
reduction of social cues, 125
references, use of, 169–70
Rehak, Bob, 107
Reid, Elizabeth M., 122
reliability, 159; *see also* verification
remediation, 32, 52, 63, 65, 103, 112, 158
rendering, 91, 113, 115
research phases, 154, 164
research question, 3, 31, 141, 152–6, 160,
    165, 167
Resident Evil, 84
ResponDesign, 143
retro-gaming, 53
reward, 39, 49, 52, 74–5, 102, 109, 135,
    137–8, 140
rhetorics, 44, 114
rich data, 160
Rig Veda, 38
risky play, 44
rites of passage, 48
ritual, 6, 20, 25, 28–9, 38, 46–8, 50,
    114, 116
Rockstar Games, 3, 113

Rogue, 79
Roguelike games, 79–80, 105, 109, 121
role-playing game (RPG), 75, 78–87,
    101, 109, 121, 123, 127–8, 130–9;
    computer role-playing game (CRPG),
    79–86; live action role-playing (larp),
    148; Massively Multiplayer Online
    Role-Playing Game (MMORPG),
    127–39; table-top roleplaying game;
    78, 127; *see also Dungeons & Dragons*
Romero, John, 104, 106, 110
Rouse, Richard, III, 94
Rousseau, Jean-Jacques, 43
rules, of game, 1, 4, 16–21, 23, 33–7, 50,
    53, 64–5, 84, 86–7, 96, 98, 100–2,
    110, 136, 150, 164–5
Rules of Play; *see* Salen, Katie *and*
    Zimmerman, Eric
RuneScape, 133–4
Russell, Bertrand, 19, 46
Russell, Steve 'Slug', 41–2
Rutherford, Rusty, 128
Rutter, Jason, 104

sacred, 38, 50
Salen, Katie, 19, 35–7, 165
sampling, 12, 53, 132, 159–63
Sanders Associates, 41, 60
Satanism, 114
Schechner, Richard, 45–7
Schiller, Friedrich, 43
Schleiermacher, Friedrich Daniel Ernst, 153
scholarly community; *see* community,
    academic
SCI model; *see* immersion, SCI model of
science fiction, 26, 42, 63, 86, 95, 114, 116
scientific writing, 169
Scrabble, 121
ScreenPlay, 158
Sears, David, 86
Second Life, 134, 140
Sega Corporation, 62, 92–4
Sega Dreamcast, 93–4
Sega Genesis, 93
Sega Master System, 92
Sega Saturn, 93
self, 11, 44–5, 49, 57, 65, 68, 85, 114, 136
Sellers, John, 56, 63
semiosis, 19
semiotics, 16
sense of wonder, 76, 87
sexualized characters, 107
shard, 130
shareware, 102–3, 105, 146
Sheff, David, 31, 56, 75–7
shell; *see* the dual model of core and shell
shikadu sedai (visual generation), 72

193